THE
RAILWAY ROUTE BOOK

Christopher Pick

A traveller's guide to the major and minor lines of the railway network of Britain.

WILLOW BOOKS
Collins
8 Grafton Street, London W1X 3LA
1986

*To my mother, who encouraged
my first railway explorations*

Title page: *No. 2* Dolgoch *pulls a train down the
valley near Abergynolwyn on the Talyllyn Railway.*

Willow Books
William Collins & Co Ltd
London · Glasgow · Sydney
Auckland · Toronto · Johannesburg

First published in Great Britain 1986
Copyright © Robert Adkinson Limited

**Designed and produced by
Robert Adkinson Limited, London**

Editorial Director	Clare Howell
Editor	Sydney Francis
Art Director	Christine Simmonds
Designer	Paul Wood, Kirby-Wood
Maps	Paul Wood

Pick, Christopher
   The railway route book.
   1. Railroads — Great Britain — Guide-books
   2. Great Britain — Description and travel — 1971-
   — Guide-books
   I. Title
   385'.0941   HE3015

   ISBN 0-00-218203-3

Phototypeset by Ashwell Print Services, Norwich
Illustrations originated by East Anglian Engraving
Limited, Norwich
Printed and bound by Sagdos, Milan, Italy

CONTENTS

Introduction

I am just old enough to remember the last years of steam on British Rail. I recall walking with my father to the end of the platform at King's Cross to admire the locomotive that was to take us north for a Scottish holiday; I remember the excitement of day trips to London that began with the rush and smell of the locomotive steaming into Bedford Midland station; there was even a short time, so I am told, when I wanted to be an engine-driver when I grew up.

Since those youthful years, I have enjoyed train travel less for a special interest in locomotives or rolling stock than because of a fascination with the journey itself and with the landscape beyond the carriage window. This book is a product of that enthusiasm and enjoyment and of my interest in the ways in which railways have knitted themselves into the social, economic and architectural fabric of the nation.

Summer 1985 was a good time to do the travelling and additional research for this book. While problems undoubtedly remain, for the first time for many years British Rail's prospects are looking good. Considerable investment is being made, at long last, in electrification schemes, new types of rolling stock and in improvements to previously unprofitable and badly served lines. The flourishing preserved steam sector is shaking off its image as merely an attraction for holiday-makers and is developing carefully-researched living museums of the steam age.

In selecting the routes I have travelled and described in the following pages, I have tried to strike a reasonable balance both between inter-city and branch-line journeys and between the competing attractions of different parts of the country. I have included many well-known scenic routes, together with some less celebrated ones, and I have also looked for lines whose history, construction, architecture or current operation is of especial interest. In addition, I have allowed myself the privilege of describing a few particular favourites of my own. I have also included as many preserved lines as possible.

The book is organized in five principal sections reflecting the five British Rail regions. Occasionally, inter-regional lines have been placed in the region that seemed most appropriate for the traveller, rather than in the BR region which actually controls the line; for instance, Norwich to Brimingham appears in the Eastern Region, while the two main lines north to Scotland are to be found one under the Eastern and one under the Midland Region. The Gazetteer lists the most important preserved lines, steam centres and railway museums throughout the country.

What the pundits say is true. It is quicker – and safer too – by rail. I hope this book will encourage readers to forsake the traffic jams and road works and begin a new exploration of Britain by train. Good travelling!

View of the north end of Sevenoaks Tunnel in about 1868, the year the South Eastern Railway's direct route from London to the Channel ports was opened.

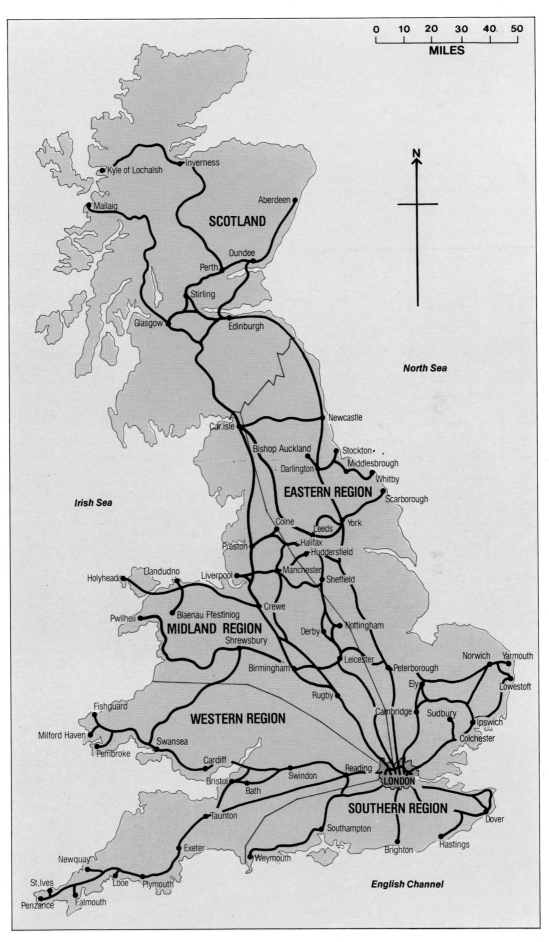

MILES
0 10 20 30 40 50

N

Kyle of Lochalsh
Inverness
Aberdeen
Mallaig
SCOTLAND
Dundee
Perth
Stirling
Glasgow
Edinburgh

North Sea

Newcastle
Carlisle
Bishop Auckland
Stockton
Darlington
Middlesbrough
Whitby
EASTERN REGION
Scarborough

Irish Sea

Colne
Leeds
York
Preston
Halifax
Huddersfield
Holyhead
Llandudno
Liverpool
Manchester
Sheffield
Blaenau Ffestiniog
Crewe
Pwllheli
MIDLAND REGION
Derby
Nottingham
Shrewsbury
Norwich
Yarmouth
Birmingham
Leicester
Peterborough
Rugby
Ely
Lowestoft
Fishguard
WESTERN REGION
Cambridge
Sudbury
Milford Haven
Swansea
Ipswich
Pembroke
Colchester
Cardiff
Reading
Bristol
Swindon
LONDON
Bath
SOUTHERN REGION
Dover
Taunton
Southampton
Newquay
Exeter
Weymouth
Brighton
Hastings
St.Ives
Looe
Plymouth
Penzance
Falmouth

English Channel

0–6–0ST No. 68005 hauls a mixed freight train on the East Somerset Railway.

4–4–0 No. 3217 Earl of Berkeley *gets to grips with*
Freshfield Bank on the Bluebell Railway.

EASTERN REGION

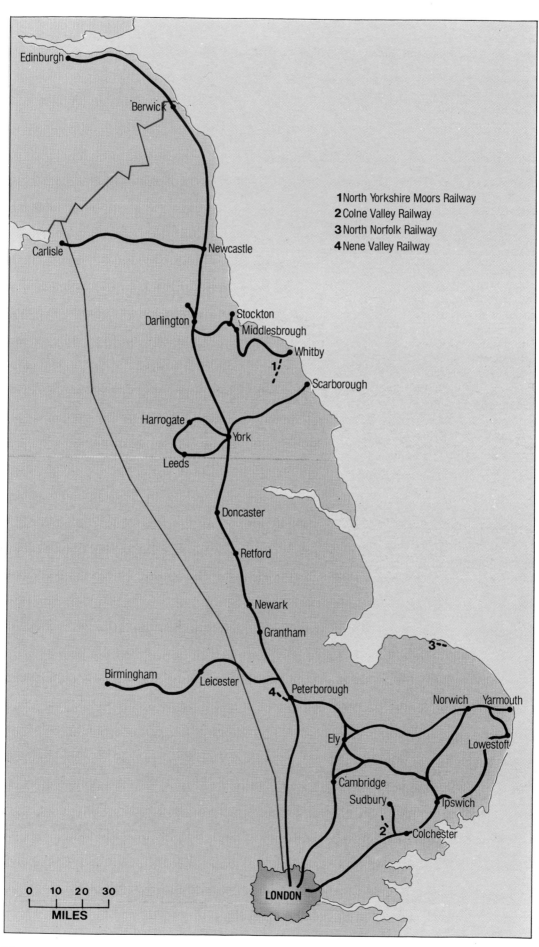

1 North Yorkshire Moors Railway
2 Colne Valley Railway
3 North Norfolk Railway
4 Nene Valley Railway

Edinburgh
Berwick
Carlisle
Newcastle
Darlington
Stockton
Middlesbrough
Whitby
1
Scarborough
Harrogate
York
Leeds
Doncaster
Retford
Newark
Grantham
Birmingham
Leicester
4
Peterborough
3
Norwich
Yarmouth
Ely
Lowestoft
Cambridge
Sudbury
Ipswich
2
Colchester
LONDON

0 10 20 30
MILES

It is fitting that this book should begin with British Rail's Eastern Region, for it was in the north-east that rail transport originated. For a century and more before the inauguration of the Stockton & Darlington Railway in 1825, a network of wagonways and rail-ways had been used to carry coal away from the mines of Durham and Northumberland. Some of the earliest experiments in steam locomotion took place in the north-east, and many of the pioneers of the railway age came from that region. Pre-eminent among them were George Stephenson and his son Robert, who, as well as building some of the first successful steam locomotives, were also responsible for surveying and constructing numerous routes throughout the country. Their celebrity, however, should not be allowed to overshadow completely the achievements of the many men of the north-east whose skills and expertise brought them responsible jobs on railways all over Britain.

Except on the journey from Stockton through Darlington to Shildon, the traveller will find little direct evidence of those early days. The Region's premier route between the capitals of England and Scotland is a fine and fast line that has seen many successful record-breaking runs.

It passes through a fascinating and varied landscape, both rural and urban, with an especially splendid stretch along the lonely North Sea coast just north of the border, and enables the traveller to see several well-known examples of railway architecture, notably the glorious station at York and the handsome Royal Border Bridge across the Tweed at Berwick.

Branch line travel is equally varied. In the north there are some dramatic journeys through rugged countryside, for instance along the lovely river Esk at the foot of the North York Moors from Middlesborough to Whitby, and straight across the Moors behind the steam locomotives of the North Yorkshire Moors Railway. British Rail's steam excursions from York to Scarborough via Harrogate and Leeds are an excellent opportunity to experience the sights and smells of the days of steam. Further south, a good number of the once comprehensive network of East Anglian lines remains, and these routes provide an opportunity to enjoy the remarkably varied landscape of Suffolk and Norfolk. Here, too, steam survives, near Peterborough (the Nene Valley Railway), in north Norfolk and at the Colne Valley Railway in the heart of the remote Essex countryside.

BR class 5 MT 4–6–0 No. 73050 near Wansford on the Nene Valley Railway in Cambridgeshire.

London to Edinburgh

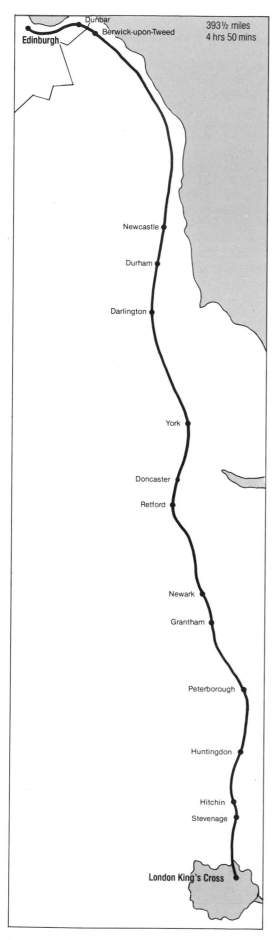

393½ miles
4 hrs 50 mins

Dunbar
Berwick-upon-Tweed
Edinburgh
Newcastle
Durham
Darlington
York
Doncaster
Retford
Newark
Grantham
Peterborough
Huntingdon
Hitchin
Stevenage
London King's Cross

The journey north from London to Edinburgh starts at King's Cross, one of the simplest and most handsome of London's termini. Lewis Cubitt, architect to the Great Northern Railway (GNR), did not favour the grandiose elaboration and display already popular with many railway companies in the early 1850s, and the design he prepared for King's Cross was entirely functional. There were to be two identical train sheds, each 800 feet long and 105 feet wide, divided by a brick wall, and covered by two semi-circular glazed roofs that reached 71 feet at their highest points. The plain brick façade on the south side, facing Euston Road, was equally simple. Two large, semi-circular glazed arcades reflected the design of the interior; there was an arched porch at ground level at which carriages drew up, and an Italianate clock tower on top re-presented Cubitt's only concession to the ornate.

The building had the additional merit of being cheap. It cost only £123,000 to construct; less, as the GNR's chairman was quick to point out to critical shareholders, than the Great Hall and portico alone at the London & Birmingham Railway's Euston terminus just along the road.

The King's Cross one enters today, more than 130 years on, is recognizably the same station, although a modern single-storey Travel Centre insensitively built in front of the magnificent façade entirely spoils the view. But the Travel Centre is less objectionable than the messy collection of kiosks and shops (nicknamed by railwaymen 'the native village') that preceded it.

Inside the station, the principal facilities such as the waiting-room and buffet are situated along the west side by what was originally the 'departure platform'. For well over twenty years after the station opened, there were only two platforms, departure and arrival, at opposite sides of each train shed, with fourteen carriage roads separating them. If there is time before the train leaves, walk to the far end of the platform and turn round to gaze at the impressive view into the twin train sheds and across to the equally majestic single-span roof of St. Pancras (see page 105), a couple of hundred yards to the right. The third, smaller, King's Cross train shed was built in 1875 to accommodate suburban services.

George Hudson

Southerners often have to be reminded that, apart from the Canterbury & Whitstable (see page 177), railways came relatively late to their part of the world, and that, at least in the early days of railway building, most of the men who provided the capital were from the north. The east-coast route is a case in point. The complex story of its construction focuses on York.

The first services from London to York in 1840 went by an indirect route, from Euston through Rugby, Derby and Normanton. North of York, railway promoters were eager to start building and develop a through service to the

Railway completed its line from Edinburgh along the coast to Berwick in 1846.

In the early 1840s, several proposals were made to build a direct route from York to London. They all met the implacable and ferocious opposition of George Hudson, the justly-named 'Railway King'. Hudson was a linen draper from York, who, equipped with a £30,000 inheritance, had set out to build a railway empire and amass a fortune. He succeeded in doing both. Hudson controlled the existing route south from York as far as Rugby; any more direct route to the capital would damage his interests. In the end, even though he tried to make the new line unnecessary by constructing a series of branch lines, Hudson lost, and the GNR started construction work in 1846. The first section to be completed was an indirect route south through Lincoln and the Fens from Doncaster to Peterborough. Then came the Peterborough to London link in 1850, terminating at Maiden Lane, north of the Regent's Canal, and finally the direct line between Peterborough and Doncaster via Grantham in 1852. Last to be built was King's Cross station, also opened in 1852.

Two years later, the various companies that had built the line between Doncaster and Berwick merged to form the North Eastern Railway which, with the GNR in the south and the North British Railway in Scotland, ran the line in alliance for nearly seventy years. In 1923, control passed to the newly-formed London & North Eastern Railway.

George Hudson of York (1800–71), linen draper turned railway magnate.

capital. The line to Darlington was finished in 1841; the next stretch to Gateshead on the south side of the Tyne three years later; and the section north from Newcastle to Tweedmouth, on the south bank of the Tweed opposite Berwick, in 1847. Railway builders were equally busy north of the border in Scotland and the North British

Mallard *leaving King's Cross with the* Tees-Tyne Pullman *in the mid-1950s. Today, the splendid train*

sheds of King's Cross remain untouched, but both track layout and signalling have been modernized.

13

North from King's Cross

Immediately the train leaves the station, it dives into Gas Works tunnel under the canal, emerges briefly, and then dives again into Copenhagen tunnel. The High-Speed Trains (HSTs) manage the steep climb out of the tunnels without any difficulty, but in the days of steam negotiating the 'Throat', as the approach to King's Cross was known, was not so easy. The tunnels were prone to flood, and the track layout was extremely complicated, with conflicting movements of mainline and local trains.

The north London suburbs flash past, with terraced rows of late nineteenth-century houses soon giving way to the more spacious inter-war developments around New Barnet and Potters Bar. Alexandra Palace, where television first went on the air, can be seen high on a hill to the left. Within a quarter of an hour, the train races through Hatfield at 100 mph plus and runs on into the gently rolling hills of the Hertfordshire countryside.

William Cubitt, the GNR's engineer (and uncle of the Lewis Cubitt who designed King's Cross), built this line for speed, with few, wide curves and, except through the north London hills where there are half a dozen tunnels in the first dozen miles, gentle gradients. Several speed records have been set on the line, including *Mallard*'s celebrated 126 mph run in 1938, a world record for steam that remains unbroken to this day. (See page 67 for the races to Scotland.)

Considerable modernization was necessary when diesel locomotives were introduced in the 1960s, notably the removal of the notorious dog-leg curve at the entrance to Peterborough station, where a speed limit of 20 mph was in force, and at Selby, where the speed limit was raised by some 20 mph. By 1973, over 80 per cent of the route from London to Newcastle had been converted to 100 mph running. That same year, two more speed records were set in quick succession, when a prototype HST reached 131 mph between Northallerton and Thirsk in Yorkshire and then, just five days later, broke the record again at 143 mph. That record still stood in 1985. But on 27 September that year the Tees-Tyne Pullman broke a clutch of other speed records, principally the world long-distance start-to-stop diesel record, achieving an average 115.4 mph over the 286.6 miles from Newcastle to London.

High-Speed Trains

The decision to introduce HSTs on the east-coast line in 1978 paid off almost immediately in terms of improved schedules (Edinburgh is now four and a half hours away from London compared with six in the 1960s) and increased passenger traffic. Since 1982, virtually all Inter-City services on the line have been operated by HSTs. In technical and marketing terms, British Rail, like any other large commercial concern, has to look well ahead. By the early 1990s, when the current generation of HST power cars will be due for costly re-engining, the sleek speed appeal of the HST services will seem old hat to regular travellers.

Faced with the choice of more of the same or electrification, British Rail chose the electrification option, and eventually managed to win government approval for the £306 million project. The HST sets will be reallocated (the jargon term is 'cascaded') to less demanding

High-Speed Trains under the functional and graceful train sheds of King's Cross. HSTs are the most recent of a succession of fast locomotives to work the line north to Yorkshire, Tyneside and Edinburgh.

routes. Electric trains will link London and Peterborough in 1987 and, if work remains on schedule, London and Edinburgh four years later. Maximum speeds on the line will remain 125 mph, although they may increase to about 140 mph if the market demands it. Even if the speed limit remains the same, BR claim that some journey times will decrease as a result of the superior acceleration of electric traction, and services should be more reliable. Maintenance and energy costs will also be reduced. In Hertfordshire the wires are already in place overhead. Electrification of the east-coast line as far north as Hitchin was completed in 1977 as part of the Great Northern Electrification of suburban lines from King's Cross.

Welwyn to Doncaster

North of Welwyn Garden City, Digswell viaduct carries the line over the tiny river Mimram. The viaduct is an imposing structure of plain brick, 100 feet high, 519 yards long and with forty arches. As with many railway structures, the best view is from the ground, not from the train.

Beyond Stevenage, the frequent towns die away, and a long run starts through fairly sparsely populated but often extremely attractive countryside. The Bedfordshire stretch is rather flat and dull, with views of cabbage and sprout fields, but after that there are water-meadows along the Ouse, and lovely rolling wheatfields around Huntingdon. Right through Grantham and Retford the line occupies a kind of borderland between the Fens, with their flat landscape and characteristically wide skies, and the gently rolling scenery of the east Midlands, with hidden villages built of mellow stone.

South of Peterborough, the train crosses a tract of Fenland known as Whittlesey Mere. Thomas Brassey, the celebrated railway contractor who built this line for the GNR, described it as a 'quaking bog', and conquered it by sinking alternate layers of faggots and peat. Then there are views of the brickfields on the right and, as you enter the city over the river Nene, of the lovely twelfth-century cathedral with its squat tower. The single, modern signal-box at Peterborough controls no less than 56 miles of the main line, and is one of only three over the route between King's Cross and Doncaster. When BR's resignalling programme is complete, just seven boxes will control the entire route to Edinburgh.

Record stretch

Beyond Peterborough, the line climbs to Stoke tunnel through the limestone ridge south of Grantham. This has always been one of the fastest stretches of the GNR line, and it was here, travelling in the opposite direction south towards Peterborough, that *Mallard* set its unbroken record. Grantham is a pleasant, unassuming market town, with the fine spire of St. Wulfram's church clearly visible from the train.

A Class 55 Deltic diesel locomotive about to leave King's Cross for the north with a night sleeper.

The land becomes flatter towards Newark, where the line passes to the right of the town. During the Civil War the townspeople stayed loyal to Charles I. The castle, parts of which date back to the twelfth century, was never taken, but was surrendered on the King's command and ruined by Cromwell's men. At Newark, as at Retford, the line passes over east-west routes between the north Midlands and Lincolnshire.

North of Retford, the train passes Scrooby, a small village where William Brewster, one of the leading Pilgrim Fathers, was born, and who worshipped at the local parish church with some of the other Pilgrim Fathers. There was once a station here, now long since closed, like all the other village halts on this line between Bedfordshire and Durham. Local stations and the unprofitable, slow-moving trains needed to serve them have been sacrificed to provide frequent high-speed, long distance services.

Doncaster has been an important railway centre since 1851, when the GNR decided to locate its locomotive and carriage works here. Jobs for 900 men became available as soon as the works opened in 1853, and by the end of the century there were erecting shops, carriage shops, repair shops and wagon shops stretching over 200 acres and providing work for more than 4,500 men. Some 3,000 staff are currently employed at the works, building the west-coast main line electric locomotives and most of BR's wagons, and carrying out overhauls. Just south of the station, the two freight yards, one on each side of the line, are all that remain of a much larger complex.

Industrial energy

The scrappy wasteland immediately north of Doncaster station signals a dramatic change of scenery. Gone is the pastoral landscape further south. In its place come vistas of collieries, pylons and, above all, power stations. The heart of the Yorkshire coalfield is not far to the west, and the presence of abundant coal and water supplies (the area is criss-crossed by rivers and canals) have made this flat rich farmland an ideal place to build the power stations needed to supply the factories and homes of the north. The

15

view of Bentley Colliery on the left and Thorpe Marsh power station on the right is quickly supplanted by two more huge power stations: Drax on the right and Eggborough on the left. Both are truly massive creations. Completed in 1986, Drax is Europe's largest coal-fired power station, with twelve cooling towers. It will burn 37,000 tons of coal every day and will have a total output of 4000 MW. Beyond Eggborough, in the far distance, a third power station, Ferrybridge, is usually visible. All three power stations get most of their coal by rail, though not via the east-coast main line. Special merry-go-round trains run a highly automated service from colliery to power station, transporting up to 1,000 tons of coal on each trip.

The line from Doncaster to York is not the original route opened in the 1840s. That went in roundabout fashion via Knottingley, some considerable way to the west, until a more direct line

(the technical term is a cut-off) was opened through Selby in 1871. Much of the cut-off was itself replaced in 1983 by a new 14-mile line, described by BR as 'the first totally new stretch of purpose-built 125 mph railway in the country', a few miles to the west. The cut-off ran directly over the new, and highly profitable and productive, Selby coalfield. If the line had remained where it was, either the National Coal Board would have had to leave unmined a mile-wide band of high-quality coal, or BR would have had to lower speeds and accept the risk of subsidence on a prestige main line. Neither option was acceptable. Instead, the NCB provided funds for a totally new line − which brought BR the added advantage of avoiding Selby swing bridge, where trains had to decelerate sharply. The new line required thirty-five structures to be built, including the twenty-six span Ryther viaduct over the river Wharfe.

The up and down platforms at York. Scissors junctions enabled two trains to be worked independently.

Extended in the 1900s, the up platform (number 4) was 1,692 feet long.

York's splendid train sheds from the north.

York

In the eyes of many the country's premier railway city, York is the home of the National Railway Museum, with its excellent collection of locomotives and rolling stock and displays on the development of railways. Here too are the Railway Headquarters Offices, built in 1906 for the NER, whose solid self-confident grandeur reflected contemporary faith in the apparently unchallengeable supremacy of the railways. But above all there is the station, the glorious station with its majestic arched roof (48 feet at its highest point), framed as you approach from the south by the city walls and the tower of the Minster behind. Inside, the principal platforms seem to curve away almost to eternity, and even when two or three expresses are loading and unloading passengers – each of the through platforms can accommodate two full-length trains with ease – they seem in perfect proportion. The splendour of the total conception is carried through to the smallest detail: for instance the iron ribs decorated with the NER monogram

and coat of arms. Recent sympathetic restoration has done much to revive the station's original atmosphere, which is enhanced when one of the BR's regular steam runs to Scarborough (see page 36) is waiting to depart.

The present York station, which opened in 1877, was built to replace a far smaller and less convenient predecessor which was sited within the city walls. This first station was built by the York & North Midland Railway as a terminus, which meant that all east-coast trains had to reverse out to continue their journey north.

That journey now leads virtually dead straight across the fertile Vale of York for 44 miles to Darlington. There is an excellent view back over the city, with the Minster and station standing out clearly, and the National Railway Museum is passed on the left. The Hambleton and Cleveland hills in the distance on the right form the western edge of the North York Moors, and the Kilburn white horse, cut in 1857, is clearly visible on Roulston Scar. Gliding is a popular sport round here.

Freight line

This is another fast stretch of line on which speed records have been set. It is also one of the sections of the east-coast route most used by freight services: in May 1984 an average of forty-five freight trains a day used the up line (that is towards London) and forty-two the down line (away from London). All manner of products are carried, often in company trains, including petrochemicals, cement, steel coils and billets, stone and fertilisers. BR runs regular, time-tabled Freightliner and Speedlink services along the entire east-coast route – one of Speedlink's regular customers is Rowntree's of York which despatches confectionery south by the ton – as well as special post and parcel trains.

Beyond Darlington, which boasts a fine station in characteristic NER style, a not especially interesting stretch of line with views of mining villages and moorland hills beyond brings the train to Durham. (Darlington's place in the history of railways is described on page 30.) The Norman cathedral and castle dominate the city, but the railway makes a dramatic impact too, striding across the river valley on a towering stone viaduct with ten arches: physical representations of two very different but equally self-confident faiths. The station at the far end of the viaduct was built in Tudor style but has been much altered.

From Durham there is a short run through mining countryside to the Newcastle suburbs. The route between Ferryhill, some way south of Durham, and Gateshead is another substantial cut-off, opened in two stages in 1868 and 1872.

Newcastle bridges

The approach to Newcastle is dramatic. Since 1905, east-coast main-line trains have normally used the 1,150-foot long King Edward VII Bridge, threading their way slowly across and swinging right to enter the station. Before that date, the only rail crossing of the Tyne was Robert Stephenson's High Level Bridge, just downstream of the later crossing – to the right if you are travelling from the south. Three railway tracks are carried on the upper deck, which is supported on the crowns of three arched cast-iron girders. Horizontal wrought-iron strings below tie the girders to the abutments and carry the lower deck, which has a 20-foot roadway and two 6-foot walkways. Stephenson devoted a great deal of thought and experiment to the design of the bridge. Had he been working a few years later, he might well have used wrought-iron for the girders rather than the more brittle cast-iron (several cast-iron girder bridges, one of them designed by Stephenson, collapsed at about this time), but in the late 1840s he still preferred the older material. That the bridge still stands, and carries a far greater volume of traffic, both rail and road, than Stephenson can ever have envisaged, is a tribute to his skill as an engineer. As one contemporary observer wrote, 'The multiplicity of column-ribs, transverse and vertical braces produces a combination of beautiful lines seldom seen.'

Queen Victoria travelled north with Prince Albert to open the High Level Bridge in September 1849. Almost a year later, on 29 August 1850, she returned to the city to open

Robert Stephenson's handsome Royal Border Bridge across the Tweed at Berwick.

An HST threads its way out of the east end of
Newcastle station. The tracks leading to the left
turn south and cross the Tyne on Stephenson's
High Level Bridge.

Newcastle Central station. Outcry and a public enquiry would have greeted the plans for the station had they been published in the 1980s rather than the 1840s, for Robert Stephenson, engineer to the York, Newcastle & Berwick Railway, and the celebrated Newcastle architect John Dobson destroyed part of the medieval city to make space for the lines. These ran directly past the castle, built in the twelfth and thirteenth centuries, which now stands isolated between two sets of tracks at the eastern end of the station. Whatever may have been lost, it cannot be gainsaid that the new building makes a spectacular contribution to railway architecture.

Newcastle Central station

Newcastle Central was the first of the grand stations of the north-east. According to one modern architectural historian, it was 'the earliest station roof where round-arched ribs were used, by themselves, to form the framework spanning the main spaces'. There are three train sheds, and the through tracks are spanned by an attractive footbridge. The street façade consists of an impressive classical portico, built in about 1860 by Thomas Prosser. Had Dobson's original plans been carried through, the entrance would have been yet more striking still, but when construction was well underway the railway's directors decided to move their headquarters south to York.

Although the main line runs north-south through Newcastle, the station was built on an east-west axis parallel with the Tyne. As a result, main-line expresses had to reverse out of the station until King Edward VII Bridge was built, when the tracks north and south of the river were linked to form a circle. This eased traffic-handling problems, especially in steam days when light engine and empty stock movements had to be fitted in between the main-line and suburban services. All the latter have now been taken over by the Tyne and Wear Metro, which can be seen as the Edinburgh express gathers speed through the northern suburbs.

After some fairly nondescript countryside, the line brushes the coast at Alnmouth, where there is a fine view of the river Alne winding towards the sea, runs inland again for a few miles, and re-emerges near the beach a little way past Bamburgh Castle. There are excellent views from the train of Holy Island, and in particular of the castle that rears up at the southernmost tip. The castle was built in about 1500 and restored at the beginning of this century by Sir Edwin Lutyens. Holy Island itself looks flat and uninteresting from the mainland, and successfully conceals its magic. Some of the earliest Christian missionaries to England founded a monastery on Holy Island or Lindisfarne, and painstakingly set down the beautiful Lindisfarne Gospels, now in the British Museum.

The view down the Tyne of Robert Stephenson's cast iron High Level Bridge from the King Edward VII Bridge, taken in the days when Newcastle was a flourishing port.

A down Flying Scotsman *thunders through Sandy in Bedfordshire one morning between the two World Wars. From 1928, the* Flying Scotsman *ran non-stop from King's Cross to Edinburgh.*

Berwick-upon-Tweed

The approach to Berwick, a few miles further on, is one of the highlights of the journey north from London. The train slows to negotiate a sharp curve, and stretched out in front of you is Robert Stephenson's magnificent Royal Border Bridge: 2,160 feet long, with twenty-eight arches 126 feet high and each with a span of 61½ feet. L. T. C. Rolt, distinguished transport historian and author of a masterly biography of George and Robert Stephenson, has written:

> Although there is nothing unique about it from an engineering point of view, there is no more romantic and evocative railway structure in the world . . . . He who would measure imaginatively the magnitude of the Stephensons' achievement and seek to recapture something of the triumph and the wonder of that heroic age of engineering, should stand upon the ruined castle keep at Berwick and gaze down that long, proud perspective of slender stone piers as the Flying Scotsman thunders across the water.

Having opened the station at Newcastle, Queen Victoria came north along the stretch of line just described to open the Royal Border Bridge, and then proceeded in the royal train to Holyrood.

What remained of Berwick Castle after the engineers and navvies of the North British Railway had smashed their way through the twelfth-century Great Hall can be seen to the left of the station, which is immediately at the north end of the bridge. Now there is another coastal stretch with deserted sandy beaches – some of the best in the country – and seagulls swooping overhead. The view at dawn from the window of the night train north is magical, as the first shafts of sunlight strike through the morning mist. The line turns inland at Burnmouth to cut across the edge of the rolling Lammermuir Hills. Shortly before the coast is regained near Cockburnspath there is a half-mile stretch of new track laid after Penmanshiel tunnel collapsed killing two men during relining work in 1979. Rather than try to re-open the tunnel, it was decided to bypass it completely; the new line took only five months to plan and build, during which time all services were diverted via the west-coast route.

The line continues along the coast through Dunbar, turns inland through rich and fertile agricultural land, and regains the coast for the last time near Cockenzie power station. Cockenzie was the destination of the first Scottish 'railway' – a wagonway built in 1722 to convey coal from the mines at Tranent, two miles inland, to the harbour at Cockenzie. The loaded wagons ran over the wooden rails down to the sea by gravity, and were hauled back by horses. Bass Rock, the small islet at the entrance to the Firth of Forth that was once used as a prison and is now a bird sanctuary, is clearly visible on the right, with the hills of Fife behind it. On the hills to the left stands a monument erected in 1824 to the 4th Earl of Hopetoun.

The first sight of Edinburgh is the bare mass of Arthur's Seat, an 822-foot volcanic hill, looming ahead, followed by Calton Hill and, on it, the National Monument and Nelson Monument. The train dives into Calton tunnels and emerges in Waverley station, sandwiched between the Old and New Towns directly beneath the castle. The present building dates from the 1890s and replaced an earlier, far less convenient structure opened in the 1840s. It has been extensively and successfully modernized, – a suitable gateway to Scotland.

Carlisle to Newcastle

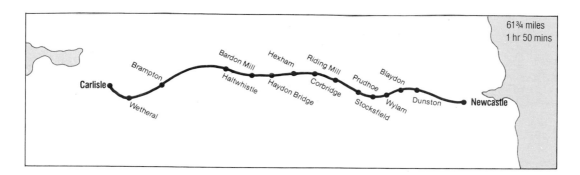

61¾ miles
1 hr 50 mins

Carlisle • Wetheral • Brampton • Haltwhistle • Bardon Mill • Haydon Bridge • Hexham • Corbridge • Riding Mill • Stocksfield • Prudhoe • Wylam • Blaydon • Dunston • Newcastle

This fine line across the roof of England has a long history. Authorized by Parliament as early as 1829, it was originally intended to be worked by horses. Construction was delayed, however, and by the time the entire route was completed in 1838 the directors of the Newcastle & Carlisle Railway had invested in two brand new steam locomotives, *Wellington* and *Napoleon*.

The line was the first to reach both of its terminus cities, preceding the main lines north by several years, and was for a time entirely isolated from the rapidly growing rail network elsewhere in the country. It also had the distinction of being the first line to cross the country virtually from coast to coast.

The route occupies another historical niche. One of the railway's early employees was a clerk named Thomas Edmondson, who, tiring of the laborious business of filling out a separate form to give to each passenger and inscribing the details of their destination in a company record book, devised a system of card tickets, a rack to hold them and a stamp to date them. This same ticket system has prevailed until the introduc-

tion of computerized ticketing in the 1980s. Edmundson moved to the Manchester & Leeds soon after on a higher salary, before setting up his own ticket-printing business.

Swinging east from the main line just south of Carlisle station, the train heads north-east and then east at the start of a long and quite steep climb towards the summit at Naworth. The first station is Wetheral, closed in 1967 but reopened in 1981. At the far end of the station the line runs directly on to Wetheral viaduct, which crosses the river Eden in five spans 80 feet wide and 95 feet high. Two more equally impressive viaducts, also built from the local Eden valley sandstone, follow before the train reaches the next station at Brampton.

The landscape is magnificent. To the left (i.e. north) of the carriage window is a pleasant, fertile and green land, with a church spire half-hidden in the trees. Only the high hills on the distant horizon provide a reminder that this is border country. In centuries past, raiding Picts and Scots swept down from the hills to loot and plunder this idyllic land.

Street House, Robert and Mabel Stephenson's cottage at Wylam, Northumberland, where their second child

George was born on 9 June 1781. Chaldron wagons ran along the wooden wagonway in front.

Wylam station towards the eastern end of the route. The Newcastle & Carlisle station house on the down line remains, but a new up platform has been built on the near side of the level crossing.

Hadrian's Wall

Beyond Brampton the hills begin to come closer. The train passes Naworth castle, built in the early part of the fourteenth century and restored after a fire in the 1840s, on the left, before reaching the ruins of Thirlwall castle, built in the middle of the same century using stone taken from Hadrian's Wall. Between Greenhead and Haltwhistle the watershed is crossed, and the Tyne is a constant companion as the line begins the gentle descent towards the east coast.

The stations on this line are thought to have been built by a Newcastle architect called Benjamin Green. A good number have survived remarkably unscathed, and are, according to one architectural historian, 'probably the oldest series [of stations] retaining most of their original features that now exist in close proximity'. Haltwhistle is an excellent example, built in a semi-Tudor style and set well back from the tracks, with the attractive arched footbridge that characterizes this line. Beyond Bardon Mill — where it is nice to see that the mill is still in operation — there are three viaducts in close succession, and views over beautifully-kept gardens which, in late summer, are full of large, ripe vegetables, ready to eat.

Hexham is a natural stopping-place if you want to break your journey. There is an excellent

The nine-arch Lambley viaduct over the South Tyne on the now closed Alston to Haltwhistle branch.

view of the abbey, built between the twelfth and fifteenth centuries, as the train enters the station. It contains beautiful medieval carvings and Roman and Anglo-Saxon treasures, and the town is pleasant to explore, with good shops and a Moot Hall. Hadrian's Wall explorers either leave the train further west, at Haltwhistle, or continue beyond Hexham to Corbridge. At Gilsland, west of Greenhead station, the line was driven through a milecastle on the Wall, resulting in considerable damage to the site. Later excavations revealed extensive Roman remains, including coins.

George Stephenson's cottage

East of Hexham, the scenery loses its drama, with lower, more gentle hills and frequent patches of woodland. Wylam, the last country station before the train reaches the Tyneside conurbation, has a central place in railway history. Here, on 9 June 1781, George Stephenson was born, and grew up in a little cottage alongside the wooden Wylam wagonway, not far from the present railway. It was on this wagonway, by then relaid with cast-iron rails, that thirty-two years later William Hedley ran his first successful locomotive, *Puffing Billy*.

Beyond Blaydon, home of the celebrated races, the Tyne becomes an industrial river, and the fields give way to power stations and slag heaps, tower blocks, terraced houses, and derelict wasteland. The line drops a little way south of the river, before turning north to join the east-coast main line just before it crosses the King Edward VII Bridge (see page 18) and enters Newcastle station.

Clouds of steam as a train leaves Newcastle Central. Compare with late twentieth-century view on page 19.

Above: *The lofty signal box with its elegantly curved brackets dominates Haltwhistle station.*

Below: *Carlisle Citadel, built in 1847 for the Lancaster & Carlisle and Caledonian Railways.*

Stockton to Darlington and Shildon

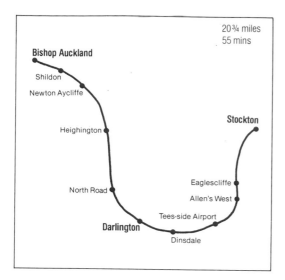

For decades the Stockton & Darlington was considered to be the 'first railway': the idea from which developed, in so remarkably short a time, the entire national system. In recent years, however, transport historians have shifted their attention both forwards and backwards: forwards five years from 1825 to the Liverpool & Manchester (see page 94), backwards to the network of rail routes that had already existed in north-east England for many decades before the 1820s.

The realization that running loaded wagons along rails was an efficient and easy means of transport was not new. Coal from the mines of Durham and Northumberland had long been transported in this way to the harbours and ports along the rivers and coast, at first along wooden wagonways, later along stronger and more stable cast-iron tracks. Nor, by the early nineteenth century, was the concept of steam power a novel one. Stationary steam engines had been in use for the best part of a century, and the first steam locomotives built by such pioneers as William Hedley and Richard Trevithick were already making fitful progress.

The directors of the Stockton & Darlington built a public railway. Other wagonways and tramways were private lines, only serving one company's collieries. But the S & D was open to the public: anyone could have their goods transported along the railways, either in their own wagon or in one of the company's wagons, on payment of the appropriate charge.

Note the word 'goods'. The S & D was not planned as a passenger-carrying line. Passengers were literally an afterthought, and indeed, until 1833 and except on the inaugural train, passengers rode in horse-drawn coaches provided by outside contractors.

Coal transport

The principal purpose of the line was to transport coal from the coalfields of south-west Durham around Shildon and Bishop Auckland to the Tees at Stockton. Since there were no waterways in the area, horses had to be used, and as a result the coal cost considerably more than coal from competing pits with better lines of communication. For some time there was doubt in the promoters' minds about whether a canal

John Dobbins' painting of the opening day of the Stockton & Darlington Railway, 27 September 1825.

Locomotion No. 1 *draws the first train across the bridge (which still stands) over the Skerne.*

A steam special run in connection with the 150th anniversary of the S & D passes Newton Aycliffe, hauled by Class B1 4–6–0 No. 1306 Mayflower and Class A3 No. 4472 Flying Scotsman.

or a railway should be built. Eventually the decision in favour of a railway was made, and George Stephenson was employed to survey the route.

As built, the line ran for some 25 miles from Witton Park Colliery 5 miles north-west of Shildon, through Darlington (which was never a terminus, despite the name of the railway) to Stockton. The westernmost portion of the line consisted of the Etherley and Brusselton inclines: two ascents and two descents with a 1½-mile level stretch between each incline. Wagons were hauled up and down by rope from a winding-engine at the top of each incline, and were attached to a locomotive at Shildon, at the foot of the Brusselton incline.

The branch to Bishop Auckland is a dead end, so today visitors who arrive by train must approach the area from the 'wrong' direction, from the coast. (The weight of freight traffic on the S & D throughout its life was in one direction only, away from the coalfields towards the coast.) One of the most interesting ways of reaching the area is to take the coastal route from Newcastle south through Sunderland, Seaham and Hartlepool. The line runs directly along the shore, with fine views out to sea and of the chemical plants as the train nears Tees-side.

The present-day line from Stockton to Darlington picks up the original route of the S & D at Eaglescliffe station and stays with it for about the next 4 miles, past Tees-side Airport as far as Oak Tree Junction, just before Dinsdale station. The landscape is flat and uninteresting, stretching out south to the Cleveland Hills and, in the very far distant west, the Pennine range. Parts of the original line into Stockton can still be traced. In the town, near St. John's Crossing where the first rail was laid, a building generally thought to have been the first railway ticket office has since been converted into a small railway museum.

Freight line

No stations were built to serve the line. Indeed, why should they have been, when carrying freight was its primary purpose, and horse-drawn passenger coaches could, and did, stop almost anywhere to pick up passengers? Inns were popular stopping-places.

The present-day line runs into Darlington Bank Top station, where it is normally necessary to change for the Bishop Auckland branch. Built in 1887, the station is a handsome building, with three light and airy train sheds; each has a semi-circular roof supported inside on elegant iron columns. One large island platform was provided, with several bays for local services, so that all the amenities could be grouped together, and internal bridges and subways were unnecessary.

The original route of the S & D ran north of Bank Top station, and the present line rejoins it shortly before entering North Road station.

Before S & D trains were diverted into Bank Top, they crossed the main line at a level crossing. It must have been amazing to see the east- or west-bound trains threading their way at right angles directly across the north-south tracks of the main line! The rest of the journey to Shildon runs along the original course of the line.

The earliest part of North Road station dates from 1842, although it was later extended on several occasions. The single platform at which the train stops is dirty and unwelcoming, with the walls covered in graffiti, but the other side of the building is a complete contrast. The station buildings have been carefully restored, and now house the Darlington Railway Museum, where *Locomotion*, the locomotive built by Robert Stephenson & Co. of Newcastle and which hauled the S & D's inaugural train, is on display, as well as an early S & D coach and many other interesting exhibits. Unlike many of his contemporaries, Robert Stephenson was both a civil and a mechanical engineer; while he spent much time surveying, planning and supervising the construction of new lines, he never lost interest in his locomotive construction company.

Heighington and Shildon

Out into the unexciting countryside, the train passes the Whiley Hill Crossing House on the right just beyond a level crossing. The building carries a plaque numbered G1 and was one of the houses the Railway built to accommodate its employees. Then, almost immediately, comes Heighington station, originally known as Aycliffe Lane Crossing. *Locomotion* was set on the tracks here when it first arrived from Newcastle, a week or two before inauguration day. On the right the little cottage now converted into a restaurant is the original booking office and accommodation for the railway clerk and his family. In front of it, at ground level and not raised as modern platforms are, a small section of the original cobbled platform is preserved.

Shildon, two stations on, was the S & D's original operations centre. Timothy Hackworth, the engineer who had been responsible for building *Locomotion* in Newcastle, moved here in 1826 to open the Railway's first repair and maintenance workshops on his appointment as Manager and Engineer to the S & D. These were on the site of what later became British Rail's Shildon Works (see below). Seven years after, the Company gave Hackworth permission to open his own locomotive construction works, while keeping his post with the S & D. These were the Soho Works, a couple of hundred yards from the present station and diagonally opposite Hackworth's attractive cottage.

Both cottage and Works are open to the public, and are well worth a visit. The cottage is furnished as it was when the Hackworths lived there, and also contains displays on local mining and on the later history of the line. The Works,

Above: *Timothy Hackworth's Soho works at Shildon as they were in 1945.*

Below: *George Stephenson's* Locomotion No. 1, *the first of four locomotives bought for the line in 1825.*

not much more than a large barn in size, contain a modern replica of *Sans Pareil*, Hackworth's unsuccessful entry in the Rainhill Trails (see page 96); a chaldron wagon of the type used to transport coal and other minerals on the S & D network (by the time the S & D was absorbed into the North Eastern Railway it owned lines as far apart as Penrith, Saltburn and Consett); and a dandy wagon – the cart that ran behind a horse-drawn train and into which the horse jumped on downhill stretches.

Locomotive works

As the S & D extended its network and traffic grew on the east-coast main line, Darlington developed in importance. The S & D moved its locomotive works there, Robert Stephenson & Co. moved down from Newcastle towards the end of the nineteenth century, and in the present century British Rail built a large number of steam and diesel locomotives in its Darlington workshops.

Nevertheless, Shildon remained very much a railway town. The Soho Works closed in 1883, but by that time the Shildon Works Company, later to become part of British Rail, was already operating. Although locomotives continued to be repaired at Shildon until 1971, the works specialized in constructing and repairing freight wagons. There were some 500 workers employed at the Works in 1894, no less than 3,400 in 1956 and 2,600 in the early 1980s. In 1982, British Rail announced its intention of closing down the Works, even though Shildon was recognized as an extremely efficient plant, and achieved regular increases in productivity.

The principal reason: surplus capacity in relation to demand. The problem was partly due to the development of custom-built wagons for specialist loads capable of high speeds, in place of the old, slow box-cars on wheels which would take almost any type of freight. Another reason was the growth of private wagon-builders who benefit from financial incentives not available to British Rail. Despite a bitter and concerted fight to maintain the Works, and the formulation of a well-researched plan to develop its full potential, in 1984 BR got its way and the Works was closed, with a loss of 86 per cent of the town's male manufacturing jobs.

Several walks have been planned round Shildon to show visitors sites of industrial and historical interest; details are available from the museum. One leads past the now-deserted BR works up the Brusselton incline. It is a fine walk, with good views of distant hills. The engine-man's house, with its S & D numbered plaque, stands at the top of the original incline, and stone sleepers can still be seen set in the ground to the side of the path.

Locomotives at the Shildon Steam Parade. Railways were once Shildon's life blood, but today the tracks to the now deserted Locomotive Works have been uprooted and the building stand forlorn.

View through the elegant and airy three-span overall roof of Darlington Bank Top station, constructed in 1887, on the east coast main line.

North Yorkshire Moors Railway

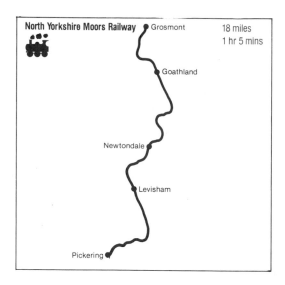

North Yorkshire Moors Railway

Grosmont

18 miles
1 hr 5 mins

Goathland

Newtondale

Levisham

Pickering

The North Yorkshire Moors line is magnificent, cutting straight across the North York Moors National Park through some of the most wild and splendid scenery that can be found on any preserved line. The line begins at Grosmont, where there are connections with the Esk Valley service, and then climbs sharply up onto the moors. At 1 in 49, the gradient is one of the steepest of any line in the country. Running across the moors, past the sinister radomes of the Fylingdales Ballistic Missile Early Warning System, the train encounters a variety of terrain: marshland, tracts of thick Forestry Commission woodland, and long stretches of purple heather that provide food and shelter for sheep and grouse. There are many excellent walks across the moors from the intermediate stations at Goathland, Newtondale (a new halt opened in 1981 to give walkers access to Newtondale Gorge) and Levisham. The final stretch is a slow descent from the moors into a more gentle land around Pickering, where the castle, originally erected in the late eleventh century but much extended, dominates the town.

In the 1820s, the citizens of Whitby wanted a railway to overcome their town's isolation. George Stephenson was called in, and he recommended the route west along the Esk to Grosmont and then south to Pickering. Today, this second section running south from Grosmont is operated by the North Yorkshire Moors Railway, while the line fron Whitby through Grosmont and on to Middlesbrough is run by British Rail (see page 34).

Ascent by water tank
Although steam locomotives were already proving themselves on regular services elsewhere in the country, for the first eleven years

LNER 2–6–0 K1 No. 200S pulls a train through Newton Dale, one of the most attractive spots on the line.

Southern Railway migrant in a northern setting: 4–6–0 No. 841 Greene King, *built in 1936, hauls a southbound train from Grosmont, where the North Yorkshire Moors Railway meets BR's Esk Valley line.*

after the line opened in 1836 horses provided the motive power. One of the principal reasons for this was the steep 1 in 10 ascent from Beck Hole to Goathland, which proved too steep for either horses or locomotives to conquer. A mile-long rope-worked incline was built. Ascending coaches were hauled up by a descending tank full of water. For the return trip the tank was emptied and pulled up by the descending coaches. However eccentric it may seem today, when the line was opened this mode of transport seems to have met with approbation. The railway's treasurer wrote of the first day of operations:

> On the signal being given three carriages loaded with passengers glided up the steep ascent with a pleasing, rapid, and easy pace; and both on going and returning many were heard to declare that the ascending and descending of the incline so far from being in any way disagreeable, was certainly as pleasant as any other part of the day's journey.

Later, a steam-powered stationary engine was installed.

In 1845, George Hudson's York & North Midland Railway took over the Whitby & Pickering line, and set about converting it to steam. This involved building an entirely new route from the floor of the Esk Valley past Beck Hole and Goathland to Moorgates high on the moor. Steam trains started to run from Whitby to Beck Hole and Pickering to Goathland two years later, but the old rope-worked incline remained in use until 1865. From Goathland there is a fascinating waymarked walk along the track-bed of Stephenson's original line, finishing at the modern railway's engine sheds at its Grosmont terminus.

In the late nineteenth century the railway moved 20,000 to 30,000 tons of roadstone from mines high on the moors every year. Remains of one working – including mineshafts, a gunpowder store and the course of railway sidings – are visible near the incline, and another tramway led down to the railway at Goathland. Further south, near Levisham station, iron was smelted in the Middle Ages, and on the moors nearby an ancient iron 'bloomery' dating back to about 100 BC has been discovered.

For decades the railway was a lifeline to the moors, especially in hard winters, when trains provided the only means of getting through the snow. But, for Dr. Beeching and those who ran the railways in the early 1960s, profitability was what mattered, even in this remote and sometimes savage part of the world, and the line between Grosmont and Pickering was closed in 1965. It reopened as the North Yorkshire Moors Railway in 1973, and now operates both steam- and diesel-powered services.

Middlesbrough to Whitby: the Esk Valley Line

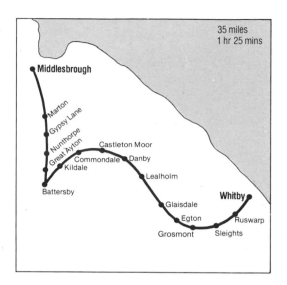

35 miles
1 hr 25 mins

Middlesbrough
Marton
Gypsy Lane
Nunthorpe
Great Ayton
Castleton Moor
Commondale · Danby
Kildale
Lealholm
Battersby
Whitby
Glaisdale
Egton
Ruswarp
Grosmont · Sleights

This line is one of the loveliest in England. After an industrial start in Middlesbrough (where the iron pointed-arch station roof was destroyed by bombs during the Second World War, although the fine iron columns with lovely swirling patterns remain), the train heads out past docks and across a narrow plain of wheatfields towards the hills of the North York Moors. The moors are the constant theme of the journey almost all the way to Whitby. The line occupies the valley of the river Esk, which cuts directly across the moors from west to east. Rugged, brown hillsides with a few fields at the lower levels climb up from the line, especially to the south, and there are good walks across the moors from almost every station, with miles of fine hilltop routes as soon as the summit is reached. The valley, by contrast, is softer and greener, the river leaping over waterfalls past unspoilt villages built from the local stone.

At first the line seems to be making straight for a single, somewhat isolated, peak known as Roseberry Topping (1,057 feet). Passing slightly to the west, it runs through Great Ayton, where Captain James Cook went to school. The schoolroom is now a small museum, but the cottage in which the explorer was brought up has been moved to Australia. The Cook monument can be seen on the top of Easby Moor above the line.

Moorland route

The present route to Whitby is all that survives of a quite large network of lines in the area. The section as far as Nunthorpe belonged to one company, the Middlesbrough & Guisborough, while the next five miles were opened in the 1860s as a connecting link by the North Yorkshire & Cleveland, which also operated the present line as far as Castleton. The Castleton to Grosmont section was planned as early as 1846, but was not opened by the NER until 1865.

LNER 2–6–0 K1 No. 2005 hauls a steam excursion through attractive moorland around Glaisdale.

Arriving and departing diesel multiple units at Whitby. The lovely harbour is to the right of the line.

Battersby was also the junction with one of the north-east's most unusual routes, if not one of the most unusual in the whole country. The 11-mile line to the Rosedale ironstone mines led across one of the wildest parts of the moors; in addition, the scarp slope had to be climbed at one of its steepest points. Here the solution was the Ingleby Incline, with an incredible maximum gradient of 1 in 5! The incline was operated from a drumhouse at the top, where a brakeman controlled the speed of the loaded descending wagons and the empty ascending ones. The line opened in 1861 and remained in operation until 1928. Much of it is now a footpath, and the layout of the incline can be seen.

North Yorkshire Moors Railway

The railway runs through Kildale and Commondale, following a small stream that joins the Esk at Castleton Moor. It continues through Danby, where Danby Lodge houses the North York Moors National Park Centre. At Glaisdale the road crosses the river over a lovely packhorse bridge right by the station; for ten years from 1866 an ironworks here produced enough to keep three blast furnaces busy. Between here and Egmont, the line hugs the river, running through a narrow gorge.

Grosmont is the junction with the North Yorkshire Moors Railway (see page 32): the

platforms of this preserved line are next to those used by the BR trains. The line from here to Whitby was part of the Whitby & Pickering Railway. It was opened in 1836, and worked by horses until as late as 1847.

The train provides an important lifeline for all the villages along the Esk Valley route. In winter, when the roads are impassable, it is often the only means of communication. Around Sleights the hills become lower and less wild, and the river begins to widen. Nevertheless, the characteristic moorland feel of the line remains until past Ruswarp, the final intermediate station. Quite suddenly, the train then rounds a bend to give a magnificent view of the thirteen arches of the Larpool viaduct, towering 125 feet above the river. The viaduct was erected in 1885 to carry the now-closed Scarborough & Whitby Railway (which has been made into a 'Trailway' for walkers).

The scenery now changes rapidly. The hills and moors have gone, almost as if they never were, and the line runs past fishing boats moored in the estuary, with good views ahead to Whitby Abbey, perched high on a headland overlooking the sea, and harbour and seaside smells all around. Whitby station is an attractive building, even though its overall roof has gone, but its tile map of the North Eastern Railway network and elegant classical façade still remain.

Steam from York

Steam from York

complete trip	106 miles	3 hrs 37 mins
York to Leeds via Harrogate	38¼ miles	1 hr 15 mins
York to Scarborough	42 miles	55 mins

Scarborough
Seamer
Malton
Knaresborough
Harrogate
York
Leeds

Having in the 1960s renounced steam whole-heartedly and, so it seemed at the time, for ever, British Rail took a good while to rediscover the simple – and potentially very profitable – fact that people, ordinary people and not merely steam buffs, really do enjoy travelling behind a steam locomotive. Now that the light has dawned, BR runs a few steam-hauled excursions on a regular timetable each summer, as well as allowing preservation and enthusiasts' societies to organize their own trips.

One of BR's regular steam excursions is from York to Scarborough. As if to prove the point that on a steam journey these days the travelling is better than the arriving, the route followed is extremely circuitous. Leaving York, the train heads first west and south through Harrogate to Leeds, and then returns to York via the main line before tackling the 42-mile stretch north-east to Scarborough. The return journey in the evening follows the same route in reverse. Both lines, York to Leeds via Harrogate and York to Scarborough, are well worth travelling in any case, even if you are unable to take one of the steam excursions.

LMS 4–6–2 No. 4269 Duchess of Hamilton *waits to head a steam excursion out of York station.*

York to Leeds via Harrogate

The branch line swings west from the main east-coast route a couple of miles north of York station (see page 17) and heads straight across the fertile Vale of York towards Knaresborough, giving good views back of York Minster and the fine station roof. The line crosses the river Nidd just before Hammerton station, and again at Knaresborough.

Knaresborough station is situated in a deep cutting, from which the train emerges straight on to a splendid four-arch viaduct. Looking back, you can see the steep streets of the town climbing up from the river bank to the thirteenth- and fourteenth-century parish church. The viaduct fits the scene perfectly, right down to its castellated parapet, even though it has been in place for only 140 years.

The attractive station at Harrogate has received many thousands of visitors who came to take the waters, and is still busy, welcoming many conference and convention guests each year. After Harrogate, the train reaches a magnificent piece of railway architecture: Crimple viaduct, for which alone the journey would be worth while. The viaduct is 624 yards long, with thirty-one arches, the highest rising to 110 feet. Unlike many viaducts and bridges, you get an idea of its splendour even as you cross it; the view back from the train a few minutes later, when there is the chance to appreciate its well-proportioned beauty, is also not to be missed.

The lines of two separate railway companies crossed at Crimple. The trains of the York & North Midland Railway ran across the viaduct; underneath, alongside the tiny Crimple beck, passed the trains of the Leeds & Thirsk line, which eventually ran from Leeds through Thirsk and Northallerton to Stockton. At first there was no junction between the two, but later a connecting line was built which swings to the right immediately it is across the viaduct and descends steeply to the Wharfe valley. It is this route which the train follows today.

Between Knaresborough and Leeds only the viaduct and a short stretch of the present line through Harrogate were not originally part of the Leeds & Thirsk line, which opened in 1849. From York to Knaresborough the line was opened in 1848 by the York, Newcastle & Berwick Railway, which was taken over by the York & Midland Railway in 1851, when through running on to the Leeds & Thirsk's line at Knaresborough began.

The line crosses the river Wharfe and its wide valley on a series of embankments and another handsome viaduct. Then it climbs steeply and runs into a deep cutting. At the far end is the magnificent entrance to Bramhope tunnel: two castellated towers, the left taller than the right, with a battlemented parapet joining them. The tunnel, 2 miles 241 yards long, was extremely troublesome to construct. Water poured in constantly (an estimated 1,563 million gallons had to be pumped out) and accidents were numerous. A memorial to the twenty-three men killed during construction was put up in Otley churchyard nearby in the shape of the north portal of the tunnel. The rest of the journey into Leeds is an uneventful one crossing the river Aire and the Leeds & Liverpool Canal.

LNWR 2–4–0 No. 790 Hardwicke *pilots Midland Compound No. 1000 on a special from York to* Carnforth *over Knaresborough viaduct crossing high above the river Nidd.*

The splendid north portal of Bramhope tunnel through the hills north of Leeds.

York to Scarborough

The line from York reached Scarborough in July 1845 (it was built by Hudson's York & North Midland), and had a rapid effect on the fortunes of this little fishing port. Visitors came in increasing numbers, and the town developed into a major resort, 'the queen of watering places'. Almost 330,000 passengers used Scarborough station in 1905, and on summer Saturdays especially the route from York was packed with special trains. On August Bank Holiday Saturday 1939, for instance, there were no less than 102 arrivals and 106 departures, and the numerous day and half-day excursions run by the railway had to be scheduled for the Sunday.

While the main line swings north-west from York station, the Scarborough route runs north-east across a flat plain towards the eastern end of the Howardian hills. The original idea of tunnelling through the hills to the river Derwent was abandoned, and instead the line meets the river west of Kirkham and follows it on an extremely twisty course as far as Malton. There is an excellent view of Kirkham Priory on the opposite bank; the Priory was founded in 1125 but most of the remains date from the following century. From Malton the line runs across the wide Derwent valley to Seamer, where there is a junction with the line from Hull and Bridlington, and thence into Scarborough.

The stations and other buildings along this line were all built by an associate of George Hudson, the architect George Townsend Andrews. A good number survive today, though many of the smaller ones are in private ownership, since all the intermediate stations except Malton and Seamer were closed in 1930, at least partly because of the difficulty of timetabling local services into a heavy schedule of long-distance traffic. Kirkham Abbey, Castle Howard, Huttons Ambo and Malton are all built of local stone, and Malton has an overall roof. Castle Howard was the station for the celebrated country house of the same name 2½ miles away. Queen Victoria used the station when she spent two nights at the house in the summer of 1850, *en route* to open Newcastle Central station and the Royal Border Bridge (see page 18).

Scarborough station must have been Andrews' pride, and no doubt Hudson's as well. Unlike many other large stations in the north-east (York and Darlington, for instance) it was never rebuilt, although it was enlarged to nine platforms as traffic increased. The famous clock tower was erected in 1884; the railway agreed to pay for an illuminated clock, which cost £15 above budget, if the Corporation would supply free gas to light it. The original trainshed and offices remain in use but four of the platforms have been demolished and the land sold for a supermarket development. The return of steam to Scarborough has resulted in the installation of a turntable, partly financed by Scarborough District Council, which is also contributing to the refurbishing of the world steam record-breaker, *Mallard*.

LNER 4–6–2 No. 4472 Flying Scotsman *heads a steam excursion out of Scarborough station.*

'West Country' Pacific No. 34092 City of Wells *hauls the Scarborough Spa Express through wheatfields near* Selby *on the second leg of its regular York-Leeds-Scarborough trip.*

LNER 2–6–0 No. 20051, built in 1949, steams through the lovely scenery past Kirkham Abbey.

London to Norwich

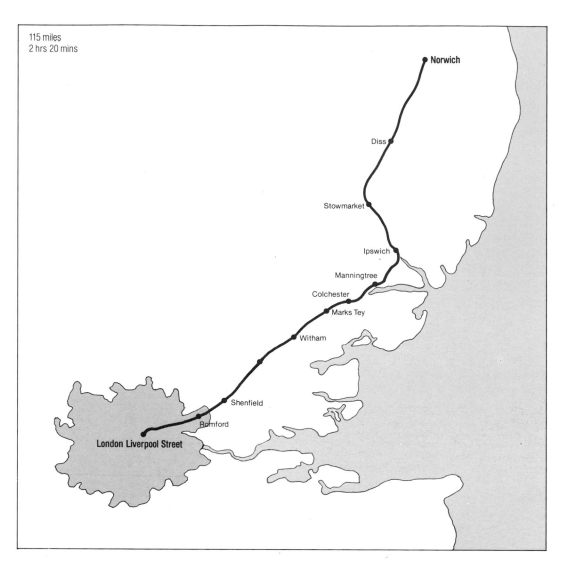

115 miles
2 hrs 20 mins

Norwich

Diss

Stowmarket

Ipswich

Manningtree

Colchester

Marks Tey

Witham

Shenfield

Romford

London Liverpool Street

Aerial view of Liverpool and Broad Street stations before the current redevelopment began. The twin train *sheds of Broad Street are on the left next to the large car park.*

The Norwich trains leave from Liverpool Street, where, during the rush hour, the whole station is thronged with people commuting between home in London's eastern and north-eastern suburbs and City offices. For many decades Liverpool Street was London's busiest station, although it has since been overtaken by Waterloo. In the early 1920s, well over 30,000 people an hour passed through Liverpool Street at peak times, and not far short of 250,000 people used the station every day. The suburban services – nicknamed 'Jazz' trains – were probably the most intensively worked in the world, and no less than 51 left between 5 p.m. and 6 p.m. each evening.

The original terminus opened in 1840 was called Bishopsgate, although it was in fact in Shoreditch, a pretty unsalubrious part of

Manningtree station on the Great Eastern line between Colchester and Ipswich in 1911.

LONDON TO NORWICH

London. Liverpool Street was planned more than 30 years later, in an attempt to bring the Great Eastern Railway nearer to the City and to develop suburban traffic. The original western trainshed opened in two stages in 1874 and 1875; the Great Eastern Hotel went up in 1884 and the eastern trainshed ten years later. All but two of the platforms, 9 and 10, were devoted to suburban traffic.

Even after a number of improvement programmes, Liverpool Street has remained a pleasing and idiosyncratic station. The footbridge winds erratically above the platforms, a relic of the days when platforms 9 and 10 extended into the depths of the Hotel basement and the way round them was even longer than it is now. Two charming little pseudo-Regency tea houses project from the footbridge. One is now used as offices, but at the other you can still find refreshment, though perhaps not in the style to which Edwardian travellers were accustomed. The western trainshed is the finer. Not awe-inspiring, like the one at St. Pancras, nor merely functional, as at King's Cross, it is by contrast delicate and welcoming in its effect. The four 76-foot high iron and glass spans are supported by double rows of cast-iron columns with frilly decorations, repeated on the staircases.

In the major redevelopment of the station which began in 1985, the western trainshed and the hotel will be preserved: a welcome reversal of a horrific plan put forward by BR in the 1970s to knock virtually everything down and build yet another towering office development. None the less, despite the restoration of the roof, much of the station's special atmosphere, which depends on the existence of so many odd nooks and crannies, is bound to be lost; a single passenger concourse is to be created, the platforms will be of equal length, and there will be more shops and cafés.

Leaving the station

From Liverpool Street, the train climbs steeply to Bethnal Green, where the Cambridge line goes off to the left, through cuttings and tunnels that, in steam days, stayed almost permanently smoke-filled. Although electrification of the suburban lines started in the 1930s, it was not finished until 1960; in a more recent scheme the main lines to Cambridge and Norwich will have been electrified by 1987.

At first the scene is typical of the inner city – depressing tower blocks interspersed with old and new terraced housing and wasteland – then the stages of London's suburban expansion become clearly visible. Stratford was the approximate boundary in the 1870s. After that there are Edwardian terraced houses around Forest Gate and Ilford, soon mixed with inter-war semis at places such as Chadwell Heath and Romford, which for long retained its separate identity as a market town and is now becoming an important business centre. Harold Heath was

developed in the 1950s. The first fields are reached around Brentwood, but, although London's sprawl ceases, new housing schemes continue in all the line-side communities to Colchester and beyond, for the population of East Anglia is expanding fast.

The Eastern Counties Railway

The line as far as Colchester was opened by the Eastern Counties Railway (ECR) in 1843, which had been planning a line to Norwich via Ipswich since 1836. Construction work was plagued with difficulties, not least the local landowners, who demanded high compensation for allowing the line to run through their estates. To make matters worse, at their engineer's insistence, the ECR built its line to a 5-foot gauge, and had to convert to the 4 feet 8½ inches that was standard on all the nearby lines the following year.

At Colchester, the ECR gave up, and decided to concentrate on its line from London to Cambridge, which gave connections to Norwich via Ely and Thetford. Another company, the Eastern Union Railway (EUR), continued the line, completing the Colchester to Ipswich stretch in 1846 and reaching Norwich in 1849. Thereupon the ECR turned hostile and did everything it could to hinder a regular London to Norwich service via Ipswich, refusing bookings at Colchester, running an irregular and slow service from Colchester to London, and even compelling the EUR to send its London passengers by steamer from Ipswich. Things improved when the ECR took control of the EUR in 1854, but even so it was not until the 1880s that this line became the principal route to Norwich.

After Colchester the line crosses the Stour estuary at Manningtree, where Flatford Mill and Constable country are only a short distance away. Then comes Brantham cutting and a short stretch through pleasant hilly country before Ipswich is reached, with views on the right of the docks and the new road bridge over the Orwell. Stoke tunnel leads into the station.

The final leg of the journey to Norwich runs straight across some of the nation's best grain country. The views across the flat land to distant horizons, occasional villages and clumps of woodland breaking up the wide hedgeless fields are never monotonous; the East Anglian landscape is subtler than it seems at first sight. Towards Norwich, the scenery becomes slightly lusher, and then the train is in the city suburbs, crossing first over the river Yare and the Thetford line (see page 45) on a viaduct and then over the river Wensum on Trowse Swing Bridge, which is being renewed as part of the electrification programme. As the train approaches Norwich Thorpe there is an excellent view ahead to the town centre with the solid twelfth-century great tower of the castle, 70 feet high and even today dominating the surrounding buildings.

The approach through the goods yard to Norwich station. The 200-foot tower of the City Hall is on the right and the stone keep of the castle, which dates from around 1160, is on the left.

East Anglian Branch Lines

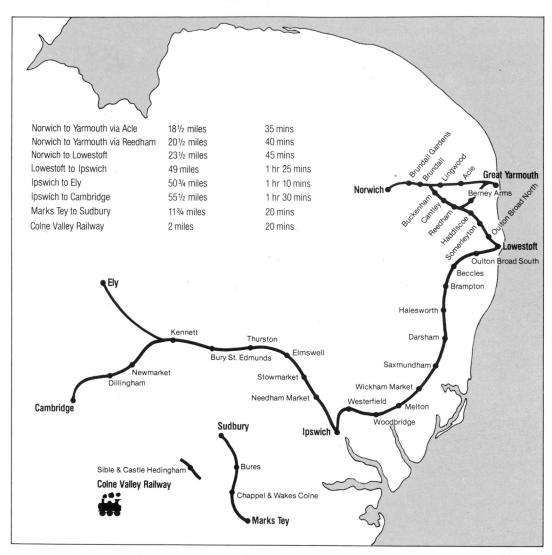

Norwich to Yarmouth via Acle	18½ miles	35 mins
Norwich to Yarmouth via Reedham	20½ miles	40 mins
Norwich to Lowestoft	23½ miles	45 mins
Lowestoft to Ipswich	49 miles	1 hr 25 mins
Ipswich to Ely	50¾ miles	1 hr 10 mins
Ipswich to Cambridge	55½ miles	1 hr 30 mins
Marks Tey to Sudbury	11¾ miles	20 mins
Colne Valley Railway	2 miles	20 mins

At one time East Anglia was full of trains: quiet rural services that made their way lazily from one little market town to the next, stopping at all the villages on the way. Not surprisingly, many of these lines have since vanished. But a good number do still remain, and provide a very pleasant way of getting to know the varied East Anglian landscape. The trains are well-used by commuters, shoppers, and school and college students, and clearly meet a genuine local need.

Norwich to Great Yarmouth and Lowestoft

British Rail calls this the 'Wherry line', in recollection of the Norfolk wherries, 15 to 40 ton sailing vessels which were the main means of transport in the area until the railways were built. It is interesting that wherries only gradually lost out to rail transport, and did not disappear completely until steam-and diesel-powered boats came into use.

The original line, Norwich to Yarmouth via Reedham, was the first railway into Norwich. It was opened in 1844 by the Yarmouth & Norfolk Railway, which became the Norfolk Railway the following year. This latter company opened an extension from Reedham to Lowestoft in 1847 before being absorbed by the Eastern Counties Railway (ECR) in 1848. At first there was not much traffic on the line, but by the 1880s Yarmouth's popularity had grown enough to justify the opening of the more direct Norwich to Yarmouth line through Acle. In the heyday of holiday resorts, from about the 1920s to the 1960s, there was very heavy traffic during the summer, with many direct trains from the Midlands and the north to Yarmouth, and today the summer still brings increased business.

Leaving Norwich, the line follows the river Yare, with pleasant views of the river and the water-meadows alongside. At Brundall, where the Yarmouth lines divide, there is a large marina, and boat-building workshops can be seen from the train. The more interesting route to Yarmouth is the longer one south via Reedham. The railway and river do not meet again until Cantley, but remain close, and gradually the arable land and patches of trees give way to marshland, with drainage ditches and boggy-looking fields. Just after Reedham, a short way from the only road bridge over the Yare between Norwich and Yarmouth, the train

Above: *Berney Arms station in the middle of remote marshland and accessible only by rail.*

Below: *The expansion of Ipswich docks has increased rail traffic to the Midlands and north.*

swings left and heads straight across the wide-open marshes. The next station, Berney Arms, has no road links at all: rail is the only means of access to the cottages, pub and mill. When the land for the railway was bought, the local land-owner made it a condition of sale that a station be built at Berney Arms and maintained in perpetuity – a condition that British Rail remains obliged to fulfil.

Now the river opens into Breydon Water on the right, with the remains of the Roman fortress of Gariannonum, now known as Burgh Castle, across on the south-west side. On the left of the train are Halvergate Marshes, one of the few sizeable stretches of undrained marshland remaining. Local farmers are now receiving financial help from the government to maintain traditional farming patterns. Joining the direct line, which runs through arable land as far as Acle and then across marshland with views of the river Bure and several windmills, the train skirts the north side of Breydon Water and enters Great Yarmouth.

The Lowestoft line crosses the Yare shortly after Reedham station and then runs alongside New Cut, a 2½-mile channel built in 1833 between the Yare and the Waveney to give sailing boats a direct link from Norwich to Lowestoft. Pleasure boats are the only traffic today. The railway joins the river Waveney and follows it through green water-meadows near Haddiscoe and Somerleyton, past Herringfleet Mill and Burgh St. Peter church on the right, to Oulton Broad. The final stretch into Lowestoft station runs alongside the Broad and the inner harbour.

Lowestoft to Ipswich

This is a lovely journey through the attractive, if undramatic, east Suffolk scenery. The East Suffolk Railway (ESR) opened the line in stages between 1854 and 1859, and built it as cheaply as it could. Cuttings, embankments and bridges were avoided whenever possible, although a swing bridge across Lake Lothing on the exit from Lowestoft had to be built. As a result, there are some surprisingly steep gradients, notably the ascent from Beccles, the long descent into Halesworth and the climb out of the town on the far side of the river Blyth.

Both Halesworth and Saxmundham further south are comfortable little market towns, centres for the surrounding villages. The Southwold Railway, which led off to the east from Halesworth, ran on a 3-foot gauge and stayed independent until it closed in 1929. An ESR branch line ran from Saxmundham to the coast at Aldeburgh: this was closed to passengers in 1966 but is still used as far as Leiston for the removal of waste from Sizewell nuclear power

station. There is a moment of magic at Woodbridge when the line runs alongside the river Deben, almost lapping the water, and passing the yachts and motor launches moored in the marina. There are lovely views of the elegant town on one side and down the estuary on the other. The celebrated Sutton Hoo ship burial was discovered only a few miles away on the far side of the river.

The East Suffolk line has always served a useful social purpose, and still does − witness the crowds travelling on the early morning train into Ipswich. But it has never made much money, if any at all, even when it carried a great deal of holiday traffic. Permission to close the line was refused in 1965, so BR pioneered Pay Trains and, in a major effort to reduce running costs, created what amounts to a basic railway in the early 1980s. Track has been modernized and singled, level crossings are operated automatically (there were no less than twenty-four in 49 miles) and Radio Electronic Token Block (RETB − see page 190) has been introduced, with fixed radio equipment in the driver's cab replacing the lineside signals. Now only three people are required to operate the whole infrastructure of this branch line, two of whom (at Lowestoft and at the junction with the Felixstowe branch) also work on other lines.

Class S15 4−6−0 No. 841 Greene King *heads a steam excursion north through the Fens past Ely cathedral.*

Ipswich to Cambridge and Ely

The principal stations along this line are all fine examples of railway architecture: solid, well-designed buildings intended to convey an image of reliability to the railway company's shareholders and passengers. Needham Market, closed in 1967 but reopened in 1971, has been described as a Tudor mansion in miniature, while Stowmarket, like many buildings in East Anglia, has something of a Dutch feel about it, with large Jacobean gables. Both these stations are built in an attractive red brick. Bury St. Edmunds is perhaps the most interesting of all. The tall twin towers, one on each side of the line, can be seen from quite far off along the track, while the 'house' part, which contains the booking-office and waiting-room, is also in a pleasing Jacobean style. At Newmarket the train now stops at a single open platform, but the old station can be seen just beyond; it is another solid red-brick building with, on the far side from the line, a magnificent façade.

To appreciate these buildings properly, it is necessary to get off the train, since each was designed to face the street; the platform view is the back view. At Stowmarket there is the open-air Museum of East Anglian Life, Bury has its lovely abbey, and Newmarket is the home of the famous stud and racecourse.

The line itself starts along the Gipping valley, sharing the route of the main line to Norwich as far as Haughley Junction. Then there is a long

Bury St. Edmunds station from the east in 1956, with its two prominent towers. The two central through tracks have now been removed.

stretch through fine arable country, with huge fields appearing to reach to the horizon, and, before Warren Hill tunnel, which leads into Newmarket, the gallops used to exercise racehorses can be seen on the left. The final part of the route to Cambridge passes through more arable land interspersed with woodland.

The Ely branch was constructed in 1879, twenty-five years after through traffic began from Cambridge to Ipswich, and runs through dank Fenland scenery, with fine views ahead to Ely cathedral. As well as local trains, the line carries a good deal of through traffic between the east-coast ports and the Midlands.

Marks Tey to Sudbury: the Stour Valley line

There are two faces to Marks Tey station. The two main platforms, through which electrified Inter-City expresses thunder, rocking everything as they pass, stand for the modern competitive railways of the mid-1980s. The third platform calls to mind the peaceful rural railway, the line curving from the platform into remote, lush country, past deep green banks with a good crop of weeds growing between the tracks. The

12-mile journey to Sudbury passes through some lovely scenery. There is a magnificent crossing of the river Colne on Chappel viaduct, 1,066 feet long with thirty-two arches – and containing seven million bricks. Next comes a pleasant stretch through a deep cutting and out into the Stour valley, with excellent views on the right towards the Vale of Dedham and over the attractive village of Bures. The final stretch runs along the river Stour and its lush water-meadows into Sudbury, where Thomas Gainsborough, the artist, was born. The town is well worth a visit.

The line to Sudbury was opened in 1849 and operated by the Eastern Union Railway until 1898, when the Great Eastern Railway bought it. An extension opened in 1865, which ran north to Long Melford and Bury St. Edmunds and west to Haverhill and Cambridge, failed to survive the cutbacks of the 1960s.

The former Colne Valley Railway can be seen leading off to the left after Chappel & Wakes Colne station. The station is also the headquarters of the Stour Valley Railway Preservation Society, which has a large collection of historic locomotives, including one of the Class N7 tanks that worked the suburban Jazz Service (see page 40), and rolling stock. Beautifully restored station buildings and items of historic interest add to the atmosphere, and it is also possible to watch work being done on the locomotives.

Sudbury station in 1911 looking north. Today the single-track line terminates here.

0–6–0T No. 40 and 0–6–0ST No. WD 190 Castle Hedingham *at the station of the same name.*

The Colne Valley Railway

Usually the long struggle to preserve a local railway and restore steam-operated services starts when closure has only recently happened. With luck, at least some of the infrastructure – track, signals, signal-boxes and station buildings and so on – will still be in place, and preservationists can concentrate on restoration work, and on the job of building up an interesting collection of locomotives and rolling stock.

It was not so on the Colne Valley line. Closure came in stages between 1961 and 1965, almost exactly a century after the line opened as the Colne Valley & Halstead Railway, and it was 1972 before anyone had the idea of bringing this quiet Essex branch back to life. A mile stretch of the by then completely overgrown trackbed between two stations was chosen for restoration, and after several years' hard work (and the obligatory battle with the planners), the line was cleared of vegetation, track was laid and a station

building and two platforms 200 feet long were built. Authenticity was the keynote right from the start of the project and, by a stroke of luck, Sible & Castle Hedingham station, one of the only two surviving station buildings, was bought shortly before its demolition, dismantled brick by brick and slowly re-erected. Later, a second station building went up, this one a near exact replica on a slightly reduced scale of Halstead station, the Colne Valley & Halstead Railway's headquarters. A footbridge from Stowmarket links the two platforms. The signal-box comes from Cressing on the Braintree to Witham branch, but is very like those built on the Colne Valley line. The latest addition is an original girder bridge over the river Colne, enabling further track to be laid.

The line is a delightful recreation of an Edwardian railway, with much authentic detail helping to give a true sense of what it was like to travel a century ago. The locomotives, rolling stock and station buildings can be visited.

49

North Norfolk Railway

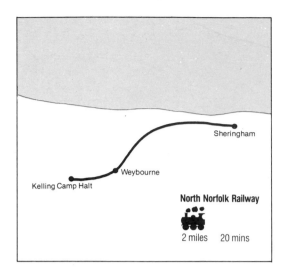

Sheringham

Weybourne

Kelling Camp Halt

North Norfolk Railway

2 miles   20 mins

junction of four lines and commonly nicknamed 'the Crewe of north Norfolk' – to Holt in 1884, with an extension to Cromer three years later. The M&GN survived Grouping in 1923 and remained nominally independent until nationalization, although the London & North Eastern Railway (LNER) took over day-to-day operations in 1936. Most of the former M&GN routes were closed in 1959, but the Sheringham branch staggered on until 1964.

Present route

The existing North Norfolk Railway occupies a short stretch of the original line. Trains leave Sheringham station and run through pleasant rolling countryside with views of the low ridge of the North Norfolk hills on the left and the sea on the right. The ascent is quite steep, with gradients of 1 in 97 and 1 in 80 – which will surprise those visitors who imagine East Anglia to be entirely flat. Beyond Weybourne, which was the Railway's terminus for many years, a short extension to a new station called Kelling Camp Halt has been built. There are plans for an eventual extension to Holt, a pleasant market town set amid the hills. As well as the ride itself, there is a small museum at Sheringham and the engine shed at Weybourne to see.

This pleasant 3-mile route is the sole surviving remnant of the Midland & Great Northern Joint Railway, which in its heyday operated a 182-mile network through the Fens and central and northern Norfolk. The area it served – the approximate boundaries were Yarmouth and Norwich in the east and Peterborough and Spalding in the west – was neither especially prosperous nor well-populated, and its services were never very successful. To compensate for low regular usage, however, there was a considerable amount of holiday traffic, especially to Cromer and to the rather more select resort of Sheringham, with through trains from the Midlands and the north. In addition, freight services brought considerable revenue, with special fish and cattle trains as well as grain, sugar beet and general goods.

The Midland & Great Northern Railway (M&GN) was formed in 1893 to take over the Eastern & Midland. This latter company had opened a branch from Melton Constable – the

Not all preserved lines are fortunate enough to have direct connections with BR. The North Norfolk occupies the original station at Sheringham, while BR trains run into a single-platform halt a short distance away. The 30-mile, hour-long trip by diesel multiple unit from Norwich runs through the heart of the Broads, crossing the river Bure at Wroxham, which is a major sailing centre. Other stations on the line include Cromer and Worsted, where worsted cloth comes from, and where, as at North Walsham, there is a fine wool church.

The signalman at Wensum Junction stands ready to pass the single-line token to the driver of GER 0–6–0

No. 564, painted in LNER livery.

0–6–0 No. 45 Colwyn *heads a train through the attractive north Norfolk hills between Sheringham and* Weybourne. The gradients on the North Norfolk are surprisingly steep.

Norwich to Birmingham

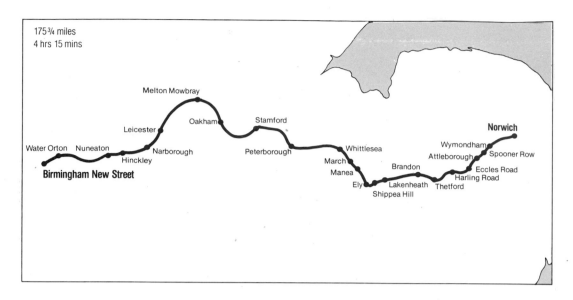

175¾ miles
4 hrs 15 mins

For variety of landscape, there can hardly be a better journey than this one across the heart of eastern and central England. The first part, from Norwich almost to Thetford, runs through gently rolling pastoral country, with wheatfields and plenty of patches of woodland. Keswick watermill, on the very edge of Norwich to the left of the line, is the first landmark. Then the two towers of Wymondham Abbey come into view as you enter the station; the church has a fine Norman nave and a magnificent fifteenth-century hammerbeam roof. Just beyond the station, a freight-only line leads off to Dereham; grain and fertilizers are the principal traffic. The line was closed to passengers in 1969, but there have been suggestions that it should be reopened. At Attleborough there is a large cider factory by the line and, between Eccles Road and Harling Road, Snetterton Racing Circuit can be seen on the right.

Beyond Harling Road the train passes through stretches of original Breckland. In the Middle Ages, these heathlands grew little more than scrub vegetation, and supported few people; as many as twenty-eight deserted medieval villages have been identified. Improved farming methods have now made the land more productive, and the Forestry Commission has established large stretches of woodland, more attractive than many of its plantations, through which the train runs to the west of Thetford. The view of Santon Downham village on the tiny Little Ouse is especially pleasant. Grimes Graves, the neolithic flint mines worked by some of the Brecklands' first settlers, lie a few miles to the north of the line.

Fenland line

Beyond Brandon, the train emerges on to the Fens, following the now wider Little Ouse for a while before running through a large poplar plantation. From here to Peterborough, over 40 miles to the west, the view is constant: a flat land of black earth broken only by drainage channels

and stretching away into the far distance under a wide, wide sky. Only Ely interrupts the view: houses scrambling up a low hill and, dominating the town, the great cathedral with its splendid west tower. The nave, which measures 537 feet, is the fourth longest in the country.

There are two more stations before the main King's Lynn to Ely line is joined. Lakenheath serves the US Air Force base a few miles to the north, while Shippea Hill is no hill at all; the *ea* ending in Fenland names originally indicated an island of firm ground that rose out of the swampy marsh before it was drained. At the junction, through trains swing on to the line for March and Peterborough, while local trains run south into Ely station, entering alongside attractive water-meadows at the foot of the town.

The route thus far opened for traffic on 30 July 1845. The eastern section as far as Brandon was built by the Norwich & Brandon Railway, which became the Norfolk Railway one month before the opening of the line, and was taken over by the Eastern Counties Railway (ECR) in 1845, while the stretch from Brandon to Ely was an Eastern Counties line right from the start. The ECR, which became part of the Great Eastern Railway when that company was formed in 1862, also built the line from Ely to Peterborough. Freight traffic began on that line in December 1846, and passenger services the following month.

The line beyond Ely

Now the train heads dead straight across seemingly endless Fenland. The scene possesses a kind of astringent beauty: field after field of cabbages, celery, beet, potatoes and other root crops, interrupted only by the washes or drains that disperse the water from this perpetually soggy land. The first two washes, which the line crosses on a sizeable bridge, are the New and Old Bedford rivers, built when the land was first drained in the middle of the seventeenth century. The view back to the massive outline of Ely cathedral is magnificent.

March was once an important railway location with seven platforms and lines to all points of the compass. This is now the sole remaining line, with the exception of a freight-only route to Wisbech. The Whitemoor marshalling yard a little to the right of the line, which once covered 68 acres and in the 1950s handled up to 7,000 wagons a day, is now virtually deserted. The line on to Peterborough crosses more Fenland and, beyond Whittlesea station, passes an enormous complex of brick works. At Peterborough the line runs underneath the main east-coast line, crosses the Nene and then climbs steeply up into the station.

The Leicester to Peterborough route, known as the Syston & Peterborough, was one of the lines George Hudson built in his unsuccessful attempt to hinder the construction of the route from York to London (see page 13). It was opened in three stages in 1846 and 1848. For the first 5 miles north out of Peterborough the minor route, which was constructed first, runs beside the main line north. The two routes part company at Helpston, where a lovely red-brick Midland Railway goods shed still stands by the track, and the Leicester line immediately plunges into a beautiful, gently rolling landscape. This is 'picture-book' England of unspoilt villages and handsome market towns, rich fields of waving corn and fine woodland groves. Stamford station is an attractive Tudor-style building in the local greyish limestone.

Stamford station, designed by the architect Sancton Wood. The weather vane on the attractive bell turret carried the initials of the Syston & Peterborough Railway.

NORWICH TO BIRMINGHAM

The castle banqueting hall and All Saints' church at Oakham in Leicestershire.

Stamford to Birmingham

Beyond Stamford the line runs beside the tiny river Chater and then at Manton Junction turns north through the Vale of Catmose to Oakham, at one point just touching the shore of Rutland Water, the largest artificial reservoir in Europe. The fourteenth-century spire of Oakham parish church can be seen from miles off, and there is also a good view of Burley on the Hill, a fine mansion that stands on the low hills overlooking the Water. The house was built in the seventeenth century and rebuilt around 1700.

Melton Mowbray, home of Stilton cheese, is the next stop after Oakham. On the way the line passes along the edge of Stapleford Park, whose owner, Lord Harborough, caused the line's surveyors a good deal of trouble when they were planning the route. There were several fights between Harborough's men and Hudson's, and the arguments delayed the opening of the central section for two years until 1848. Past Melton

Mowbray and the junction with the former Nottingham line, now partly used as a test track, the line runs near the river Wreake and joins the Midland main line at Syston, a few miles north of Leicester station.

The final leg of the journey to Birmingham is the least interesting. The line, which branches off the Midland main line south of Leicester, was opened in 1864 as the South Leicestershire Railway. There is some undistinguished countryside as far as Nuneaton, where the west-coast main line is crossed and then on to the outskirts of Birmingham. At Whitacre Junction the line passes a large waterworks on the left and then, running alongside the river Tame, Hams Hall power station on the right. The line into Birmingham New Street station passes through an area of mixed housing and industry, including the Metro-Cammell works where some of BR's rolling stock is built, with a fine view of the city centre just before the station is reached.

Wymondham Abbey, a landmark on the line to the west of Norwich. The octagonal tower at the front was formerly a central crossing tower belonging to the Abbey now destroyed.

Nene Valley Railway

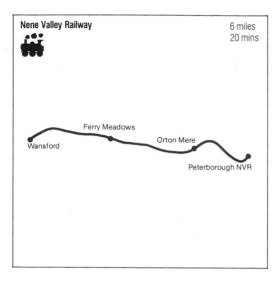

Nene Valley Railway   6 miles
       20 mins

Wansford   Ferry Meadows   Orton Mere   Peterborough NVR

The Nene Valley Railway is unique among preserved lines in Great Britain. Among the substantial collection of locomotives and rolling stock the visitor can see not only well-known British examples but also a wide variety from continental Europe. Sweden, Norway, Denmark, Germany, France and Italy have all contributed, so that a ride on the railway can have something of an exotic feel about it. There is also a sizeable collection of industrial locomotives, those workhorses of the railway system, rarely seen and even more rarely appreciated by the travelling public, which were used for hauling such raw materials as iron ore, coal or sugarbeet to and from factories and mines.

It is hard to pick out the stars of the collection. There is *Britannia,* the first of British Railways' Standard Locomotives, built in 1951; *92 Squadron,* one of the Southern Railways's light Pacifics designed by O. V. Bulleid; the *French Nord* 4–6–0, which hauled the boat trains to and from the French and Belgian channel ports; the German class 64 and the Swedish B class 101. The favourite of many people, however, is *Thomas* (named after Reverend Awdry's famous engine), which spent its life working at the Peterborough Sugar Factory. Among the rolling stock are two Wagon–Lits, a *Brighton Belle* Pullman saloon and numerous freight wagons.

Peterborough's first railway

The 5½-mile line just to the west of Peterborough was formerly part of the Northampton & Peterborough Railway that ran roughly southwest through Oundle and Wellingborough to Northampton. George Stephenson surveyed the line, which opened on 2 June 1845. It was the first railway to reach Peterborough. Through trips to London were possible, but the journey was extremely time-consuming. The fastest train took nearly two hours to reach Northampton, just over 42 miles away; and it took another three hours on to Euston from there. Peterborough only achieved its direct link with

the capital five years later when the Great Northern Railway (GNR) opened (see page 13), by which time the Northampton line had been absorbed by the London & North Western Railway.

After the Second World War, the line, like so many other branch services, could not compete with cars, buses and lorries. Passenger numbers dwindled, and passenger services were withdrawn in 1965, followed by freight services eight years after that. Already, however, the Peterborough Railway Society was in active existence. After five years' hard labour a Light Railway Order was obtained, and trains ran again.

The principal station, called Wansford, is at Stibbington, an attractive village just off the A1. The wooden building on platform 2 came from Barnwell, 12 miles down the line, while the rest of the station is newly built. The train heads to the west first, through Wansford Tunnel, which is 1,848 feet long, before the engine runs round at Yarwell Mill, the junction with the former branch to Market Harborough, and returns through Wansford station. Next comes a level-crossing over the old Great North Road, followed by Wansford signal-box, one of the largest preserved boxes in operation in Britain, before the line crosses the river Nene twice to run through Ferry Meadows Country Park, were there is a station. The stretch between the two river crossings passes near Durobrivae, a Roman town served by Ermine Street. The Norman tower visible is that of Castor church. The following mile is along an embankment above water-meadows to Orton Mere station, and then comes the latest extension, 1½ miles to the new station near the city centre, Peterborough NVR. A Museum of World Railways is planned to open nearby in 1988.

The French Nord 4–6–0 No. 3628 brings a two-coach train out of Wansford tunnel.

Above: *Passengers wait on a wet day to board visiting Pullman coaches at Wansford station.*

Below: *Wansford station at the turn of the century with a GNR train from Stamford in the bay platform.*

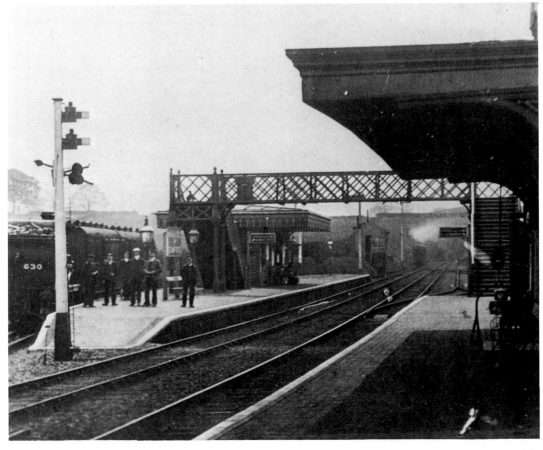

MIDLAND REGION

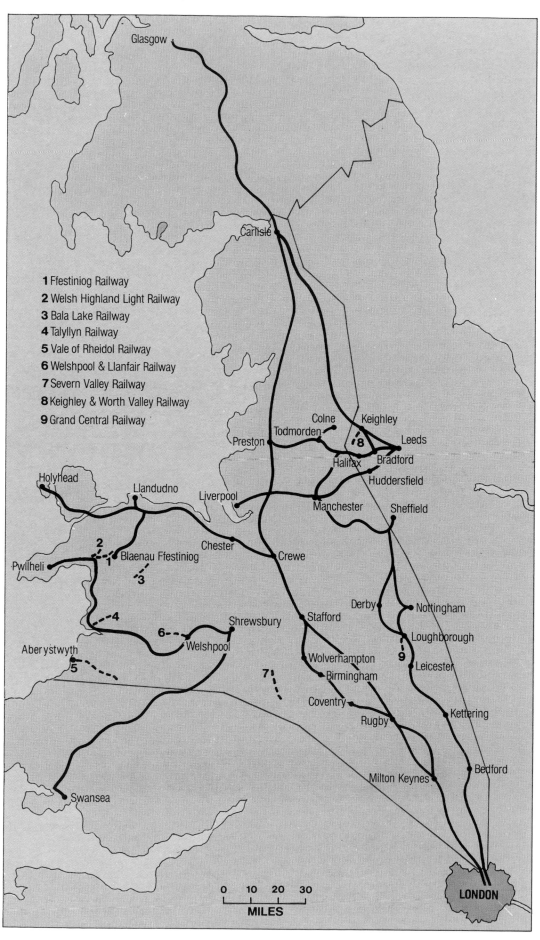

1 Ffestiniog Railway
2 Welsh Highland Light Railway
3 Bala Lake Railway
4 Talyllyn Railway
5 Vale of Rheidol Railway
6 Welshpool & Llanfair Railway
7 Severn Valley Railway
8 Keighley & Worth Valley Railway
9 Grand Central Railway

Glasgow

Carlisle

Colne   Keighley
Todmorden
Preston   8   Leeds
         Halifax   Bradford
                   Huddersfield
Holyhead
Llandudno
Liverpool   Manchester   Sheffield
2   Blaenau Ffestiniog
1   Chester
Pwllheli   3   Crewe
                                Derby   Nottingham
                         Stafford   Loughborough
         4   9
6   Leicester
Aberystwyth   Welshpool   Shrewsbury   Wolverhampton
5   7   Birmingham
                              Coventry   Kettering
                                   Rugby
                                             Bedford
                         Milton Keynes
Swansea
                    0   10 20 30
                         MILES

LONDON

58

Of all British Rail's Regions, the Midland is the most diverse as far as both its landscape and its history are concerned. When it opened in 1830, the line between Liverpool and Manchester became the first fully-fledged public railway in the world, operating a regular service of locomotive-hauled passenger trains: the route remains much the same today. So too does George Stephenson's impressively engineered line from London to Birmingham, the first long-distance inter-city line and the first main line to reach the capital city, along which electric locomotives now race at speeds of 100 mph and more.

In the south of the Region, the landscape offers quiet pleasures: the gentle rolling south Midlands plain, for instance, where the line to Birmingham keeps close to the canal which it eventually supplanted, and the idyllic Severn valley, which can be enjoyed during a ride on the Severn Valley Railway, one of the liveliest and most successful of the independent steam lines. Further north, the hills and mountains provide plenty of drama. The run through the Lune Gorge and the ascent of Shap between Lancaster and Penrith are not to be missed, while the various trans-Pennine journeys follow majestic routes through the hills, passing splendid moorland, foaming rivers and handsome stone built villages.

For the committed railway enthusiast, as well as for those who simply enjoy a holiday trip on a train, the lines of north and mid-Wales can hardly be surpassed. There is a dramatic conjunction of railway and ocean both along the north Wales coast on the Chester to Holyhead route and on the Cambrian Coast line from Shrewsbury to Pwllheli, often threatened with extinction but now apparently secure, at least for the forseeable future. There are attractive inland routes: the line from Llandudno to Blaenau Ffestiniog, which pushes into the high Welsh mountains, and the trip across the heart of the remote and lovely mid-Wales hills from Shrewsbury to Swansea. But above all there are the numerous steam-hauled narrow-gauge lines, most originally built to transport minerals mined high in the mountains, and which today carry holidaymakers on often breath-taking and precipitous journeys through magnificent scenery. The survival and continuing appeal of lines such as the Ffestiniog and the Talyllyn, to name but two of the most celebrated, is a tribute to the persistence, devotion and physical stamina of those who set about their preservation.

Poster issued by the Midland Railway in the 1890s to show the extent of its services.

London to Glasgow

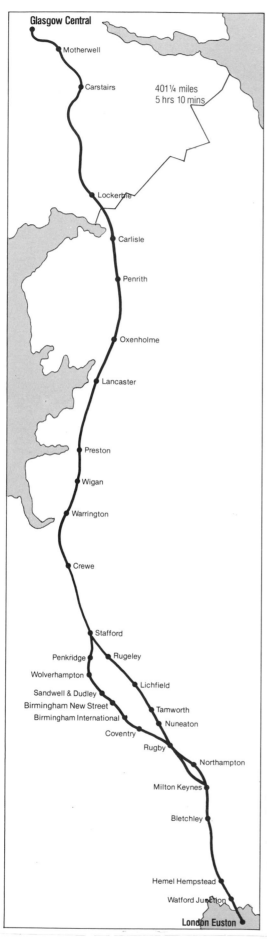

Glasgow Central
Motherwell
Carstairs
401¼ miles
5 hrs 10 mins
Lockerbie
Carlisle
Penrith
Oxenholme
Lancaster
Preston
Wigan
Warrington
Crewe
Stafford
Penkridge   Rugeley
Wolverhampton
Sandwell & Dudley   Lichfield
Birmingham New Street
Birmingham International   Tamworth
Coventry   Nuneaton
Rugby
Northampton
Milton Keynes
Bletchley
Hemel Hempstead
Watford Junction
London Euston

Today's Euston is a functional, anonymous building of the late 1960s, with little or nothing of interest to hold the traveller's attention. The Euston of yesterday was the first terminus of the first long-distance main line in Great Britain, and hence in the world, but nothing of any significance now remains. Lost is Philip Hardwick's magnificent Doric arch which triumphantly symbolized the birth of the railway age – lost despite an influential last-minute campaign to save it, and even though the demolition contractor was willing to number the stones and re-erect the arch elsewhere at his own expense. Gone, too, are Robert Stephenson's plain and elegant train sheds with their glass and iron roofs and Philip Hardwick's splendid Great Hall and board room.

No one disputes that the old Euston had grown, as one modern historian has put it, 'hideously and chaotically', making it unsuitable for a late twentieth-century railway. What is still vividly regretted, almost a quarter of a century later, is that the best parts of the old terminus were not incorporated into the new station, and that an outstanding piece of architecture and an important part of history no longer exists.

The London & Birmingham Railway
Built by Robert Stephenson, the London & Birmingham was a venture the like of which had never before been undertaken. No less than 112 miles of railway were to be driven through sometimes awkward country, by an almost totally inexperienced workforce which could supplement its muscle-power with only a few rudimentary tools, and which was supervised by almost equally inexperienced contractors. The difficulties were immense. Even though he had the support of an able team of assistant engineers, it must have seemed to Stephenson, who was not yet thirty years old, that he had to be everywhere at once; the burden was enormous.

Considerable earthworks were required, for the line ran through three ranges of hills – the heights almost immediately north of the terminus, the Chilterns and the Northamptonshire uplands south of Rugby – and Stephenson insisted that, except on the exit from Euston, the ruling gradient should be no more than 1 in 330. At all the major works, apart from Watford tunnel, Stephenson had to take direct control when the difficulties of the job defeated the contractor. At Wolverton, one part of the embankment gave way under the weight of soil tipped on it, and later another part caught fire.

The tunnels at Blisworth and Kilsby, both in Northamptonshire, took so long that the opening of that part of the line had to be delayed, and for several months passengers were conveyed from Denbigh Hall, north of Bletchley, to Rugby by coach. At Blisworth the problems were water and the instability of the clay. Pumping engines had to be installed to cope

9.50 a.m. on platform 13 of the now vanished Euston station, and passengers arrive for the Royal Scot.

with the powerful springs and large retaining walls built, in places over 2 feet thick.

Things went even worse at Kilsby. Here there were quicksands and the first shafts were quickly flooded. Stephenson sank a new line of shafts across the hillside, built cross-headings to the flooded shafts, and set up pumping engines. It was nineteen months before the thirteen engines, which extracted no less than 1,800 gallons a minute, had cleared the quicksand and work on the tunnel could resume.

An army of navvies

An unprecedented army of men gathered to build the line. One estimate suggests that a minimum of 12,000 navvies was employed, with as many as 20,000 at times. There were 1,000 at Kilsby and according to L. T. C. Rolt the great majority were living in:

crazy turf-thatched huts which they built themselves. The Ox Greet at Kilsby became the stage for wild saturnalia with which the villagers dared not interfere. Barrels of beer were rolled out of the inn on to the green, where the navvies danced and fought each other or wagered their money on dog fights and cock fights. When a gang felt hungry they would buy a beast from a local farmer, cut it up on the green, and bear away on forks or shovels carried over the shoulder great joints of meat to be roasted over their encampment fires.

Robert Stephenson (1803–59) who built many of the earliest rail routes and locomotives in Britain.

Lithograph by J. C. Bourne of the construction of Kilsby tunnel. Candles were often the only light source.

Recent research has rehabilitated the navvy's image, and such 'randies' or pay-night celebrations were occasional rather than every-day events. For the most part, the navvy's life was a grim one, of hard physical labour in unpleasant conditions, with the very real risk of death or injury, and unsoftened by luxury of any kind.

The London terminus

The first plan had been to build a terminus at Camden Town, on the far side of the Regent's Canal from the city, and it was only after work started on the rest of the line that a new site 1½ miles further south at Euston Square was fixed when the previously reluctant landowner, tempted by the prospect of increasing land values, finally agreed to sell. The new terminus involved a steep ascent, 1 in 66 at its steepest, worked from the opening of the line in 1837 until 1844 by stationary engines at Camden Town. These hauled the carriages up on a cable.

The original passenger buildings at Euston may not have survived, but a remarkable complex of buildings near the goods yard at Camden Town has. Glance to your right as the train crosses the Regent's Canal, and you may just see a handsome warehouse fronting the water. This was the Interchange Warehouse. Freight wagons entered the upper floors of the warehouse from the now closed sidings behind, barges came in by water, and goods were transferred directly from one to the other.

The Great Hall at Euston, opened in May 1849. The staircase at the far end led to a gallery and offices.

Contrary to common belief, the coming of the railway did not immediately put the canals out of business. Goods still had to be distributed locally from the railhead, and until the development of road transport this was done by barge, where there were canals, and by horse. If you have time to spare in London, it is worth nosing around the Camden Lock area, for as well as the Interchange Warehouse a remarkable group of stables and warehouses erected during the mid-nineteenth century by the North London Railway survives, many still with the original fittings intact. On the right beyond the warehouse the Roundhouse can be seen. Built in 1847 as an engine shed, it was sold in 1869 because it was too short for the locomotives then in use, and had a varied career before becoming a theatre in the 1960s. It is presently being converted to a black cultural centre.

The train gathers speed through Primrose Hill tunnel and races through London's north-west suburbs. For the traveller making his, or her, first trip by train, as was the frequent experience on this line, the sudden plunge into darkness must have been quite alarming. The author of a contemporary guide wrote that the transition:

> excites considerable surprise; one moment we are in the midst of day – in the next the train is surrounded with a midnight darkness, which is scarcely penetrated by the rays of the dim lamps suspended at the tops of the carriages.

Direct City link

The countryside is reached beyond Watford tunnel, and from there to Rugby the landscape is undistinguished but pleasant. Stephenson built his railways as direct inter-city routes, in contrast with George Hudson of York, who routed his lines through as many population centres as possible. As a result, there are few settlements of any size between Watford and Rugby, except for Milton Keynes, which is a child of the 1970s. Stephenson's line has met the test of time well, accepting much faster running than he can ever have envisaged. Electrification (completed to Liverpool and Manchester in 1966 and to Glasgow in 1974) brought extensive works – principally the installation of overhead conductor wires, relay rooms and feeder stations for the power supply; modifications to bridges and tunnels to ensure clearance; and station modernization – but it is still recognizably Stephenson's line along which we travel today.

The line passes Berkhamsted castle on the right and soon after enters Tring cutting, 2½ miles long and 57 feet deep at its lowest point. To create the cutting, navvies removed no less than 1½ million cubic yards of chalk, all wheeled in barrows along planks precipitously laid down the sides of the cutting. The London & Birmingham established its locomotive works 21 miles further on at Wolverton, formerly a small

A southbound train silhouetted against the evening sky of the south Midlands.

village. LNWR locos were also built there for a short period, but after 1865 the works handled only carriage and wagon construction and maintenance. Currently some 2,000 people are employed at the works overhauling and refurbishing electric multiple units. Before the introduction of dining-cars towards the end of the nineteenth century, express trains halted at Wolverton for a short meal break.

Through the Watford Gap
The railway and the Grand Union Canal run close to one another from Watford until, beyond Milton Keynes, they are joined first by the M1 (the first of Britain's long-distance motorways just as the Birmingham line was the first long-distance railway) and then by the A5. This last is the oldest route of all, for it follows the Roman road connecting London and Holyhead. After the 1½-mile Blisworth cutting (the canal runs through the hills in a tunnel), all four draw close together to run through Watford Gap. Then comes Kilsby tunnel, 1 mile 666 yards, and the train enters Rugby station 4 miles later, little altered since it was rebuilt in 1896.

At Rugby the line divides. Today's northbound expresses run along the Trent Valley line, opened in 1847, through Nuneaton and Lichfield to Stafford. Shortly before Stafford is reached, the line crosses Shugborough Park. The Earl of Lichfield struck a bargain with the Trent Valley Railway: he would allow the line across his land if, in keeping with the follies that already decorated the estate, the railway

company provided appropriately ornate tunnel entrances and a bridge. The results, according to a recent guide, 'form some of the most remarkable decorative features on any railway'. The western tunnel entrance resembles the gateway of a Norman keep, the eastern portal is in Egyptian style, while the Lichfield Drive Bridge is a low arch with Ionic columns, surmounted by three plinths bearing a lion, a seahorse and the Lichfield arms.

Stephenson's original route into Birmingham runs through Coventry and Birmingham International, a new station serving the airport and Exhibition Centre. New Street station was opened in 1854 and extensively altered to form a major interchange in the 1960s. The original terminus at Curzon Street seems to have been too small almost from the start, and was relegated to freight usage after 1854. The site has been redeveloped, but at least the triumphal Ionic entrance arch does survive.

The Grand Junction Railway
By the time a service of through trains from London to Birmingham began on 17 September 1838 the next stage north had already been operating for fourteen months. The 82½ miles of the Grand Junction Railway were planned to link the London & Birmingham with the Liverpool & Manchester at Newton-le-Willows (see page 94), so giving a direct connection between the capital and the rapidly industrializing north. George Stephenson and his former pupil Joseph Locke were to have shared responsibility

Rugby station, photographed about ten years after it was rebuilt by the LNWR in 1886. It remains *remarkably unchanged today, with a fine lofty overall roof and lengthy platforms.*

for the Grand Junction route, Locke taking the southern section and Stephenson the northern. Jealousies and disagreements arose on Stephenson's part, and he eventually withdrew, leaving Locke in control of the entire line.

The Grand Junction marked the debut of the railway construction career of Thomas Brassey. Having won the contract for a short stretch of line near Wolverhampton, he went on in the next thirty-five years to built 1,700 miles of railway in Great Britain, and another 2,800 abroad, often in co-operation with Locke.

The present route north from Birmingham runs through what was once the heart of the Black Country but is now rapidly becoming derelict and overgrown. There are views over canals (Birmingham's canal network is more extensive than that of Venice), and the line also passes Matthew Boulton's Soho Foundry, opened in 1762 to manufacture James Watt's steam engines. The original Grand Junction route, which by-passed the centre of Wolverhampton and is now a freight-only line, is rejoined just north of Wolverhampton station.

Crewe

Leaving the Potteries to the east, the line runs through pleasant flattish countryside to Crewe. Crewe is a creation of the railway age. The Grand Junction Railway built a country halt in a tiny village, Monks Coppenhall, near a manor house called Crewe Hall. On 30 June 1837, just four days before the first trains ran on the Grand Junction, two new lines were authorized from Crewe to Chester (see page 68) and from Crewe

to Manchester, and Crewe's career as a major railway junction was launched. The Grand Junction moved its carriage and wagon works to the town in 1843; locomotive construction began in 1845 and soon, under LNWR control, the works became 'the most comprehensive and integrated railway workshops anywhere in the world', making their own steel and, from the steel, locomotives, rails and all the mechanical equipment needed to run a railway.

Crewe was a true company town. The population, 184 before the railway arrived, rose to 4,491 in 1851 and to over 43,000 at the turn of the century, when 10,000 were employed in the works. Everything – schools, roads, houses, churches, sewers – was provided by the LNWR, and in return the company expected, enforced and on the whole received absolute loyalty.

Crewe remains a very important railway centre. Over six million people change trains there every year, and another million start or finish their journeys at the station. Each weekday 133 Inter-City expresses, 162 local trains and 120 freight services pass through, and 3 million parcel bags and 1.1 million mail bags are handled a year. The works, BR's largest in terms of staff, are the main locomotive overhaul works in the country, taking responsibility for all the west-coast main line fleet of electric locomotives and most types of main line diesel-electric locomotives. In summer 1985 Crewe station was shut for seven weeks for a major modernization programme, in which track and signalling were renewed and replaced. The oldest signals were 100 years old, and most dated back to 1938. One benefit is that trains can now pass through the station at 80 mph instead of the previous maximum of 20 to 30 mph.

Towards the Lake District

North of Crewe, there is another country section, on which the line crosses the Shropshire Union Canal and then the river Weaver twice. The second crossing, at Dutton north of Northwich, is a fine red sandstone viaduct, 440 yards long and 60 feet high, the only major construction project on what was otherwise an easy line to build. Now the wide Mersey plain is entered, and the view is mostly industrial through Warrington and Wigan to Preston, which boasts a handsome station built in 1880.

The line from Newton north to Preston was opened on 31 October 1838 by the North Union Railway, and the section on from Preston to Lancaster on 25 June 1840 by the Lancaster & Preston Junction Railway. The two quickly quarrelled, and at one time in 1842, although through services were maintained between London and Lancaster, passengers had to get out at one station in Preston and walk to the other, while the trains were run empty through a connecting tunnel. Eventually, the LNWR leased the Lancaster & Preston in 1859, while the North Union part of the line came under the joint control of the LNWR and the Lancashire & Yorkshire.

The view of the long, remote hills of the Forest of Bowland on the right between Preston and Lancaster provides a foretaste of the journey to come on what is one of the most splendid and scenic stretches of main line in the country. Shortly after Lancaster, where the immense twelfth-century stone tower castle can be seen, there is a good view over Morecambe Bay, with the hills of the Lake District beyond. After Carnforth, where the locomotive sheds to the left of the line have been converted into a museum of steam known as Steamtown, the line climbs as the hills begin to close in. Leighton Hall, built in the late eighteenth century, can be seen on the left.

The Kendal and Windermere line branches off at Oxenholme, and a couple of miles before Oxenholme station is reached the hills open up to give a lovely view of Kendal. Now a climb starts which, though less celebrated than the ascent of Shap that follows, is almost as steep, and in bad weather could be quite as difficult. There are splendid views of the mountains, with Whinfell Beacon in the foreground; the line crosses Dockray viaduct, 370 feet long with six spans, and then the viaduct of the former line from Sedbergh and Ingleton can be seen to the right of the line.

Ascent to Shap Summit

Nothing can equal the experience of travelling behind a mighty steam locomotive as it roared through the Lune Gorge and then struggled up the 4-mile 1 in 75 ascent to Shap Summit, 916 feet above sea level, having picked up a banking engine at Tebay. The modern experience is anesthetized; it is all too easy and comfortable, so much so that sometimes the driver has to brake for the speed restriction on Shap Summit.

Tebay was once a thriving railway community, the men working in the railway sidings or on the station, which served both the main line and the branch over the Pennines to Barnard Castle in County Durham, or driving the six banking engines that assisted the trains to the summit. Now there is virually nothing; the branch closed in 1962, the station six years later. The Lune Gorge is spectacular, with the Borrowdale Fells to the left and the Howgill Fells to the right. In contrast, view from Shap, reached after a couple of cuttings, is of bare wind- and rain-swept moorland.

After the freight branches to granite and cement works at the Summit have been passed, the line begins the long descent, mostly across open moorland with views to the Lake District hills to the left, although there is a more pastoral stretch along the river Leith. Two viaducts are crossed, the Lowther, in the grounds of the now demolished Lowther Castle, and the Eamont,

Joseph Locke's twenty-arch viaduct over the river Weaver, the only major piece of structural engineering on the Grand Junction Railway.

The new erecting shop at Crewe Works built during the 1930s. The LNWR workshops at Crewe made machinery of all kinds, not just locomotives.

from which Dalemain House, home of the first chairman of the Lancaster & Carlisle Railway, can be seen. From Penrith it is an unexciting run alongside the river Petteril into Carlisle.

Lancaster & Carlisle Railway

The Lancaster & Carlisle opened its line on 15 December 1846. The company remained independent until 1859, when the LNWR leased the line, full amalgamation following twenty years later. Both George Stephenson and Joseph Locke put forward proposals for the route. Stephenson, as always, favoured the easiest route that would avoid gradients, even if it meant going a long way round; on this occasion he suggested a barrage across Morecambe Bay, from which the line would run along the coast through Whitehaven to Carlisle. Locke preferred going 'up and over' the hills, although his first proposal did include a 1¼-mile tunnel under Shap Fell. He argued that the time trains lost on the ascent would be compensated on the descent and also foresaw, perhaps better than Stephenson, that locomotives would continue to grow in power and capacity.

The directors of the Lancaster & Carlisle eventually chose Locke's route, and went on to select Thomas Brassey to build the line. It was a happy combination. The immense work was completed in little more than two years by an army of navvies at one time nearly 10,000 strong. Over 500 men alone worked on Shap cutting for two years, removing 350,000 cubic yards of debris. Brassey built mud huts, a school and a church for his men, but even so there were disturbances from time to time, and attacks on local people. In February 1846 opposing groups of English and Irish navvies rioted in Penrith. Because so many lines were being built elsewhere, Brassey had to pay high wages to his men, who even went on strike briefly for more pay.

The Caledonian Railway

It was at Carlisle Citadel station that the Lancaster & Carlisle and the Caledonian Railway met, the latter carrying the line along a route planned by Locke across the border, through Annandale and the Clyde Valley and into Glasgow. This route also lost its drama with the vanishing of steam. Having crossed the Eden just beyond the station, and run briefly along the edge of the Solway Firth, where there are fine views back to the Lake District hills, the train starts a long ascent through Lockerbie and alongside the Annan towards the summit at Beattock (1,051 feet). The line climbs close to the A74 trunk road from the south and follows a Roman road, for this route north was used by the Romans and there are many ancient sites nearby.

Past Beattock summit, the train snakes down the long descent to Carstairs, running alongside the infant river Clyde, tiny here in comparison with the grandeur it attains in Glasgow. It is desolate country, although some of its bleakness has been tempered by the large stretches of recently planted woodland. Tinto, a conical hill on the left set in gentler, more pastoral country, heralds the approach of Carstairs, where the lines for Edinburgh and Glasgow divide.

The final 29 miles to Glasgow are along the Clyde valley, first through pleasant countryside and then into an industrial landscape, now partly abandoned by the heavy industries that brought Glasgow its prosperity. Just before the line crosses the Clyde, the site of the Caledonian's first terminus is passed at Bridge Street Junction. It was not until 1879 that the Admiralty gave permission for a bridge over the river, enabling the Caledonian to erect its splendid Central station. The recent sensitive modernization has retained the best features of the building, including the magnificent front, the steel trussed roof and the wooden booking offices. The celebrated destination indicator, which used linen blinds printed with station names and inserted manually into windows, has gone, to be replaced by the largest electronic travel information indicator in Europe.

Racing to the border

The honour of achieving the first Anglo-Scottish rail link went to the west-coast route when the Caledonian opened its line north from Carlisle on 15 February 1848. Although the North British line from Edinburgh to the border (see page 13) had already opened, it was another two years before the Tyne and the Tweed were bridged and through trains could run on the east-coast route. Within a month, the Post Office switched London to Edinburgh mail to the west-coast route and rivalry between the two for Anglo-Scottish traffic continued for many years.

In 1888, during the first of the two celebrated series of Great Races to Scotland, the time taken to reach Edinburgh from London on each line was reduced considerably. The west-coast companies, who had the longer and more difficult route, reduced running time from 10 to 8½ hours, while on the east-coast it fell from 9 to 8¼ hours. On individual journeys during the period of the races, much quicker times were achieved. (See page 182.)

Stanier Class 8P 4–6–2 No. 46229 Duchess of Hamilton *prepares to head out of Carlisle.*

London to Glasgow express in the Cumbria fells near Shap. Today's electric locomotives manage the steep ascents between Lancaster and Carlisle, and over Beattock to Glasgow, without difficulty.

Crewe to Holyhead

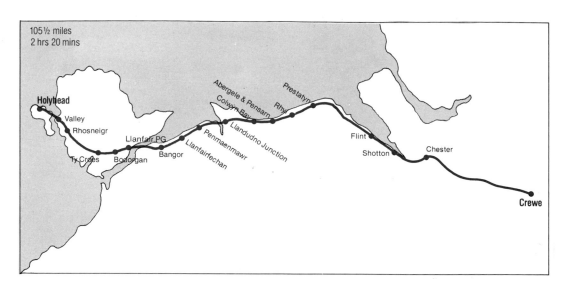

The first section of this route, from Crewe to Chester, crosses the broad Cheshire plain and for much of the way follows the Shropshire Union Canal. Beyond Chester, where there is a fine Italianate station with twin towers guarding the arcaded entrance, and Shotton, where the steel works can be seen on the right, the line runs along the shore of the widening Dee estuary. When it reaches Point of Ayr, at the tip of the estuary, the line swings west and hugs the coast virtually all the way to the Menai Straits.

There is an especially fine stretch after Penmaenrhos tunnel where the trains sweep past the edge of Colwyn Bay and another around Penmaenmawr, where the line runs along a tiny coastal strip between the sea and the mountains, directly underneath the massive outcrop known as Penmaenmawr Mountain (1,300 feet). The views inland are good on a fine day, with the peaks of Snowdonia standing out clear and high. Once the Straits have been crossed, the final stretch through southern Anglesey is not especially interesting, though it is fun to pass through the famous station at Llanfairpwllgwyngyllgogerychwryndrobwll-llantysiliogogogoch – the longest station name in the world – which was closed in 1966 and reopened in 1973.

The Britannia Bridge over the Menai Straits as Stephenson built it.

Irish packets in Holyhead harbour. Holyhead was chosen by the government as the port for the Irish Mail *because it gave the longest land route, trains being faster than steamers.*

The Chester & Holyhead Railway

The Chester & Crewe Railway built the line from Crewe to Chester, although three months before it opened on 1 October 1840 the Grand Junction, which had already built the main line north through Crewe, took that company over. Authorization for the line to Holyhead took longer to be granted, for there were prolonged discussions about where to site a new harbour and which route the railway should take to get to it. The choice eventually fell on Holyhead and the coastal route, and the Chester & Holyhead Railway, which had engaged Robert Stephenson as its engineer, was given the go-ahead in July 1844.

It was neither an easy nor a cheap line to build. Tunnels had to be driven through shale and slate, and two bridges had to built, over the river Conwy and across the Menai Straits. The line opened in three stages. The first trains ran from Chester to Bangor on 1 May 1848. Three months later, locomotives having been shipped across the Straits, a service began to operate between Llanfair PG and Bangor. But it was not until 18 March 1850 that the new Britannia

Bridge (so called because the central pier rested on the Britannia Rock in the middle of the Straits) between the mainland and Anglesey opened, and a through service could be instituted. By this time, the Chester & Holyhead had run out of money, and the line was worked by the newly formed London & North Western Railway (LNWR), which now controlled the west-coast route from London to Glasgow. The LNWR bought the line in 1859.

The arrival of the railway did much to develop towns such as Prestatyn, Rhyl and Llandudno, increasing numbers of holiday visitors arriving during the second half of the nineteenth century. Most of the line between Chester and Llandudno was quadrupled in the early years of the twentieth century (it has since been reduced to two tracks again), and Rhyl station was rebuilt at the same time, being given three long platforms, fast passing lines in the centre, a covered footbridge and carriage sidings. The line carried – as it still does – a good deal of passenger and main traffic *en route* to and from Ireland and a substantial amount of freight.

Tubular bridges

The two bridges are the highlights of the journey. Initially, Stephenson worked on the crossing of the Menai Straits, and then built the smaller and less difficult bridge over the Conwy in order to try out his ideas. Today, however, it is Conwy that best preserves his original conception, since the Britannia Bridge over the Straits was badly damaged by fire in 1970.

Stephenson's initial proposal for a bridge of two cast-iron arches 105 feet above high water was rejected by the Admiralty because of the danger that the masts of sailing ships would collide with the spandrels. There were no such risks with Telford's road crossing nearby, built a quarter of a century earlier, since this was a suspension bridge.

Stephenson then devised a bridge consisting of two wrought-iron beams, each of which contained a rectangular tube large enough to accommodate a train. The tubes were continuous, each 1,511 feet long, and would be mounted on masonry piers on each shore and on the Britannia Rock. It was a controversial design, the more so since Stephenson was considering dispensing with suspension chains, and a worrying time for him, as his railway bridge over the river Dee in Chester had recently collapsed, killing five people and almost ruining his reputation. L. T. C. Rolt quotes Stephenson in his biography:

> 'It was a most anxious and harrassing time with me', he admitted . . . afterwards. 'Often at night I would lie tossing about seeking sleep in vain. The tubes filled my head. I went to bed with them and got up with them. In the grey of the morning when I looked across the square it seemed an immense distance across to the houses on the opposite side. It was nearly the same length as the span of my bridge.'

At Conwy, a similar design was proposed, but with a single span of 400 feet instead of the four totalling 1,380 feet over the Straits. The easier crossing at Conwy was tackled first. The tubes were prefabricated nearby and during March and April 1848 the first one was floated into the river on pontoons and lifted into position by hydraulic presses. The first train crossed the bridge on 18 April, and by the next winter the second tube was in place.

Attention now focused on the Britannia Bridge. The tube for the up line was floated out and lifted in two sections between June 1849 and January 1850, not without considerable drama on the first occasion when the tube threatened to break loose and be swept out to sea. The down line tubes were positioned during the summer of 1850, after the up line was already in use.

Today the crossing of the Menai Straits lacks the excitement of Stephenson's original construction, although the views up and down the Straits, denied to generations of earlier travellers, are magnificent. When the bridge was rebuilt in the early 1970s, the tubes, which had been considerably distorted by the heat of the fire, were not replaced. Steel arches were substituted, and the train crosses on an open deck, on top of which a road deck has been placed to relieve the pressure of traffic across Telford's bridge. However, the original masonry towers, decorated with lions intended to represent the strength of the bridge, have been retained.

Though it is much shorter, the bridge over the Conwy does supply the genuine experience. Three bridges can be seen from the platform of Llandudno Junction station. On the left is Stephenson's tubular bridge, the entrance designed like a castle keep with arrow slits and battlements and two battlemented turrets alongside; in the centre is Telford's original road bridge; and on the right a modern road bridge. Behind all three run the walls of the magnificent late thirteenth-century castle, one of the most superb fortifications in the country. The train leaves the station, crosses the first part of the estuary on an embankment (there are fine views south to Snowdonia), and then plunges briefly into tubular darkness, before emerging and running along the castle walls. A journey not to be missed!

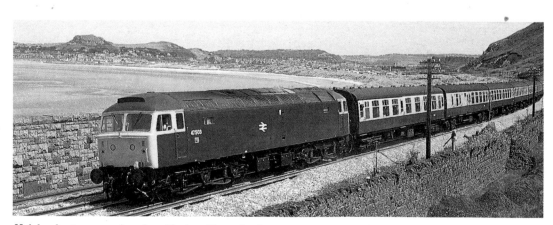

Holyhead express running alongside the wide sands of the North Wales coast near Penmaenmawr.

A steam excursion crosses the Dee just beyond Chester station. A girder on Robert Stephenson's original bridge here broke into three in May 1847, eight months after it was opened.

Llandudno to Blaenau Ffestiniog

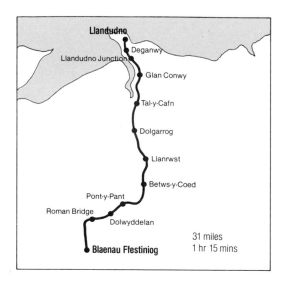

31 miles
1 hr 15 mins

This splendid line runs through magnificent scenery from the coast at Llandudno south along the valley of the river Conwy and then up into the hills and slate mountains around Blaenau Ffestiniog, where a new station, opened in 1982, is shared with the Ffestiniog Railway (see page 74). The trip is well worth making for its own sake, as well as being a useful link with the Cambrian Coast line (see page 82).

The branch to Llandudno from the main line to Holyhead was opened in 1858 and leased by the LNWR four years later. Llandudno station was rebuilt and enlarged in 1897 to cope with the increasing number of visitors to the town; today

it looks rather sad, but still comes alive during the summer season.

The route south from Llandudno Junction was opened in three stages. The Conway (note the anglicized spelling) & Llanrwst's section was opened in June 1963, but the company had been taken over by the LNWR only two months after building began: the LNWR was determined not to let any rival companies on its patch. The extension to Betws-y-Coed was opened to freight services in 1867, and to passenger trains the following year. The LNWR hesitated for some years before tackling the final stretch: construction would be expensive and tunnels inevitable, but there were potential profits in the form of slate traffic. Nor was the company sure whether to construct a standard-gauge line or to opt for a narrower gauge like the other slate tramways in the mountains. In the end, standard gauge was chosen, and the line finally opened in July 1879, the permanent station in Blaenau being completed two years later.

Conwy estuary

There are lovely views of Conwy castle on the stretch between Llandudno and Llandudno Junction. Then the line runs up the estuary, alongside the river and pleasant water-meadows. The hills begin to close in as the train approaches Betws-y-Coed, where the Conwy Valley Railway Museum is situated in the old goods yard alongside the line. There is a purpose-built museum with displays on the history and development of

Blaenau Ffestiniog with the former GWR station in the middle distance and surrounded by huge grey slate workings. The station was the terminus for the line from Bala, opened in 1882 and closed in 1961.

Conwy castle with the modern road bridge over the Conwy, Telford's suspension bridge and, on the far left, *the castellated entrance tower of Stephenson's rail bridge.*

railways, especially in North Wales, and some standard- and narrow-gauge locomotives and rolling stock.

Beyond Betws-y-Coed, the line climbs steeply, twisting and turning to win every advantage from the land and minimize the sharpness of the ascent. There are five tunnels, four of them short, on this part of the line, a seven-arch stone viaduct and no less than seventeen bridges. The scenery becomes increasingly Alpine, with farms and little streams tucked into folds in the hillside, and magnificent distant views of the highest Snowdonia peaks, including Glyder Fawr (3,279 feet) and Snowdon (3,555 feet).

The line climbs higher and higher, then plunges into the deep darkness of Ffestiniog tunnel, 2 miles 338 yards long. The other side is a startling contrast. Whereas the northern slopes were a mixture of greens and browns, with wild flowers in spring and a wonderful range of colours in autumn, Blaenau Ffestiniog lives in a world of grey. Grey is the colour of the houses and streets, and above the settlement tower massive, unfriendly mountains of grey slate. The train runs past the old station into the new terminus, where it is possible to change trains for the Ffestiniog Railway, and a freight-only line leads south to Trawsfynydd nuclear power station.

Welsh Narrow-Gauge Lines

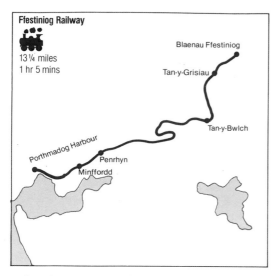

Ffestiniog Railway
13¼ miles
1 hr 5 mins

Blaenau Ffestiniog
Tan-y-Grisiau
Tan-y-Bwlch
Porthmadog Harbour
Penrhyn
Minffordd

Ffestiniog Railway

The rock-bottom essence of volunteering on the Ffestiniog was hard physical work; shovelling, digging, wheeling a barrow, hauling out tree-trunks, cutting down branches, pulling out nettles and brambles by hand, tipping out loads of ballast, carrying heavy rails and sleepers .... There were a great many who came a few times, and a few who came a great many times.

To a greater or lesser extent these words, written by an historian of the Ffestiniog venture, apply to all preserved steam lines, which in the early years depend for ultimate success on the willingness of their supporters to undertake any task, no matter how menial or boring, in pursuit of what for years seems an unattainable objective. They apply with great force to the Ffestiniog Railway; the line had been closed for eight years when a preservation society was formed, and then a period of no less than twenty-eight years elapsed before the original aim, to resume running between Porthmadog and Blaenau Ffestiniog, was achieved.

To begin with, a word or two about the early history of the line, which is the oldest of the narrow-gauge lines in Wales still in operational existence. It was opened in 1836, having been built so that, except for the last ¾-mile across the cob at Porthmadog, there was a continuous downhill gradient from Blaenau Ffestiniog. On the downward journey, wagons laden with slate from the quarries around Blaenau were simply worked by gravity, without any additional motive power. Horses hauled the empty wagons on the return journey.

Steam haulage was introduced in 1863, but it was another six years before the Ffestiniog's most famous locomotive, the 0–4–4–0 *Little Wonder,* was delivered. There had been suggestions that the line should be doubled, to cope with increasing traffic on the 1 foot 11½ inch gauge line. *Little Wonder* was developed in response to this situation. A double-boiler arti-

culated locomotive with twin fireboxes, it was twice as powerful as anything that had previously been able to negotiate the steep twists and curves of the route.

Until 1881, the Ffestiniog was the only railway to Blaenau. In that year, the London & North Western Railway (LNWR) opened its line to the town, and two years later the Great Western Railway (GWR) branch from Bala was completed. Increased competition, and the gradual fall in demand for slate as other, cheaper roofing materials began to be used, brought about the slow decline of the line. Tourist traffic helped prospects between the wars, but by 1945 the company had run out of money, and all services ceased the following year.

When the volunteers set to work eight years later, they found a track overgrown with a jungle of vegetation but, underneath, 'the foundations of a finely engineered railway', as the Ministry of Transport described it. In 1955, services across the cob from Porthmadog to Boston Lodge began to operate; in 1956 the route was extended to Minffordd; and in 1958 it reached Tan-y-Bwlch, 7½ miles up in the mountains. It was subsequently extended to Dduallt in 1968.

The switchback climb up to Tan-y-Bwlch through magnificent scenery and with superb

2–6–2T Mountaineer, *built in the USA and used in France during the First World War, at Boston Bridge at the south-east end of the Cob.*

0–4–4–0T Merddin Emrys, *built by the Ffestiniog Railway in its own locomotive works in 1879, hauls* a down train through magnificent scenery below *Dduallt.*

views into the hills and back to the estuary and the coastline was a far finer and more exciting journey than the trip on many other preserved lines. But the Ffestiniog's supporters remained unsatisfied: Blaenau was still their goal. New problems arose, and to solve these problems a group of people formed whose activities and resolution have become part of Ffestiniog folklore. They were the 'Deviationists'.

The principal problem was the British Electricity Authority (BEA), the forerunner of today's Central Electricity Generating Board. The BEA proposed building a pumped storage electricity scheme, which would have involved flooding the line north of Moelwyn tunnel. The Festiniog Railway Company (for technical and financial reasons the original company formed in 1832 to operate the line never went out of existence, and remains in control today) resisted, but lost, and had to wait until 1971 before financial compensation was finally agreed.

The Deviationists would not accept defeat and abandon the aim of reaching Blaenau. Eventually a new route was agreed with the electricity authorities, and construction began in 1965 at

Dduallt. There followed thirteen years of hard labour. If the opening of the earlier sections of line had been difficult, this part was backbreaking. An entirely new line had to be carved out of the rock, most of the work being done by volunteers at weekends and during annual holidays. A new Moelwyn tunnel had to be constructed, this one 295 yards long. Above all, there was the dramatic spiral just beyond Dduallt, where the line twists back on itself in order to gain height.

When the Deviation was opened to Tan-y-Grisiau in 1978, there remained only the final 1¼ miles into Blaenau Ffestiniog, opened in 1982, to a brand-new station shared with trains on British Rail's line through the mountains from Llandudno (see page 73). As the line emerges from Moelwyn tunnel the views are of a bleaker, less pastoral landscape than before, with moorland and a reservoir stretching out to the slate peaks.

Although the Ffestiniog's route is now complete, the Railway continues to develop. Attention is being directed towards restoring the historical 'feel' of the line and to training volunteers for skilled jobs such as driving locomotives.

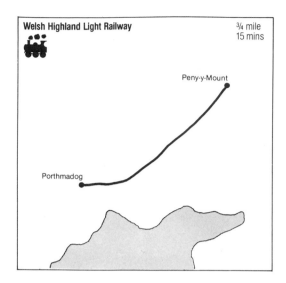

Welsh Highland Light Railway

3/4 mile
15 mins

Peny-y-Mount

Porthmadog

Welsh Highland Light Railway

The title of this short but fascinating line commemorates a longer narrow-gauge line (the gauge was 2 feet) that ran through the mountains, carrying both holiday-makers and cargoes of slate for trans-shipment to the Cambrian main line at Porthmadog.

The original Welsh Highland Railway, which opened in 1923 and closed fourteen years later after the Festiniog Railway had tried but failed to make a go of the company, was itself the result of the merger of two older railways. These were the North Wales Narrow Gauge Railway, which completed its line from Dinas to Rhyd-ddu on the western slopes of Snowdon in 1881, and the ponderously named Portmadoc, Beddgelert & South Snowdon Railway Company, which took over an existing tramway from Porthmadog worked by horses and began to build a northward line through Beddgelert to Rhyd-ddu (or South Snowdon, as it was un-nationalistically named). The PB & SSR ran out of money and abandoned the works, which were finished, with some alterations from the original plan, by the Welsh Highland Railway. A new terminus south of the Cambrian coast line at Porthmadog was also constructed, as well as a link line to the Festiniog Railway's Harbour station.

One of the highlights of a journey on the original route was the spectacular view of Aberglaslyn Pass. Two short tunnels in quick succession suddenly brought the line out on to a ledge high above Afon Glaslyn, from which the line descended steeply into a third tunnel. This was not the only attractive part of the trip. Further north, there was the lovely valley of the Gwfrai and the girder bridge over Afon Treweunydd, and everywhere there were spectacular cuttings and curves as the line kept a precarious foothold on the mountainside.

The present line runs near, though not on, the southernmost portion of the original Welsh Highland line. The idea of reviving the route germinated in 1961, and the present Welsh Highland Light Railway Company was formed three years later. But it took well over a decade of frustrating negotiations and, on the whole, frustrated hopes before the first locomotive was delivered in 1975 and the first track laid the following year. Even so it was not until 1980 that the first services began to operate. The frustration arose principally because of the difficulty of winning the commitment of the County Council to reopen the original route from Porthmadog to a point between Beddgelert and Rhyd-ddu.

Diesel locomotives worked the trains for the first three seasons, and were joined by a steam locomotive in 1983. From the terminus the line curves past Gelert's Farm Works (where the Railway's machine shop, carriage shed and loco shed are to be found), towards the original course of the Welsh Highland Railway. The sidings where slate was loaded from the WHR's narrow-gauge wagons to the standard-gauge wagons of the main line can be seen on the right. Before the train reaches the terminus at Pen-y-Mount, there are views up the Croesor valley, with Cnicht (2,265 feet) dominating the scene.

Karen, *the Welsh Highland Railway's first steam locomotive, built in Bristol in 1942.*

Cnicht seen through the point levers at Pen-y-Mount.

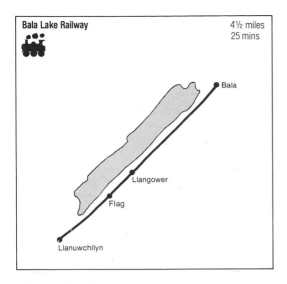

Bala Lake Railway

4½ miles
25 mins

Bala

Llangower

Flag

Llanuwchllyn

Bala Lake Railway

The Bala Lake Railway is a narrow-gauge railway that runs along the track of a former standard-gauge route. The present-day 4½-mile line through attractive scenery at the edge of Lake Bala occupies part of what was the GWR's line from Ruabon on the English border across the mountains to the coast at Barmouth. The line, originally built by a number of different small railway companies, opened throughout in 1869; the Bala & Dolgelly Railway (B&DR), which was responsible for 17¼ miles including the stretch along the lake, was taken over by the GWR in 1877.

For some time it was touch and go whether this route or the former Cambrian line through Welshpool and Machynlleth (see page 82) would be chopped, but the line was finally closed in 1963, eight years before the idea of a new, private line was mooted. In contrast with many other private lines, services got off the ground pretty quickly, and in 1972, the following year,

the first trains ran on a 1¼-mile line from Llanuwchllyn, to the south-west of the lake. Since then the line has been extended twice, and now finishes a short walk from Bala town centre. There are plans for another extension around the end of the lake to the Dolgellau road.

Llanuwchllyn remains the principal station. When Rheilffordd Llyn Tegid Cyf, to give the Bala Lake Railway Company its proper title, was set up, the station building at Llanuwchllyn was the only remaining Bala & Dolgelly station structure. It has since been enlarged, using bricks from dismantled stations to preserve the style of the original building, and a Cambrian Railway platform canopy has been added. The signal box and frame date from 1896, by which time the GWR was already in charge.

From Llanuwchllyn the line runs through open fields and then along the lake to the first station, which has the curious name of Flag. The name dates from the time when the B&DR built a private station here for one of its principal shareholders, Sir Watkin Williams Wynne. Sir Watkin's house was on the far side of the lake; when he arrived at the station a flag was hoisted to signal a boat to come and fetch him.

The next station, Llangower, is in an attractive spot beside the lake. Then comes a short section away from the foreshore through meadows and along a deep cutting before the line returns to the lake shore on an embankment. Another cutting intervenes, and then there are lovely views once more across the water as the town comes into sight. The final station is reached around a long right-hand curve.

In the first few years, the line, which was built to a gauge of 1 foot 11½ inches, was worked by diesel locomotives. Steam locomotives have been operated since the mid-1970s, however, and the hour-long two-way trip through pleasant country is very popular with visitors.

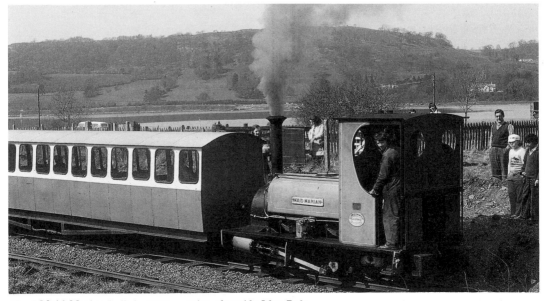

No. 5 Maid Marian *built in 1903, running alongside Llyn Bala.*

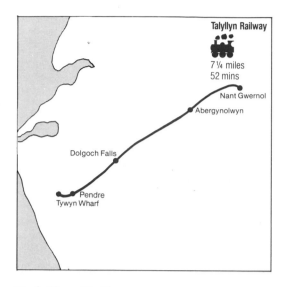

Talyllyn Railway

7 ¼ miles
52 mins

Nant Gwernol
Abergynolwyn
Dolgoch Falls
Pendre
Tywyn Wharf

Talyllyn Railway

Now well into its second century, the Talyllyn Railway has operated a service every year since 1866. That it has done so is principally the result of the efforts and faith of two men: Sir Haydn Jones and L. T. C. Rolt. Jones bought the Railway from its original owners in 1911, and despite sharply declining passenger and freight traffic did not break his pledge to keep the line open during his lifetime.

On Jones' death in 1950, Rolt, an engineer and writer whose superb biographies of George and Robert Stephenson and Isambard Kingdom Brunel are often quoted in this book, assembled a group of enthusiasts who together formed the Talyllyn Railway Preservation Society: the first railway preservation society in Great Britain, and possibly in the world. The Society operated its first services in 1951, and today the Railway is a flourishing concern, attracting over 65,000 visitors a year.

One further person has to be thanked for the survival of the line. That is the parliamentary draftsman responsible for drawing up the bill by which the railways were nationalized in 1948. For some reason, one assumes the obscurity and virtual dereliction of the route, the Talyllyn Railway was not named, and so remained in private hands after nationalization.

Slate was the original purpose of the line, which was built in 1865 to carry slate from the hills above Abergynolwyn to the main Cambrian line at Tywyn (see page 84). Passengers were also carried, mainly quarrymen travelling to and from work, although there were some tourists right from the start. The gauge chosen was an uncommon one of 2 feet 3 inches; there have been only two others with that gauge in the country, both long since vanished.

Steam locomotives have worked the line from the start. The two ordered for the opening of the line were not supplemented until the Preservation Society took over, and while the present fleet contains four additional steam locomotives

in all, the original duo, *Talyllyn* and *Dolgoch*, are still proudly at work on the line.

The spick and span line the visitor travels on today is the product of a great deal of hard work, most of it by voluntary labour. By a stroke of good fortune, two of the locomotives of one of the other 2 feet 3 inch gauge lines, the Corris Railway only 15 miles distant at Machynlleth, had not been removed, even though the line had closed three years before; these were bought and worked while *Talyllyn* and *Dolgoch* were being renovated. Rolling stock has been repaired (three carriages and a brake van also date from the opening of the line) and additional items have been bought; track was first made safe and later renewed; Wharf station was substantially rebuilt, with a new track layout and an additional platform constructed; the engine shed at Pendre station was rebuilt and the workshops developed (repairs are undertaken on behalf of other preserved lines as well as the Talyllyn's own stock); and of course all the day-to-day work of repair and maintenance has to be tackled in order to ensure safe running.

The Society's most substantial project, completed in 1976, has been the ¾-mile extension at the eastern end of the line from the former terminus at Abergynolwyn to Nant Gwernol. Originally, only goods and mineral trains ran over this final stretch which passes through some magnificent countryside.

Wharf station

Services start at Wharf station in Tywyn, close to the BR station. The name Wharf signifies an exchange point, not with water-borne transport, but with the standard-gauge Cambrian Railway. The station buildings occupy the former yard where rows and rows of slates were stacked, awaiting the wagons that would carry them to builders' yards in virtually every expanding Victorian suburb in the country. As well as a booking office, shop, café and so forth, the station buildings house the Narrow Gauge Railway Museum, which has a fine collection of locomotives and rolling stock, and displays on the slate industry in north Wales.

The next station, Pendre, is reached almost immediately after a steep ascent. After this, the line runs out into the countryside, and there are fine views ahead to the mountains. There is a steep climb beyond Hendy Halt, at 1 in 71 one of the steepest on the entire line, as the train enters the lovely valley of Afon Fathew. Past Rhydyronen the line continues to climb along the edge of the valley to Brynglas, where there was once a wool mill. Cadair Idris comes into view now as the train makes for Dolgoch, where the spectacular falls and ravine should not be missed; the walk around the Dolgoch estate makes a pleasant break from the ride on the train. Dolgoch viaduct, just before the station, has three arches and rises 51 feet above the gorge.

The next section, which brings the train to Abergynolwyn, runs through Forestry Commission plantations before emerging on to the bare mountain just before the station. The village nearby has shops and an interesting small Quarry Museum. The final stretch runs through woodland, past a waterfall and then around Afon Gwernol gorge to Nant Gwernol station.

0–4–0T No. 6 Douglas, *presented to the Talyllyn Railway in 1953, crossing Dolgoch viaduct and almost* *hemmed in by the trees growing on the banks of the stream below.*

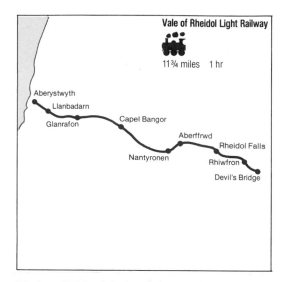

Vale of Rheidol Light Railway

11¾ miles   1 hr

Aberystwyth
Llanbadarn
Glanrafon
Capel Bangor
Aberffrwd
Rheidol Falls
Nantyronen
Rhiwfron
Devil's Bridge

Vale of Rheidol Light Railway

Despite British Rail's decision to stop using steam locomotives during the 1960s, and the unfriendly attitude it adopted even to steam-hauled excursions for a number of years thereafter, one steam railway remained in its hands. This signal honour is held by the Vale of Rheidol Light Railway, which runs for 11¾ miles from the coast at Aberystwyth inland along the Afon Rheidol to Devil's Bridge.

The line opened for traffic in 1902. Taken over by Cambrian Railways eleven years later, it then became part of the GWR in 1922 and of British Railways at nationalization. On several occasions, especially during the 1960s, British Rail threatened to close the line. By the 1980s, however, it had become an established and successful tourist attraction, and British Rail's earlier policy of neglect, which allowed stations to deteriorate and failed to care for rolling stock and locomotives, had long since been reversed.

The line was built on a 1 foot 11½ inch gauge with two purposes in mind: to bring lead from the mines in the Rheidol valley to the coast and the main line, and as a tourist attraction. Over the years, it is the second function that has come to predominate, and from 1937 freight was no longer carried.

The journey starts from the main-line station in Aberystwyth, where steam locomotives occupy platforms alongside diesels bound for Shrewsbury and London. When the line's original terminus was given up in 1968, the Vale of Rheidol trains were transferred to the platforms once used for the now-closed Carmarthen branch. Leaving the town, the line crosses the river Rheidol and runs along the river valley in beautiful scenery for some 5 miles. Then the ascent starts: 480 feet are climbed in only 4 miles at a gradient at times as steep as 1 in 50. It is a magnificent journey with breathtaking curves that only a narrow-gauge line can achieve, through a lovely tree-filled gorge, especially delightful in spring and autumn. The finale is a sharp bend to the left that brings the line to Devil's Bridge, built in the twelfth century, and the series of spectacular waterfalls beyond.

A unique sight on a British railway: a narrow-gauge locomotive with the driver wearing a regulation BR cap. No. 8 Llewellyn climbs slowly through wooded country along the vale of Rheidol.

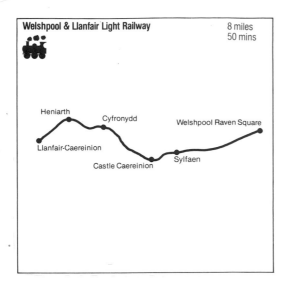

Welshpool & Llanfair Light Railway — 8 miles / 50 mins

Heniarth · Cyfronydd · Welshpool Raven Square · Llanfair-Caereinion · Castle Caereinion · Sylfaen

Welshpool & Llanfair Light Railway

This delightful line, which runs for 8 miles through some of the most attractive countryside of the English-Welsh borderlands, carries far more passengers today than ever it did in its earlier life as part first of Cambrian Railways and later of the GWR. After many schemes and years of planning, construction got under way in 1901, and the line opened two years later. An unusual gauge of 2 feet 6 inches was selected, and the Cambrian Railways operated the line with rolling stock and locomotives provided by the Welshpool & Llanfair Light Railway Company. At Grouping in 1923, the route became part of the Great Western Railway.

There were no minerals underneath the gently rolling hills of Montgomeryshire, as the county was then known, nor was there any industry. Instead, the purpose of the line was to serve the agricultural community: to bring farm produce and people from the villages into Welshpool, the local market town, where the station was shared with the main line to the Cambrian coast (see page 82). Passenger usage fell sharply in the mid-1920s, when a competing bus service – also operated by the GWR – was introduced, and passenger services ceased entirely in 1931. Freight services were maintained until 1956, although in the last few years only one train a day ran in each direction.

The line was re-opened in 1963 as a private concern and was worked by *The Earl* and *The Countess,* the two Beyer Peacock 0–6–0 side tank locomotives purchased in 1903 for the first opening of the line. For a short while the original terminus was used, but in August 1963 the local council completed its purchase of the section of line running through Welshpool, along the streets of the town and of alleyways at the back of houses. At first, the eastern terminus was at Castle Caereinion; in 1972 the line was re-opened to Sylfaen, and in 1981 the Railway's biggest project was completed when the extension to Welshpool Raven Square, on the edge of town, was opened.

From Raven Square, the line climbs steeply – the gradient is an amazing 1 in 29, which would be virtually insuperable for any standard-gauge locomotive – up Golfa Bank. Then there is a delightful stretch with sharp curves and good views as far as Cyfronydd, where the railway meets Afon Banwy, following it and the main road between Welshpool and Dolgellau into Llanfair Caereinion.

As well as *The Earl* and *The Countess,* the line now boasts an interesting collection of locomotives from many different parts of the world. The first international arrival was from the Austrian Tyrol, and since then engines running on the line have come from Antigua, Sierra Leone and Finland.

Sir Drefaldwyn *at an ungated crossing near Golfa Bank. The locomotive, whose name translates as* 'Montgomeryshire', *came to the W & L from a line in south-east Austria.*

Shrewsbury to Pwllheli

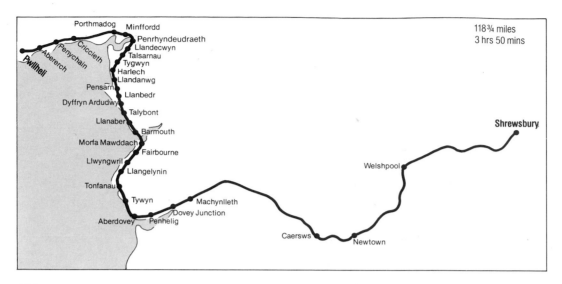

This journey takes the traveller through some of the most attractive parts of central and north Wales. To begin with, mountains are the theme as the line cuts across the Cambrian range, finding a route between some of its highest peaks. Then an estuary section brings the train out on to the coast, and from Aberdovey nearly all the way to the terminus at Pwllheli there are fine sea views, with some dramatic estuary crossings and, to the east and north, the distant prospect of the mountains of Snowdonia.

British Rail calls this route, and the connecting line south along the coast from Dovey Junction to Aberystwyth, the Cambrian Lines, in recollection of the company that operated much of them. The Cambrian Railway was the largest independent Welsh railway company when it was absorbed into the Great Western Railway in 1922, the year before Grouping. The Cambrian had been formed in 1864 from a number of small companies, three of which were already operating the present line from Buttington, just east of Welshpool, as far as Machynlleth. The line beyond Machynlleth was promoted by the Aberystwith & Welch Coast Company (sic) and was opened piecemeal between 1863 and 1867. The A & WC itself was taken over by the Cambrian Railway in 1865.

A northbound class 47 diesel passing through Shrewsbury station beneath a semaphore signal gantry.

Above: *The view as a Shrewsbury train swings on to the bridge over the Mawddach estuary.*

Below: *The view north across the Mawddach estuary towards Barmouth and the summit of Diffws.*

Risk of closure

Until the 1960s, a surprisingly large number of lines found an often difficult way through the hills and mountains of central and north Wales. The Cambrian Lines are almost the only survivors − and until the mid-1980s even their survival was very much at risk. A closure notice was served on the line north of Dovey Junction in 1971, and after that a prolonged twilight prevailed, in which the line became caught in a spiral of decline.

Despite quite heavy use by local inhabitants (almost 40 per cent of journeys in 1980 were by schoolchildren) and by the summer influx of visitors, operating costs far exceeded revenue. The backlog of costly maintenance work grew year by year, additional speed restrictions had to be imposed at various points, over and above the already low limit operating throughout the line, and the unattractive diesel multiple units used and the lack of through services beyond Shrewsbury did not help to attract more passengers. And then there was the bridge across the Mawddach estuary at Barmouth, which had to be closed between October 1980 and May 1981 after it was discovered that teredo worms (a rare species of marine worm) had been attacking the timber piles.

In January 1985, however, things took a turn for the better when BR announced a package of improvements, costing a total of £4.7 million. The entire line west of Shrewsbury is to be controlled from a single operations centre at Machynnlleth under Radio Electronic Token Block (described in detail on page 190) and level crossings will be automated; new, faster and more comfortable 'Sprinter' diesel multiple units will be employed on the line; and there is to be a daily through train between London and Aberystwyth using a specially adapted locomotive. These improvements are due to take effect by 1987, and will, it is hoped, attract more business to the line.

Jacobean station

The journey starts in splendid style at Shrewsbury station, built in 1848 in Jacobean style with a handsome façade and a tall clock tower. Originally, the building had two storeys, but in 1903 the whole station was raised and a third storey was added underneath the existing two in the same style. The platforms extend over the river Severn, which almost encircles the city, and a walk to the far end of one of them is rewarded with a fine view of both the river and the castle, originally Norman, but much altered and rebuilt since then.

Shrewsbury was never a Cambrian station. The first 18 or so miles of the trip are along what were originally the metals of the Shrewsbury & Welshpool, which was later operated jointly by the GWR and the LNWR, and until the closures in the 1960s only trains for Aberystwyth regularly ran via Shrewsbury. The line passes rich dairy country at first, with good views southwards the Stiperstones and Long Mynd with their characteristic conical peaks, before joining the river Severn shortly before entering Welshpool. Now the hills gradually become higher, and there are views of distant peaks as the train runs through Newtown and on to Caersws over the river and then the Montgomery Canal. This is just the kind of lush peaceful country that tempts many people to get off the train and explore, but, except for the three places just mentioned, the thirteen intermediate stations between Shrewsbury and Machynlleth, a distance of over 60 miles, were closed in the 1960s. Since the line is to benefit from substantial investment, there must surely be a case for reopening some, despite the operational difficulties this could cause on a single-track line.

David Davies

Caersws is the start of high mountain country and of one of the most dramatic stretches of the entire route: the long climb to the summit of Talerddig (693 feet). The original aim had been to make directly south-west for Aberystwyth. But no feasible route around the mass of Pumlumon (2,427 feet) could be found, and a more northerly route was selected. Even that was not easy. At Talerddig a cutting 120 feet deep

had to be gouged out of solid rock; for a time it was the deepest cutting in the world. David Davies, the contractor, preferred a cutting to a tunnel because he could use the stone for bridges further west along the line.

Davies was a classic example of a Victorian who made good through his own efforts. He started life as a sawyer and finished it as a builder of bridges and docks and owner of many coalfields in south Wales. This was among the first lines he built. 'I often feared this would be the rock of my destruction, but with hard work and Heaven's blessing it has proved to be the rock of my salvation,' he is quoted as saying when the line was completed.

The mountainous stretch continues for some time, the line running alongside Afon Iaen. Then the hills begin to get lower, and the countryside softer, as the descent to the Dovey valley starts. Soon the train is running alongside the Dovey in fertile countryside, through Machynlleth and on to Dovey Junction.

Dovey Junction sounds as if it should be a busy station. The reality is a wooden platform with a waiting-room set in the middle of grassy marshland, with no access by road. Trains along the Aberystwyth branch follow the southern side of the Dovey estuary, while those of Pwllheli cross the river on a largely timber bridge, the first of several along this stretch of line. Now there is a fine run along the edge of the estuary, the track squeezed between the hillside and the shore. Seawalls and four short tunnels through headlands had to be built to bring the line to Aberdovey.

Coastal route

Now, finally, the sea is reached, and you scarcely lose sight of it for the next 47 miles to Pwllheli. From Aberdovey to Tywyn, where the terminus of the Talyllyn Railway (see page 78) can be seen on the right, the line crosses the flat coastal plain, with views to distant hills on the right. Soon, however, the mountains reach straight down to

The deep cutting hewn through the rock at Talerddig.

Portmeirion, the Italianate village built by the architect Clough Williams-Ellis in the 1920s.

the sea and at Friog the line climbs to a narrow ledge poised above the water; at one point an avalanche shield protects the tracks from falling rocks. On a clear day, the houses of Barmouth can be seen from northbound trains as they descend to the shore again at Fairbourne, where a 12-inch gauge miniature railway has its terminus.

Morfa Mawddach, Welsh for Barmouth Estuary, is where the Pwllheli line met the former Cambrian line along the estuary to Dolgellau, which closed in 1965. Beyond it is one of the highlights of the trip: the crossing of the estuary on the magnificent 121-span bridge. The view up the estuary towards Cadair Idris (2,928 feet) to the south and Diffwys (2,462 feet) to the north is magnificent, with peak after peak rolling back from the water's edge.

All but eight of the spans are of timber. The steel spans of the bridge, which can also be crossed on foot, can be opened to allow shipping through, although that rarely happens nowadays. After the infestation by marine worms had been discovered, the bridge was repaired in two stages. In May 1981, diesel multiple units were allowed to cross. Five years later all the timber piles had been encased in concrete, and the bridge was opened to locomotives.

Barmouth to Pwllheli

Beyond Barmouth the line follows the shore again, with views towards Snowdonia and, to the west, of the Lleyn Peninsula. It turns inland for a time, before regaining the coast near Llanbedr, where the deserted buildings of a Royal Aircraft Establishment are passed close to the line. Now Harlech Castle dominates the view, the station lying immediately in its shadow. The castle was built by Edward I between 1283 and 1290 and, for four years in the early fifteenth century, it was occupied by Owain Glyndŵr and his men. Moving away from the coast, the line makes for the timber bridge over Afon Dwyryd. Portmeirion, Sir Clough Williams-Ellis' Italianate village, can be seen on the opposite side of the estuary.

Past Minffordd, where the Ffestiniog Railway (see page 74) crosses above the present route, the line rolls on to another wooden bridge, across the estuary of Afon Glaslyn. The views here are spectacular. Porthmadog is something of a railway centre. As well as the BR line, there is the terminus of both the Ffestiniog Railway and the Welsh Highland Railway (see page 75), although the three lines do not meet.

The line returns to the coast near Criccieth, where the great castle was raised in the first half of the thirteenth century, and runs for almost the entire final stretch along the shore, through Butlin's holiday camp at Penychain and into Pwllheli. In good weather it is possible to see a long stretch of the coast to the south, perhaps as far as Barmouth, with, as always in this part of the country, the high mountains standing out above the coastal plain.

Shrewsbury to Swansea

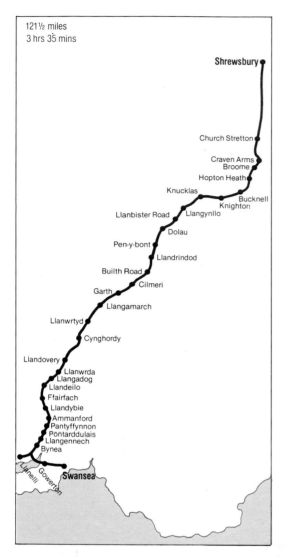

121½ miles
3 hrs 35 mins

Shrewsbury

Church Stretton

Craven Arms
Broome
Hopton Heath
Bucknell
Knucklas
Knighton
Llangynllo
Llanbister Road
Dolau
Pen-y-bont
Llandrindod
Builth Road
Cilmeri
Garth
Llangamarch
Llanwrtyd
Cynghordy
Llandovery
Llanwrda
Llangadog
Llandeilo
Ffairfach
Llandybie
Ammanford
Pantyffynnon
Pontarddulais
Llangennech
Bynea
Llanelli
Gowerton
Swansea

'The country through which the line passed was a succession of mountains and valleys, affording some of the most romantic and beautiful scenery anywhere to be met with, but with a small and scattered population.' Thus one of the first railway magazines described the Central Wales line, and it is not a judgement with which any present-day writer could disagree. The landscape remains as attractive and remote as ever it was when the first trains ran the full length of the route in October 1868, and the line still serves a succession of small market towns and lonely hamlets, although the population of this part of rural Wales is slowly increasing.

How is it, then, that the Central Wales line – nowadays commonly and more persuasively called the Heart of Wales line in marketing literature – has managed to survive, when lines running through busier areas have been axed by the dozen? Rumour has it that, when BR put the line up for closure in 1967 (they had already done so once before in 1962), the matter was discussed in Cabinet: the line, one minister pointed out, runs through several marginal parliamentary constituencies, and voters in central and west Wales are known for their willingness to change sides . . . . But the route still exists, and is operated under a Light Railway Order, which permits simplified signalling and other operating requirements and imposes a limitation on the number and speed of trains.

An investment programme announced in April 1985 involves the introduction of a new signalling system. Instead of passing the key tokens that permit them to enter a single-line section of track to a signalman, drivers will use instruments on station platforms to deposit and withdraw the

Knucklas viaduct, a memorial to its age, built by the engineer Henry Robertson.

A Heart of Wales train winds through the fine countryside around Sugar Loaf Mountain. A trip on this line takes the traveller through some of the least known and most attractive parts of inland Wales.

tokens. The instruments will be linked electronically to ensure that only one train is permitted on to one section of track at a time. A number of level crossings will also be automated.

Llanelly Railway

The first sections of the line were built at the southern end, and by 1858 the Llanelly Railway was operating a 30½-mile route from Llanelli north-east to Llandovery. In the north, around Shrewsbury, the London & North Western Railway (LNWR) was in expansionist mood, and was wanting in particular a direct link to the mining regions of south Wales and to the west Wales ports. Independent companies began to push southwards stage by stage. In 1862, when the Central Wales Railway got into financial difficulties because of unexpected construction problems at Knucklas viaduct and Llangynllo

tunnel, the LNWR stepped in with funds, providing in return locomotives and rolling stock for the new line.

By 1868, the LNWR had effectively taken control of the line from Craven Arms south to Llandovery: the next section to Llandeilo was a joint LNWR and Great Western Railway (GWR) route, followed by a GWR stretch to Pontarddulais and Llanelli, over which the LNWR had running rights. The northernmost portion, from Shrewsbury to Craven Arms, was also in joint ownership, while the direct line from Pontarddulais to Swansea was built by the LNWR.

The Central Wales line shares the first 20 miles of the 121-mile journey to Swansea with the Shrewsbury–Hereford–Newport route. From Shrewsbury (the station is described on page 84) the train runs through lush Shropshire

Carreg Cennen castle, a formidable stronghold perched on an outcrop 300 feet above the Towy valley.

countryside, with views of the Caer Cardoc range on the left and Long Mynd on the right. There is a long ascent to Church Stretton and then a descent to Craven Arms, where the Central Wales line branches off to the south-west. The train halts just beyond the station for the guard to operate the points.

Border country

The train is now running through the Marches, the borderlands between England and Wales that were once hotly disputed; the lineside villages seem peaceful and timeless, as if their way of life has hardly changed for centuries. The town of Knighton, which is a focal point for walkers on the long-distance Offa's Dyke Path, is in Wales, while its station is in England. Stretches of the original Dyke, built in the eighth century as a defensive rampart, can be seen high on the hillside to the right of the train.

The line continues alongside the river Teme as far as Knucklas, where there is a magnificent view from the station ahead to the viaduct, 190 yards long, with thirteen arches. Castellated turrets guard the approach at each end. The village nestles at the foot of the viaduct, and on the hillside above the ruins of Knucklas Castle can be seen. The line climbs from Knucklas, plunges into Llangynllo tunnel, and reaches the summit on the far side.

Beyond Llangynllo station comes a lovely stretch along the side of the Lugg valley to Llanbister Road and then through a cutting in the hills to Dolau, in the middle of a wide valley. The edge of Radnor Forest is visible to the left. Llandrindod Wells, the next station but one, was one of several spa towns to benefit from the construction of the railway. In the last years of Victoria's reign as many as 80,000 visitors arrived each year, most of them by train, to take the waters and restore themselves to health. Not so many come now (and few of them by train), but the town is still an important tourist and conference centre.

Builth Road is the next stop. The Central Wales line used to cross the Cambrian Railways' Mid-Wales line from Brecon to Llanidloes and Moat Lane here on a steel girder bridge. An hydraulic lift was used to transport passengers' luggage between the two stations. In the small engine shed at Builth Road were housed the two engines that helped trains up the long ascent to Llandrindod Wells.

Sugar Loaf tunnel

Immediately after the station the line crosses the river Wye and then runs through two short tunnels into Cilmeri, where a monument to Llewelyn the Last, the final member of a long line of Princes of Wales, can be seen on the right.

Now the line follows Afon Irfon through Llangamarch and Llanwrtyd, two small spa towns, and then begins the steep climb up to Sugar Loaf Mountain (1,098 feet) and Sugar Loaf tunnel.

When the line was built, the tunnel gave a great deal of trouble; the rock was unstable, and large quantities of water had to be pumped out. It has always been a dank and miserable place. One steam-locomotive driver recollects:

If it was a warm day going through the tunnel it was enough to smother you with the fumes and you were glad to get out. Even on a cold winter's night you'd be perspiring in the tunnel and sometimes you had to put your coat over your head because it was that hot. They say the roof of the Sugar Loaf was too low . . . on to the chimney stack. . . . [The tunnel] was hard graft and the perspiration was dripping off you and you were soaking wet and especially when you were on the bank engine in the rear . . . you had to come down and face the wind, you know, no shelter at all. It's a wonder to me that we all never caught pneumonia.

The far side of the tunnel opens up to some of the best views on the entire trip: behind is the conical Sugar Loaf, in front the Black Mountains range and, further off, the Brecon Beacons. There is fast running down a 1 in 60 descent to the lovely brick and stone Cynghordy viaduct over the river Bran, built on a curve. A wooded section brings the train to Llandovery, where the line enters the Tywi valley, accompanying the river on a long section through pleasant, though less spectacular, countryside to Llangadog, Llanwrda and Llandeilo. Beyond Llandeilo, Dinefwr castle can be seen; the great tower was built between 1150 and 1250, although the 'summerhouse' addition on the top was put up in the eighteenth century. Now the train leaves the Tywi, runs for a short while alongside the tiny Afon Cennen and then climbs briefly before joining the Loughor in Ammanford.

The wild uplands have been well and truly left behind now, and the line enters an industrial landscape. There are several mines near Ammanford, and at Pantyffynnon, just over a mile further south, a freight-only line serving three collieries comes in on the left and another joins from the right. Central Wales trains used to run directly from Pontarddulais into Swansea Victoria along the LNWR extension opened in 1867. Since it closed in 1964, they have reverted to the original route via Llanelli, running towards the town alongside the widening Loughor estuary. At Llanelli, the train reverses and runs along the main line (see page 146) into Swansea.

Cynghordy viaduct, south of Sugar Loaf Mountain,
100 feet high with eighteen brick and sandstone arches.

Severn Valley Railway

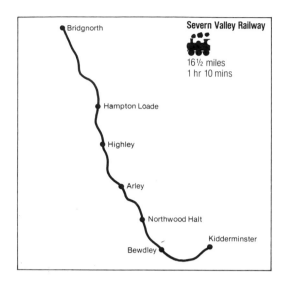

Severn Valley Railway

16½ miles
1 hr 10 mins

Bridgnorth

Hampton Loade

Highley

Arley

Northwood Halt

Bewdley

Kidderminster

This is one of the finest preserved lines in the country. First and foremost, it is a line on which a proper journey can be made: a trip of more than 16 miles through delighful countryside along the river Severn. Second, there is a substantial collection of locomotives and rolling stock, with examples from several different companies and periods of twentieth-century railway history. And, third, there is the special atmosphere of a Great Western line to be enjoyed; that sense of doing things correctly and with the style that only a successful, self-confident institution like the GWR could generate and that, nearly forty years after the Railway vanished at nationalization, is maintained on this efficiently-run line.

The Severn Valley Railway started as an independent concern, like many other lines. It originally ran for 40 miles from Shrewsbury to Hartlebury, north of Droitwich in Worcestershire, where it met the Oxford, Worcester & Wolverhampton Railway (OW&W). Authorization to build the line was granted in 1853. Construction only started in 1858, however, by which time the OW&W (the initials were said to stand for Old, Worse & Worse) had leased the line, and the first trains ran in 1862. The GWR absorbed the line during the 1870s, and from then until nationalization in 1948 only the familiar and much-loved chocolate and cream coaches and green locomotives of the GWR were to be seen running on the rails. The line may have seemed rather like a narrow-gauge northern outpost of the GWR, but it was very much a part of the Great Western network, which covered a large part of the West Midlands and the border counties.

Closure under Beeching
The Severn Valley remained an archetypal country railway. Four trains ran the length of the line each day, with sometimes a few more on the southern stretch below Bridgnorth, and there was some freight, principally agricultural

products and coal from the colliery at Alveley. The link route from Bewdley to Kidderminster, built by the GWR in 1878, made connections to and from Birmingham easier. Inevitably, when the planners and accountants reviewed the British Railways network in the early 1960s under the leadership of the now notorious Dr. Beeching, the Severn Valley line was a clear candidate for closure. The main part of the line was closed in 1963, although passenger services between Bewdley and Kidderminster survived until 1969 and freight ran north to Alveley Colliery until 1970.

Again in 1970, the first steam services were run by the fledgling Severn Valley Railway over 4 miles of track between Bridgnorth and Hampton Loade. Four years later services were restored from Hampton Loade to Bewdley, and in 1984 an extension to a brand-new terminus at Kidderminster was opened, partly financed by a highly successful share issue.

These bare facts conceal an enormous amount of hard work. Track, rolling stock and locomotives had to be purchased, restored and properly maintained and improved. Stations had to be brought back to their original condition, and maintained in as pristine a fashion as possible. Passenger facilities of every kind had to be organized. The existence of the line had to be publicized and its attractions constantly reviewed in order to keep up with public tastes. And, last but not least, the trains themselves had to be run safely and to time. Considerable training is needed for these responsible tasks, the bulk of which are done not by paid employees but by volunteers working at weekends and during their holidays.

The lure of steam: a glowing fire and track ahead. The engine is 4–6–0 No. 7819 Hinton Manor.

Above: *4–6–0 No. 7812* Erlestoke Manor *which was restored in the SVR's works, leaving Bewdley.*

Below: *The General Manager's Saloon at platform 2 of Bridgnorth station.*

SEVERN VALLEY RAILWAY

Bridgnorth station

This part of the Severn Valley has few roads, and so the journey takes you through countryside that would otherwise remain completely cut off. The line begins at the attractive little market town of Bridgnorth, set on a ridge of sandstone hills. The station, which is also the site of the Railway's locomotive shed and workshops, is in the Lower Town, close to the banks of the Severn.

There is a steep climb up out of the station, and the line runs high above the river along Oldbury viaduct. Then comes a gentle descent through pleasant farmland to Stern's Cottage, where the river is rejoined and followed for 4 miles to Hampton Loade. The journey continues through a woodland stretch, past the sidings that are the only remnant of Alveley Colliery, and over a steep ascent and descent to Highley station. The river again accompanies the line to Arley, generally recognized as the most attractive station on the railway. Soon afterwards the train crosses the river on the Victoria Bridge, a beautifully restored piece of mid-Victorian industrial art.

The line runs past reservoirs and into the Wyre Forest, through Northwood station (unless someone asks to get on or off, for the halt is a request stop), and along the wide river valley to the lovely town of Bewdley with its eighteenth-century houses. The final leg of the route to Kidderminster turns away from the river, running near a safari park and through Bewdley tunnel before ascending to the new station at Kidderminster built in traditional GWR style next to the British Rail station.

Rolling stock

A good number of the passenger carriages used on the line are not British Rail stock from the 1950s or 1960s, but are more interesting examples from earlier periods. Normally, two trains run in the chocolate and cream livery of the GWR; one in the post-Grouping London Midland & Scottish Railway's crimson-lake, and one in British Railway's carmine and cream of the 1950s.

Enthusiasts will have their favourite among the large stock of locomotives. It is worth looking at two locomotives from the GWR, *Hagley Hall* and *Hinton Manor*, both of which took part in the special steam trains laid on to celebrate the 150th anniversary of the GWR in 1985, and *RAF Biggin Hill*, one of the famous 'Black Fives' to enter service between 1934 and 1950 and one of the last steam locomotives to run in 1968, having been selected to take part in the Farewell to Steam tour on 11 August 1968. Also well worth looking out for is *Leander*, built at Crewe works in 1936 and one of the celebrated Jubilee Class 5XP 4–6–0s introduced by the LMSR in 1934.

2–8–0 No. 8233, built in 1940 by Sir William Stanier for the LMSR, crosses Victoria Bridge over the Severn.

The same standard heavy freight locomotive, 2–8–0
No. 8233, heads a train out of Bridgnorth station.

Liverpool to Manchester

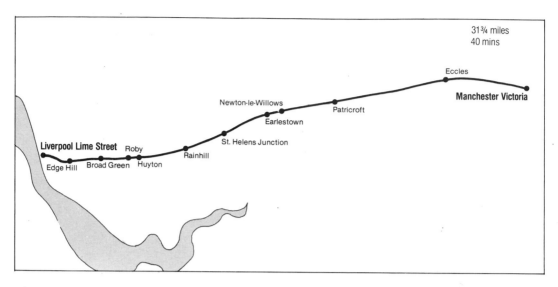

31¾ miles
40 mins

Eccles

Manchester Victoria

Newton-le-Willows

Patricroft

Earlestown

Liverpool Lime Street · Roby

St. Helens Junction

Rainhill

Edge Hill · Broad Green · Huyton

Liverpool to Manchester

This, it must be admitted immediately, is not at all a scenic route. But it is an essential journey for anybody with any interest at all in the history of railways: essential not only for sentimental reasons but also because, more than 150 years on, it is still possible to capture a good deal of the original atmosphere of the line.

It is important to be clear about the way in which the Liverpool & Manchester marked the start of the railway age. The line was not the first railway ever, nor was it even the first public railway. That distinction goes to the Stockton & Darlington (see page 26). It was, however, the first line to possess all the characteristics of a modern railway: that is, it employed mechanical power to haul timetabled passenger services over a double-track route with defined intermediate stations. Its predecessors had done some of these things, but not all of them; and the instantaneous success of the Liverpool & Manchester Railway meant that its successors all modelled themselves on the same pattern.

Wapping tunnel

Except for a short stretch at each end, the present-day line runs over the very route that George Stephenson built. Lime Street is now the Liverpool terminus, although the original freight terminus at Wapping (later known as Park Lane) was only closed as recently as 1966. Wapping was reached through a steep 1¼-mile tunnel built on a 1 in 48 gradient, along which wagons were wound by a stationary steam engine installed at the top of the incline at Edge Hill. Passengers embarked and disembarked at Crown Street, which was reached by a short tunnel from Edge Hill.

The tunnel to Wapping, which took three years to build, became one of the fashionable sights of town as soon as the public was admitted in July 1829, fourteen months before the line opened. A contemporary writer, James Scott Walker – evidently an enthusiastic protagonist of the railway since he dedicated his work, *An*

Accurate Description of the Liverpool and Manchester Rail-way, to George Stephenson – described a visit. The visitor found himself

within a vast vaulted passage, above twenty feet in width, which, without break, winding or lateral excavation, rings far and near with the voices of passengers and waggons. His footing is pleasant, dry and spacious, the road being formed of sand is as smooth as a bed left by a summer sea, and the double lines of rail-way in the middle, rising about an inch above the level, and in continuous and parallel lines, serve at once to guide his course and to convey an idea of interminable distance . . . . He is pleasingly surprised to find that his situation is by no means

Replica of Robert Stephenson's Rocket *built at Springwall near Newcastle. This locomotive took part in the restaging of the Rainhill Trials in 1979.*

*A diesel-hauled train enters Olive Mount Cutting, its
70-foot high rock walls thick with vegetation.*

gloomy, for the sides and roof of the vault being white-washed, have a cheerfulness and even warmth of appearance which he could not have anticipated.

Walker was so enraptured with the finished tunnel that he failed to do justice to the immense and difficult work involved in its creation. Hundreds of men laboured in the most appalling conditions for three years, equipped only with primitive tools. There was danger from subsidence, from flooding, and from the simple fact of darkness: candles were the only form of lighting available at the time.

Edge Hill

The modern departure from Lime Street, while not as steep nor perhaps so fantastic to modern eyes, is nevertheless most impressive. A gloomy, cavernous tunnel, built for the opening of Lime Street in 1836, ascends almost immediately from the end of the platforms. As the train climbs slowly up to Edge Hill, it is easy to imagine how eerie this underworld must have seemed in the days of steam. There is a fine view back to the glass and iron trainshed of Lime Street, best appreciated from the front of a descending diesel multiple unit.

At Edge Hill the passenger coaches were attached to, or detached from, their locomotive. To begin with, trains consisted of either first-class or second-class coaches, and were not mixed. To quote our fulsome guide once more, marking 'the commencement of the open Railway' were 'two beautiful Grecian columns, built of chequered brick, with pedestals and capitals ornamented with stone'. Ornament was 'combined with utility', for the columns served as chimneys for the furnaces of the two winding engines in the Crown Street and Wapping tunnels. In addition, a bridge built in Moorish style linked the two engine houses. The present Edge Hill station was also opened in 1836.

The line soon enters Olive Mount Cutting, which, even though the line has been quadrupled, still takes the breath away almost as much as it did that of the first travellers. The rock walls tower 70 feet above the train, green with damp and vegetation. The 2-mile cutting, through which, in 1830 at least, 'the carriages thunder like fabled chariots of the gods', leads into a long stretch which runs through the Liverpool suburbs.

Rainhill Trials

There is nothing now to distinguish the level stretch of track on which in October 1829 the celebrated Rainhill Trials took place, but undistinguished as it may seem now there can hardly be a more significant spot on the entire railway network in Britain. The directors of the L&M staged the trials, not principally to decide which design of locomotive should be used on the line, but to determine whether to use locomotives at all or instead a system of stationary engines placed at intervals along the track. (One contemporary estimate suggested that no less than 54 fixed locomotives would have been needed to haul carriages and wagons over the 30-mile track.) In the event, there could be no doubt. Robert Stephenson's *Rocket* lived up to its name, more than fulfilling the requirement that it should haul a train of three times its own weight the equivalent of the distance from Liverpool to Manchester and back at a speed of 10 mph, and in doing so proved the case for locomotive haulage conclusively.

Shortly before Earlstown station, the line crosses the Sankey viaduct over Sankey brook and the former St. Helen's Canal, now filled in. This railway viaduct, 60 feet high and with nine arches, was another novel feature of the line: 'the picturesque appearance of vessels under sail, far below the feet of the traveller, wending their way through a rich and undulated country, conveys an impression to the mind at once pleasing and sublime.'

Accident memorial
Past Newton-le-Willows station and just after the M6 motorway crosses the line, the train runs underneath a second road bridge. Look carefully

Contemporary etching showing the crowds who assembled on the Moorish arch at Edge Hill to watch the Duke of Wellington and other assorted VIPs leave *on the inaugural trip of the Liverpool & Manchester Railway in 1830. Rocket is at the head of the train on the left.*

The Passenger Enquiry Office at Manchester Victoria, c. 1910, which became the eastern terminus of the Liverpool & Manchester in 1844.

to the right as you pass under the bridge, and you should just catch a glimpse of a marble monument attached to the base of the bridge. The monument commemorates another railway first – the first victim of a railway accident.

William Huskisson, a prominent Tory politician and MP for Liverpool, was killed here on the day the line opened. The train had halted, and Huskisson was standing with others on the track talking to the Prime Minister, the Duke of Wellington, who was seated in a carriage. *Rocket* came up on the other track and, although most people managed to scramble out of the way, Huskisson became confused, and fell in *Rocket*'s path as he was trying to climb into the Prime Minister's carriage. He died later that evening.

After a few miles, the train starts its journey across Chat Moss, a curious heath-like area of stumpy trees and vegetation still only partly cultivated. In Stephenson's day it was a quaking, seemingly bottomless bog, an unconquerable obstacle, so the sceptics said, across which a line could never be laid. Stephenson proved them wrong, as he had so many other doubters in the past, though not without considerable efforts.

His idea was to float a kind of raft of heather and brushwood across the bog; eventually, he believed, if enough material were piled on, the raft would stabilize, and the tracks could be laid. This duly happened, although at the Manchester end a bank had to be built up by tipping wagonload after wagonload of spoil into the sticky, black mire.

Station museum

The last leg of the journey runs through Eccles and Salford into central Manchester, where the present-day journey terminates at Manchester Victoria station. Remarkably, the original terminus at Liverpool Road survives, and now forms part of the Greater Manchester Museum of Science and Industry. The buildings were restored in the 1980s to their original external appearance, while inside as few alterations as possible have been made in order to accommodate the Museum's exhibits.

The station agent's house is the oldest on the site; built in 1808, it was later bought by the railway. In the passenger building, both the first- and second-class booking halls survive; the former now looks as it did in 1830, with a Victorian family buying tickets from the clerk, and a railway policeman looking on. A warehouse built in 1830 with a capacity of 10,000 bales of cotton and carriage sheds built during the 1860s can also be seen.

97

Lines across the Pennines

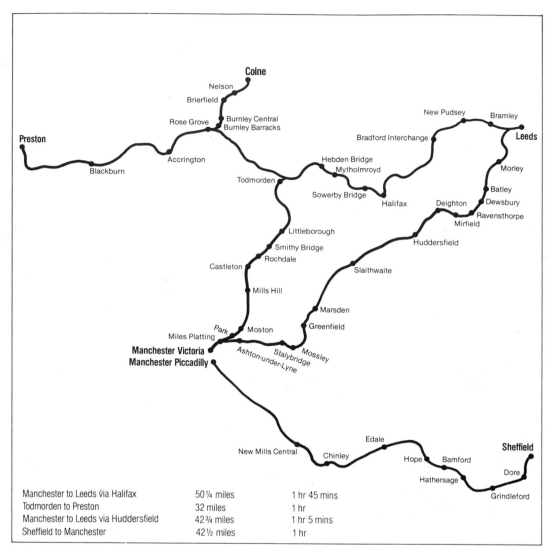

Manchester to Leeds via Halifax	50¼ miles	1 hr 45 mins
Todmorden to Preston	32 miles	1 hr
Manchester to Leeds via Huddersfield	42¾ miles	1 hr 5 mins
Sheffield to Manchester	42½ miles	1 hr

The Pennines were among the first major physical obstacles to confront railway surveyors and engineers. Well-used canals and coaching roads already connected the large towns that lay east and west of the chain, and with railway networks rapidly developing on either side, attempts to drive a line across the Pennines were soon made. Four routes were opened in the 1840s and early 1850s, and a fifth was constructed almost at the end of the century. Of these five routes, four remain open today, and each provides an interesting journey through often spectacular scenery.

Manchester to Leeds via Littleborough and Halifax

This was the pioneer trans-Pennine line, and it followed well-established lines of communication. To the west, it ran along the narrow gorge between Littleborough and Todmorden, next to the Rochdale Canal which had been constructed in 1804. To the east, the key was the river Calder, whose banks had long supported a number of sizeable industrial communities such as Hebden Bridge, Sowerby Bridge and Halifax.

The route also had the advantage of being relatively low; the watershed was only 537 feet above sea level.

A route had been proposed as early as 1824, but the Manchester & Leeds Railway (M&L) was not incorporated until 1836. It survived for eleven years before becoming part of the larger Lancashire & Yorkshire network in 1847. Work began in 1837 under the supervision of George Stephenson. The stretch from Manchester to Littleborough opened in July 1839, and on the other side trains began to run from Normanton to Hebden Bridge, via Wakefield, Mirfield and Elland, in October 1840. From Normanton, the M & L's trains ran over North Midland metals into Leeds. The delay in the opening of the through line was caused by the Summit tunnel, which was not ready until March 1841.

The first few miles from Manchester Victoria to Rochdale are not especially exciting, although the Pennines can be seen clear ahead, and the line runs close beside the Rochdale Canal. Stephenson built part of this stretch on a 1 in 155 gradient, much steeper than his normal practice. Beyond Littleborough, a pleasant town sheltering under the Pennine summits, the line enters a gorge, hemmed in tight with the road and the canal, with hills towering above. Then comes the tunnel, 1 mile 1,125 yards long, followed on the eastern side by another stretch of valley which brings the line to Todmorden, where it strides across the canal and the town on an extremely impressive viaduct. Stephenson remarked of his tunnel: 'I don't think there is such another piece of work in the world. It is the greatest work that has yet been done of this kind.' In 1985, the tunnel was closed for nine months after a fire, and passengers travelled between Littleborough and Todmorden by bus.

The next 15 miles are along the twisting Calder in company with the river and the road. The station at Hebden Bridge has been attractively restored to its original appearance when the Lancashire & Yorkshire built it in 1909. At Milner Royd Junction beyond Sowerby Bridge, where Branwell Brontë started his brief career as a railway clerk in 1840, the original line turned east towards Wakefield; today's trains turn north-east, running to Halifax and Bradford.

The line through Halifax, which had previously had no through services at all, was opened in 1852, and three years later the town acquired a fine classical station, fully in line with its pretensions as a commercial and civic centre. Beyond Halifax, the line continues through hilly country to Bradford, with two tunnels and two viaducts *en route*. The train reverses at Bradford, from where it is a short journey through Pudsey to Leeds.

Above: *Westbound freight train at Sowerby Bridge. On the hill is Wainhouse Tower, 270 feet high, built in 1871 as part of a dye works but never used.*

Below: *Locomotives wait to take a train at Manchester Victoria during the last week of steam on British Rail.*

The imposing façade of Manchester Victoria, built in 1909 for the Lancashire & Yorkshire Railway, recently cleaned and restored to reveal its original splendour.

Todmorden to Rose Grove

This 10-mile link route has had a curious recent history, with BR seeming deliberately to run down the line, only to undergo a last-minute change of heart. Local passenger services stopped in 1965, when the last of the intermediate stations was closed, and from then on the only passenger train to use the line was a daily service between Leeds and Blackpool. In 1976 even that was withdrawn in winter. Freight traffic was re-routed as well. By 1983 there were no regular trains at all in winter, and BR had to run an empty diesel multiple unit over the line simply to keep the track circuits in working order. Closure seemed inevitable.

In 1984, however, a regular service between Leeds, Preston and Blackpool was instituted, and this impressive route can again be enjoyed. There are even plans to open a new station at Burnley. The route follows the river Calder as it cuts across the Pennines, through some remarkably wild and craggy country. The line swings north-west from the Halifax to Littleborough route (see above) in the centre of Todmorden and immediately starts to climb steeply, leaving the terraced hillside streets of the town behind. Kitson Wood tunnel and the thirteen-arch North Wood viaduct come before the summit at Copy Pit (749 feet), and there are another two tunnels on the descent to Burnley. At Gannow

Junction, just before Rose Grove station (where there are neither roses nor groves to be seen), the line joins the Colne to Preston route. The remaining 30 miles west to Preston are undistinguished, except for Blackburn station, which has an impressive overall roof.

North-east of Rose Grove, the line to Colne passes through Burnley on a striking viaduct that dominates the town centre. Beyond Colne there was another trans-Pennine link to Skipton (see page 112), closed in 1970. The Copy Pit route was opened by the Manchester & Leeds in 1849, and the link with the East Lancashire's line through Blackburn to Colne was made the following year.

Manchester to Leeds via Stalybridge and Huddersfield

This route follows the river Tame in the west and the Colne in the east. Work was started in 1845 by the Huddersfield & Manchester Railway & Canal Company, which had been formed the previous year when the Huddersfield & Manchester Railway bought the canal. But by the time the Standedge tunnel had been built and through trains had started to run, on 1 August 1849, the London & North Western Railway had taken over.

The route out of Manchester as far as Stalybridge is primarily industrial. Beyond, the line runs up into the heart of the Pennine hills, with the Huddersfield Canal always in sight at the valley bottom. When the route was being planned, the decision was taken to keep as close to the canal as possible; indeed as early as 1825 it had been suggested that the canal should be filled in and track laid through the Standedge canal tunnel. The landscape here is not pretty in the traditional 'chocolate-box' sense of the term. Handsome would be a better description; the hills are wild and remote, the stone towns and villages with their tall mill buildings ordered and friendly, each a natural complement of the other.

From Greenfield a little branch nicknamed the Delph Donkey ran down the valley to Delph. At Diggle, the train plunges into Standedge tunnel, emerging 3 miles and 66 yards later just short of Marsden. The first Standedge tunnel was built as a single bore; a second single bore was constructed in 1871, and then a double bore in 1894. All four remained in use until 1966, when the original single bores were closed, having first been used for experimental work on the Channel tunnel scheme. Water troughs were installed in the twin bores in 1878, the tunnels being almost the only level stretch of track on the route where the steam trains could take on water.

Construction of the initial tunnel was a mammoth task that took over three years. Nearly 2,000 men were employed when work was at its

Banking engine at Copy Pit summit in 1966.

Shortly before the end of steam, a mixed freight train struggles up the western slope of the Pennines near

Diggle before plunging into Standedge tunnel along what is now the principal and fastest trans-Pennine link.

101

most intense, and at one time thirty-five faces were being excavated simultaneously. The canal tunnel, which runs immediately beneath the rail route, was used to bring up materials and remove debris, shafts being driven between the two.

On the Yorkshire side there is a steep descent through the Colne valley, where the arrival of the railway helped the cloth industry to spread from Huddersfield out to the smaller settlements. The magnificent station at Huddersfield is approached through two short tunnels. It is well worth sparing some time to look at the station. The interior, including the roof, was rebuilt in 1886. The exterior, which dates from 1847, is stunning; Sir John Betjeman described it as 'the most splendid station in England'. The central part of the façade consists of a portico with eight Corinthian columns, linked on each side by a colonnade leading to two smaller pavilions, also adorned with columns. The southern pavilion carries the coat of arms of the Lancashire & Yorkshire, the northern one that of the Huddersfield & Manchester Railway & Canal Company. The local council now uses the central building for civic events.

Beyond Huddersfield station the train runs across the Huddersfield viaduct, only 53 feet high but 663 yards long, and then heads for Leeds via Mirfield, Batley and Morley, where there is a further lengthy tunnel. This route was built by the Leeds, Dewsbury & Manchester Railway and was opened on 31 July 1848.

LMS 5MT 4–6–0 No. 5305 heads a steam excursion through the Peak District hills near Chinley on the southern Sheffield to Manchester route.

Sheffield to Manchester

This is the southermost trans-Pennine route, and was the last to be built, being opened by the Midland Railway to freight traffic in November 1893 and to passengers the following year. The line heads out of Sheffield alongside the river Sheaf, sharing the tracks with the main line to London (see page 109). Immediately after Dore Junction, where the London trains swing south, the line enters Totley tunnel, at 3 miles 950 yards the second longest tunnel in the country. According to David Joy, a modern historian of Yorkshire railways, by the 1890s, when the line was being built,

> Engineering techniques had . . . greatly improved, but the work ran into almost insuperable difficulties through encountering vast amounts of water. At one stage 5 million gallons a day were pumped from the headings, excavations having to be stopped altogether for weeks at a time.

Beyond the tunnel, the line runs along the Hope Valley through a fine mountainous landscape. Hope and Edale are both popular places with walkers and climbers, and just before the train enters a second lengthy tunnel the brooding summit of Kinder Scout (2,031 feet) dominates the view to the right. After Cowburn tunnel, 2 miles 182 yards long, the scenery gradually becomes softer and eventually suburban, as the line runs into the outskirts of Manchester along the river Goyt. Beween Chinley and New Mills, the route from Buxton (another scenic line well worth travelling along) and the Peak Forest canal can be seen on the opposite side of the valley. The final stretch into Manchester Piccadilly is through a mixture of nineteenth- and twentieth-century industry, now sadly semi-derelict.

The Woodhead route

This trans-Pennine line also ran between Manchester and Sheffield, but by a more northerly route, crossing the summit through the Woodhead tunnel west of Penistone. The line was built by the Sheffield, Ashton-under-Lyne & Manchester Railway, which in time became part of the Manchester, Sheffield & Lincolnshire Railway, itself renamed the Great Central in 1897 (see page 120). Work started in 1838, and passenger and freight trains began to run in 1841, although through journeys were not possible until work on the Woodhead tunnel was complete in December 1845.

As well as the tunnel, 3 miles 22 yards long and the longest in the country at the time it was built, there were two majestic viaducts on the Lancashire side, Etherow and Dinting Vale. Originally both had wooden arches, which were replaced by cast-iron girders after about twenty years. On the Yorkshire side, the line descended to Penistone and then ran down the Don valley to Sheffield.

The thousand or more men who built the tunnel lived in huge encampments on the wild moorland, enduring bitter weather and filthy living conditions. The work was dangerous; twenty-six men lost their lives, and 140 more were injured. The first tunnel was rapidly followed by a second bore, completed in 1852. An electrification scheme was started in the 1930s. When it resumed after the Second World War, a new double-bore tunnel had to be built, as the existing tunnels, now almost a century old, were too small to accommodate the overhead wires. Electric working began in 1954, but already competition from road transport was increasing, and the railways were being rationalized. Passenger services were withdrawn from the line through Woodhead tunnel in 1970, although freight services survived until 1981.

Above: *Freight train at Torside on the Lancashire side of the Pennines on the now closed Woodhead route from Manchester to Sheffield.*

Below: *The magnificent colonnaded façade of Huddersfield station, considered by many to be the most imposing station exterior in Britain.*

London to Sheffield

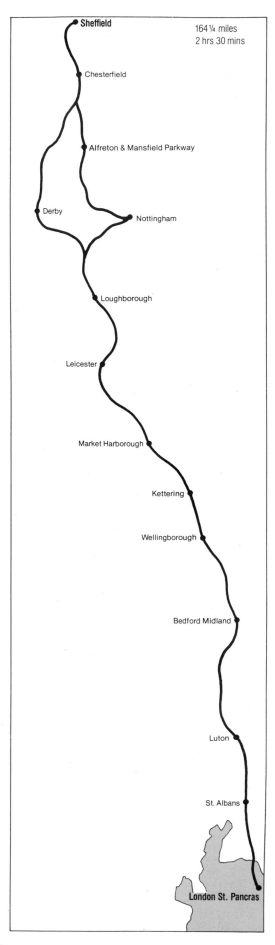

Sheffield

164¼ miles
2 hrs 30 mins

Chesterfield

Alfreton & Mansfield Parkway

Derby

Nottingham

Loughborough

Leicester

Market Harborough

Kettering

Wellingborough

Bedford Midland

Luton

St. Albans

London St. Pancras

Can there be a more noble and spectacular station, both in overall plan and in detail of execution, anywhere in the world than St. Pancras? The roof is one single, glorious arc of glass, 689 feet long, 240 feet wide and 100 feet high at its apex: the largest single-span roof in the world when it was built. The platforms and booking-hall are still mercifully free from the obtrusive clutter of equipment and passenger facilities that spoils the sense of balance and space in so many other stations. The marvellous wood-panelled linenfold booking offices with their little statues of railwaymen have been allowed to remain (though not without a struggle). Most of the original detail has survived unspoilt: the frieze of coloured diamond-shaped tiles along the side walls is still in place, as are the plaques of the Butterley Iron Company, Derbyshire (deep in Midland Railway territory), at the base of every third of the iron ribs they manufactured to support the roof.

W. H. Barlow built the train shed in 1868. Sir George Gilbert Scott's Midland Grand Hotel, constructed five years later along the Euston Road frontage of the station, could hardly represent a greater contrast. Where the train shed is simple and functional, the hotel is rich and ornate, with battlements, turrets and pinnacles and a splendid 270-foot clock tower. Inside, there is decorative ironwork on chandeliers, radiators and columns, carved oak doors, marble-faced walls and a magnificent Grand Staircase climbing the height of the building.

Every modern convenience was provided for the guests, many of whom were Midlands and northern industrialists come to the capital on business. There were electric bells, 'ascending rooms', as newly-invented lifts were called, and even dust chutes. Unlike the station, however, the hotel has suffered a decline. Converted to offices in the 1930s, it housed the headquarters of British Transport Hotels and later BR's catering division (it was apparently a splendid place to work but very inconvenient), and since 1983 has been almost empty, awaiting new tenants. What a magnificent possibility for a Victorian-style hotel!

Midland Railway terminus
The Midland may have come late to London, but when it did arrive it was determined to make Londoners notice its presence. For by 1868 the Midland Railway (MR) was nearly a quarter of a century old and in the top rank of railway companies, with a dense network of lines in the Midlands and north. At first, the Midland had run into Euston over LNWR metals from Rugby. Increasing traffic and serious delays made that unsatisfactory, and in 1857 the MR opened a new line south from Leicester through Kettering and Bedford to Hitchin, from where the Great Northern line into King's Cross (see page 12) was shared. The new route brought

The Midland Grand Hotel, Sir George Gilbert Scott's Gothic masterpiece. The roof of Barlow's plainer but equally splendid train shed extends behind the hotel, while on the right the façade of King's Cross is visible.

only a short-term improvement. Business was booming on the GNR route, and both companies were carrying more and more freight, especially coal; in 1862, 2,383 Midland freight trains and 961 passenger trains were delayed south of Hitchin; and the GNR was requiring the Midland to triple its annual minimum payment of £20,000 if the line between Hitchin and King's Cross were quadrupled.

By now, the Midland wanted a permanent base in London, free from the vagaries of rival companies. The obvious solution was to build a new line and a new terminus. Parliament gave its consent in 1863, and freight services began in 1867, passenger trains in 1868.

Building the line
The new line from Bedford to London was the first to benefit from mechanization. According to David Brookes, historian of the railway navvies:

> The contractors . . . mustered an impressive number of steam-driven machines, consisting in 1866 of eight locomotives and fifty-one stationary and portable engines and cranes; a large proportion of this equipment worked at and around St. Pancras.

It was the entrance to St. Pancras, and in particular the crossing of the Regents Canal, that posed one of the most considerable problems on the line. The decision here, in contrast with King's Cross and Euston, was to go over the canal and then to stay at the same level, rather than drop down to street level, which would have presented locomotives with a steep and awkward climb as they left the station. As a result, St. Pancras was built 12 to 17 feet above the Euston Road. Underneath the platforms at ground level is a huge area which was mostly used for storing beer brought by train from the breweries of Burton-upon-Trent, in the heart of the Midland's home territory. The unit of measurement used to position the iron columns that supported the train shed roof was the length of a beer barrel.

Just beyond the station, part of St. Pancras Old Churchyard had to be razed to accommodate the line, as well as several thousand slum houses in Agar Town and Somers Town. There was a public scandal when skulls, bones and open coffins were seen scattered about, and the dead had to be reverentially reburied, supervised by a young architect's assistant named Thomas Hardy. Less concern seems to have been voiced about the fate of the ten thousand or so slum-dwellers whose homes were destroyed.

Sheffield was never the Midland Railway's principal destination, nor that of the London, Midland & Scottish Railway (LMSR) which succeeded it. Regular expresses ran from St. Pancras to Manchester or Leeds, and from Yorkshire to Scotland along the Settle to Carlisle line (see page 110). After nationalization, the lines from Euston and King's Cross became the principal routes to Scotland, and St. Pancras trains were gradually cut back to Sheffield. At one time, indeed, there was a suggestion that St. Pancras should close altogether. That danger has now receded. Since autumn 1982, High-Speed Trains (HSTs) have been operating Inter-City services to Sheffield, via Derby or Nottingham. In 1983, electrification of the line as far north as Sharnbrook was completed, although it was only early in 1984, after a prolonged industrial dispute, that the new driver operation only trains between London and Bedford came into full service.

North London
On the other side of Primrose Hill tunnel, the train passes West Hampstead. The GLC once nursed a grand plan to build a transport interchange here with the nearby main line from Euston, the North London line (see page 168), bus and underground.

Beyond Mill Hill are the first green fields, although the countryside is fairly uninteresting until the other side of Bedford. A few miles short of Bedford, the line passes Ampthill, a delightful small Georgian town deprived of its station since the early 1960s, and then burrows through a gentle ridge of sandstone hills, on top of which stand the ruins of Houghton House, Bunyan's House Beautiful in *Pilgrim's Progress*. Almost immediately after, the view on the left is of brick fields and chimneys, while on the right the Redland Stone Company has a rail terminal.

The line crosses the meandering Ouse in Bedford and then re-crosses it another six times in the 7 miles north to Sharnbrook. This is pleasant pastoral countryside with gently rolling low hills. The Midland built this section of line on the cheap, and so, instead of tunnelling through the summit just north of Sharnbrook, a 60-foot cutting was constructed, with a 1 in 120 ascent from the north. When the line was quadrupled during the 1880s, a tunnel just over a mile long was built to accommodate the new tracks. The Wymington Deviation, as the new stretch was called, is used today only by freight services.

Kettering to Leicester
Kettering station was rebuilt in about 1890 in an attractive orange-pink terracotta; the awnings on the island platform with their lovely ironwork survived from the original station put up when this stretch of line was constructed in 1857. Beyond Kettering, the former direct line to Nottingham branches off to the right. This route, which leads across the Northamptonshire and Leicestershire iron-ore fields, was opened in 1879 (for freight) and 1880 (for passengers) to

George Stephenson (1781–1848).

take direct Nottingham-London expresses and freight, principally iron-ore and coal. Part of the line survives as a freight route, passenger services having been withdrawn in 1966.

The stretch through Corby to Manton Junction, where the line meets the east-west Peterborough to Leicester line (see page 54), carries agricultural products, steel tubes and aggregates; further north it is used as a British Rail test track. There has been pressure to re-open passenger services to Corby, but the electrification required would make this a major investment. The line between Kettering and Manton Junction crosses the valley of the river Welland on the dramatic Harringworth viaduct, the longest in Britain discounting those in London: 1,275 yards long, 60 feet high, with eighty-two 40-foot arches. There are two tunnels as well, each more than a mile long.

The scenery on the 27-mile run from Kettering to Leicester is classic English shire-land. The fields remain small, with hedges that have survived for generations (in contrast with the land further east), small patches of woodland and comfortable, traditional villages. This is some of England's best hunting country. Beyond Leicester, the view is of a scrappier, more industrial land as the line follows the Grand Union Canal into Loughborough and then, to the north, the river Soar.

Thomas Cook

The city of Leicester produced no locomotive-designers or railway-constructors. It did, however, produce the first travel agent and excursion-organizer: Thomas Cook (1808–92). Cook's first venture was in July 1841, when about 500 people paid a shilling each for a return ticket to a temperance rally in Loughborough, travelling in twenty open coaches.

Cook's business expanded rapidly. Within five years he was organizing pleasure trips to North Wales and Scotland; through tickets to Belgium and France were introduced in 1855, a tour to America took place in 1866, and a world tour six years later. But Cook's first trip to Loughborough was by no means the first railway excursion; almost a year earlier the Nottingham Mechanics Institute had run an outing to Leicester.

Midland Railway

Beyond Leicester, we are in the territory of the Midland Counties Railway (MCR), one of the three companies that amalgamated to form the Midland Railway in 1844. (The others were the Birmingham & Derby Junction and the North Midland.) The MCR opened its line from Derby to Nottingham in May 1839, and an extension south to Leicester a little less than a year later. The two lines met at Trent Junction, just north of the crossing of the river Trent.

Although you would not realize it now, for no trace of the buildings survives, there was a busy interchange station at Trent Junction until it closed on New Year's Day 1968; almost a

GWR Castle Class 4–6–0 No. 4079 Pendennis Castle *heads a steam excursion at Sheffield.*

The lovely island platform awnings at Kettering with their attractive decorative iron-work, erected in 1857 and retained when the station was rebuilt in 1890.

hundred trains a day called there in 1961. There was never a settlement, though, just a few railwaymen and their families living in railway cottages. Having passed Ratcliffe-on-Soar power station on the right (which is supplied with coal by merry-go-round trains) and crossed the river, trains routed via Nottingham branch off to the east, those calling at Derby to the west.

Nowadays the lines running north along the river Erewash from Trent Junction lead to Toton marshalling yard, and are used by freight only; with the advent of through freight services the yard, like many others around the country, is no longer as busy as it once was. Having called at Nottingham, the Sheffield trains loop back to the Erewash valley above Toton and follow it north to Clay Cross. The Midland Railway opened the southern part of the Erewash valley line in 1847, and the extension to Clay Cross fifteen years later. The line had an immediate and dramatic impact on the area, greatly increasing the output of both coal and iron.

Derby

Derby was the Midland Railway's centre of operations. Its locomotive and carriage works were located here, the latter in particular contributing to the company's distinguished reputation. Midland passengers were always carried in considerable comfort and style. A new 60-foot dining car, divided into a smoking lounge,

dining-room, pantry and kitchen, was introduced in 1892, while during the first half of the 1870s third class accommodation was introduced, and then second class abolished.

The Derby tradition continues. British Rail's carriage workshops build and overhaul most of BR's locomotive-hauled coaches, including all of the most modern HST coaches. The locomotive works, which can be seen on the right across several sets of tracks from the station, manufacture all British Rail's bogies, and are responsible for overhauling HST power cars. It is also possible to catch a glimpse of the original sixteen-sided engine shed of the North Midland Railway, built in 1840. The Railway Technical Centre, passed on the left as the train enters Derby from the south, carries out research and development work; the ill-fated Advanced Passenger Train was developed here, as well as many more successful innovations such as Radio Electronic Token Block (see page 190) and paved concrete track.

Beyond Derby, we follow the line George Stephenson built for the North Midland Railway as far as Chesterfield. The line was opened as far as Masborough (Rotherham) on 11 May 1840, and extended to Leeds on 30 June the same year. Stephenson's route quite deliberately missed Sheffield out. His brief was to link Derby and Leeds, and in his opinion the hills around Sheffield made access to that city too difficult.

The transit shed at St. Mary's goods depot, Derby, in 1911. These were the days when anything and *everything was sent by rail.*

Derby station in 1911. Robert Stephenson's light iron trainshed was partly destroyed by bombing in 1941, the remainder being demolished in 1952.

Down express for Sheffield running over points at Ambergate, 1911, near the junction of the Sheffield line and the route that ran over the hills to Buxton.

Leaving Derby, the train runs through pleasant pastoral country along the river Derwent as far as Ambergate, passing through Belper in a fine, deep stone cutting. The landscape becomes rather more hilly, with distant views of high peaks. Clay Cross tunnel (1 mile 26 yards), just before the junction with Erewash valley line, has a splendid castellated north portal. Clay Cross town sits on top of the tunnel.

George Stephenson

Passing through Chesterfield, there is a good view of the fourteenth-century parish church with its well-known crooked spire. George Stephenson spent his last years at nearby Tapton House, in Chesterfield, overlooking the line. Here he tended his gardens and the exotic fruit in his hothouses, and saw to the affairs of the local mines, ironworks and limeworks he had purchased with a group of friends. Of this final contented phase of a turbulent life, his biographer L. T. C. Rolt has written:

> He remained to the last a simple man, hating only the pompous and pretentious. On his frequent journeys between Chesterfield and Ambergate he took a

childish pleasure in flourishing his free pass and being ushered deferentially to a first-class compartment. Yet . . . when no passenger train was due, he would cheerfully clamber into one of a train of empty coal-wagons bound from Ambergate to Clay Cross and be trundled away perched quite contentedly on an extemporized plank seat.

The line to Sheffield

Beyond Chesterfield, the original North Midland line branches off to the right, while the Sheffield train follows the direct line, which the MR opened in 1870. It is easy to see why Stephenson shunned this route. The line climbs steeply through a rocky landscape before plunging into Bradway tunnel (1 mile 267 yards long), from which it emerges at Dore Junction, where the Sheffield to Manchester line is joined (see page 102). From here it is a few miles through the Sheffield suburbs and along the fast-flowing river Sheaf into the city centre. Sheffield station was rebuilt in 1904 when the existing magnificent arcade and covered cab drive were added.

Settle to Carlisle

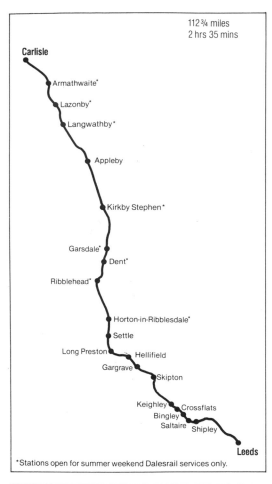

112¾ miles
2 hrs 35 mins

Carlisle
Armathwaite*
Lazonby*
Langwathby*
Appleby
Kirkby Stephen*
Garsdale*
Dent*
Ribblehead*
Horton-in-Ribblesdale*
Settle
Long Preston
Hellifield
Gargrave
Skipton
Keighley
Crossflats
Bingley
Saltaire
Shipley
Leeds

*Stations open for summer weekend Dalesrail services only.

'Perhaps nowhere in the kingdom has nature placed such gigantic obstacles in the way of railway engineers as have been encountered over the 72 miles lying between Settle and Carlisle'. These were the words with which a newspaper greeted the completion in 1875 of the Midland Railway's new line through some of the most difficult and desolate terrain in England.

A ride along the route today confirms the truth of that contemporary observation. Even on the most benign summer's day, the land seems wild and uncompromising, while winter brings fog, persistent rain and often deep drifts of snow. To conquer this land, the engineers, and more particularly the many navvies who found employment here (5,863 in 1871 according to the Midland's own figures), had to build. Tunnels, embankments, cuttings, viaducts and bridges in unprecedented numbers sprang up across a land more bleak and less hospitable than any yet crossed by iron rails.

The motives behind this intense labour were commercial pride and rivalry. The influence of the Midland Railway spread well beyond its base in central England; it had running powers and lines as far apart as south Wales, the West Country and the coast of East Anglia. But one thing it had always lacked: a direct route to Scotland. North of Ingleton, Midland traffic had to travel over tracks owned by the rival London & North Western Railway (LNWR), which, per-

Settle to Carlisle at its most impressive. Midland Railway compound No. 1000 pilots LMS Jubilee No.

5690 Leander *over Ribblehead viaduct amid the winter's snows.*

haps not unnaturally, gave priority to its own business. The Midland's coaches were attached not to expresses but to the slowest services or, worse still, to a clanking coal train; connections were missed, and travellers compelled to wait on remote and draughty station platforms until they could continue their journey.

New route north

This situation was not to be endured: a third route to Scotland must be built. In 1866, the Settle & Carlisle Railway Bill received the Royal Assent, whereupon the Midland had an attack of cold feet and tried to drop the project. Elaborate negotiations with other railway companies followed, an Abandonment Bill came before Parliament – and failed. Now, like it or not, the Midland had to go ahead.

The line took the best part of six years to build, and cost just under £3.5 million, in contrast with the original estimate of £2.2 million. Its course was planned to take advantage of the natural contours of the land. Key rivers were the south-flowing Ribble and the north-flowing Eden. Following their valleys would provide a relatively easy ascent (the aim was to avoid gradients of more than 1 in 100). The intervening few miles of moorland around Aisgill – the wildest spot on the line – could be crossed by a series of viaducts and tunnels.

The work was never less than hard, and often literally back-breaking. One engineer reported:

I have known men blast the shoulder clay like rock, and within a few hours have to ladle out the same stuff from the same spot like soup in buckets. Or a man strikes a blow with his pick at what he thinks is clay, but there is a great boulder underneath almost as hard as iron, and the man's wrists, arms and body are so shaken by the shock that, disgusted, he flings down his tools, asks for his money, and is off.

Huge quantities of soil, rubble and stone had to be shifted: 100,000 cubic yards were removed to form a cutting near Horton, and more than twice that amount was used for an embankment near Mallerstang. Nor was the weather kind. Rainfall was well above average, in what is in any case an extremely wet part of the country, high winds threatened the masons as they clung to the piers of the viaducts, and in winter there was the inevitable snow and ice.

Dramatic route

While the 22 miles of the line north from Settle are the most dramatic part of the route, to gain the full flavour of the countryside, and so appreciate the gradual change in the landscape from pastoral valley to windswept moorland, the journey is best started at Leeds.

Even as you leave the station, there is a view ahead to distant hills on the horizon. The train soon leaves the suburbs behind, and runs

Blea Moor signal box, one of the loneliest outposts on the rail network.

through well-wooded countryside along the river Aire and the Leeds & Liverpool Canal. Fine mill buildings are visible at Shipley, Saltaire (a model settlement built by the mill-owner Sir Titus Salt in the 1850s), and Bingley. Bingley Five-Rise, the famous staircase of five interconnected locks, can be seen just above the line to the right. At Keighley, the BR platforms are next to those serving the Keighley & Worth Valley Railway (see page 118).

Skipton is a fine example of a Midland Railway station, solidly constructed of stone and with well-preserved glass and iron awnings. Only its size suggests that it has seen busier days.

The line from Leeds to Skipton was built by the Leeds & Bradford, and opened to Skipton in 1847, with an extension, now closed, across the Pennines to Colne in Lancashire (see page 100) the following year. The next section north-west to what is now known as Settle Junction and then on to Lancaster was built by the North Western Railway (unofficially but always referred to as the 'Little' North Western to avoid confusion with the LNWR) and opened throughout in 1850. It was this line that gave West Yorkshire a direct link with the west-coast route to Scotland, and eventually caused so many disputes about running powers that the Midland built its own route to Carlisle.

Settle

Superficially, the scenery over the next 15 miles to Settle seems much like the land south of Skipton. But already the high hills and moorland are closing in, and the fertile strip of valley narrows all the time.

At Settle Junction, just short of the town, the line divides, the Lancaster branch running off to the left while we head north. At one time there were no less than three stations named after Settle: Settle Junction has long since closed, while the station on the Lancaster line is now called Giggleswick.

In the days of steam, the line ahead was no joke for the novice or unprepared fireman, for the relentless ascent meant furious and constant shovelling to keep the steam pressure high. This is still the case, as the Settle to Carlisle is one of the BR lines on which steam excursions are run quite regularly.

Rail ascents can be misleading. On quite a steep climb it is perfectly possible to look through the window and wonder what all the fuss is about: the train hardly seems to be climbing at all. The natural comparison with what a walker or motor car can tackle is totally misleading. For a train composed of seven or eight or more heavy coaches and an equally heavy locomotive, a gradient of 1 in 100 is already steep; the ideal is far less. Only the coming of electric locomotives, which take their power from the national grid, has finally conquered the problem.

The Dales

Beyond Settle, hills rear up on each side of the line, with dry stone walls climbing through the lower sheep-scattered fields to the windswept tops. The famous Three Peaks of the Dales come into view: to the left of the line first Ingleborough (2,373 feet) and then, beyond Ribblehead viaduct, Whernside (2,419 feet); on the right, Pen-y-Ghent (2,231 feet).

Horton, whose station we rush through at some speed, is the principal rendezvous for walkers and climbers in the area. All the local stations on this stretch of line were closed in 1970, although they are reopened on some summer weekends when the successful 'Dales-rail' service operates.

Ribblehead viaduct

A few miles beyond Horton, the train begins to slow down for the approach to one of the greatest of all engineering achievements on the line: the Ribblehead viaduct. Because of the state of the viaduct's fabric, the line across it has been singled, and a speed restriction of 20 mph imposed. The twenty-four limestone piers of the viaduct, 104 feet high and 1,328 feet long, stride out across Batty Moss. The campers and walkers often seen beneath, at least in summer months, are completely dwarfed; good though the view of the viaduct is from the train, seen from the moor the structure is even more impressive.

It took five years to build the viaduct (each pier had to be sunk 25 feet into the ground). During this time a large community of navvies recruited from many parts of the country and their families grew up. Their group of huts was nicknamed Sebastopol. A contemporary reporter observed that the settlement

> resembled the gold diggers' villages in the colonies. Potters' carts, drapers' carts, milk carts, greengrocers' carts, butchers' and bakers' carts, brewers' drays, and traps and horses for hire, might all be found, besides numerous hawkers who plied their trade from hut to hut.

The Midland had their offices there too; and stores and stables, public houses, shops, even a hospital, a post office, a mission house and 'day and Sunday schools' were also built. Two missionaries were appointed to the line, and the daughter of one organized a concert that raised funds to buy a library of 200 books. 'But, despite all these conventionalities, the spot was frequently most desolate and bleak.'

Such comforts, for all that they may not have alleviated the misery of the weather and the harshness of the labour, had been virtually unknown thirty years before, when large numbers of new lines were being built. But, by the 1870s, Britain was a highly industrialized nation, and there were many alternative sources of employment for skilled craftsmen, and for

Above: *The long, slow ascent past Mallerstang signal box towards Ais Gill on the southbound journey.*

Below: *Headed by a 2–10–0 No. 92051, a mineral train runs over Dent Head viaduct in August 1967.*

unskilled labour as well. Perhaps, too, a social conscience had evolved since the earlier days of cut-throat competition between railway companies. Similar colonies could be found further north near Blea Moor tunnel and at the summit of Aisgill Moor.

Blea Moor

Climbing all the time, surrounded by views of ridge after ridge of hills piled on each other, the train passes Blea Moor signal box and heads straight for the tunnel mouth.

What a work the tunnel was! Tramways were built from Batty Moss and from Dent, to the north, to bring materials up, and no less than seven stationary engines were used, five of them positioned at the top of the ventilation shafts to haul up debris excavated by the tunnellers below and to send down bricks and mortar used to line the tunnel. Coal had to be imported to power the engines, and dynamite for blasting.

The train emerges 2,629 yards later and almost immediately crosses a second splendid viaduct, Dent Head, over the tiny river Dee, 591 feet long with ten arches. Arten Gill viaduct follows next (660 feet long, 117 feet high, with seventeen spans), then Dent station, at 1,145 feet above sea level now the highest station in England, before the train plunges into Rise Hill tunnel, 1,213 yards long. There is much new forestry planting around Dent.

Garsdale station is 2 miles from the north end of Rise Hill tunnel, in a completely isolated spot. The village it was built to serve lies 3 miles off. This was also the junction with the Hawes branch, closed in 1959, and an equally impressive piece of engineering with two viaducts and a tunnel; at Hawes it met an NER branch that ran through Wensleydale from the east-coast main line at Northallerton. Just south of Garsdale station water-troughs were set in between the rails so that locomotives could take

2–10–0 No. 92220 Evening Star *crosses Lunds viaduct north of Garsdale.*

A diesel-hauled freight service runs through Dent station, the highest railway halt in England.

A steam excursion crosses the twelve-arch Dandry Mire viaduct, 681 feet long and 50 feet high, north of *Garsdale where the Hawes branch once led off to the east.*

on additional water without stopping; for some time the troughs were heated to stop them freezing in winter. The water ran off the fells and was collected in a 43,000-gallon tank.

Aisgill summit

Now the train approaches the final climb to the summit at Aisgill. Dandry Mire viaduct is crossed, and then comes Moorcock tunnel, Lunds viaduct and Shotlock Hill tunnel. At Dandry Mire the original intention was to build an embankment, but for two years the peaty bog swallowed wagonload after wagonload of earth and rubble until the engineers admitted defeat and constructed a viaduct instead.

Just past the site of Aisgill signal box the line is, as it were, up and over, for Aisgill viaduct crosses a beck that flows north into the river Eden. From now it is downhill all the way – a long way, however, and just as difficult an ascent for southbound trains as the one for trains travelling north – and the country remains wild and unforgiving, with the long, brooding Mallerstang ridge just above the line to the left.

Birkett tunnel follows, 424 yards long and driven through a geological wonderland of different rocks. Beyond, the views are of a softer and greener land, with the Eden valley stretching out into the distance. To the north and north-east, however, the hills of the Pennine chain remain.

The descent into the valley continues past Kirkby Stephen, where there is no longer a station, and Appleby, where the station still exists. There are two viaducts and a tunnel between the two stations, and still more of each

as the line runs through increasingly pastoral country towards Carlisle.

Now the river Eden, soon quite wide and fast-flowing, is our companion, and in the distance the outlines of the Lake District hills can be seen to the west. Near Appleby, Harter Fell and the long ridge of High Street (2,359 and 2,719 feet respectively) are visible; further north, probably around Langwathby, Saddleback or Blencathra (2,847 feet) should come into view.

From the edge of Carlisle the line runs along the tracks of the Newcastle to Carlisle route (see page 22), which by the 1870s was owned by the North Eastern Railway, and enters Carlisle station. True to form, the LNWR would not permit the Midland to utilize its lines.

Fight for survival

No one doubts the magnificence of the Settle and Carlisle line. But, at least on British Rail's part, there have long been doubts about its viability. Having run down services for many years (quite deliberately in the opinion of some people), in November 1983 British Rail served formal Notice of Closure – ironically on the very day that west-coast main line trains to and from Scotland had to be re-routed because of a derailment. Since then, many organizations and individuals have become involved in a lengthy battle to keep the line open. Public hearings are due in spring 1986, and it seems unlikely that even if closure is confirmed it will go ahead before the end of 1986.

Three main arguments are put forward in favour of keeping the line open. They are concerned with railway strategy, regional and local needs, and tourist potential.

The strategic argument, which turns on the value of a third route north to the border, is the weakest. BR has long since decided to concentrate investment on the main east-coast and west-coast lines. Through services from London to Scotland via Settle and Carlisle have not run for many years, and the Nottingham to Glasgow expresses were re-routed via Manchester and Preston in 1982. In timings the Settle route cannot compete with the electric services on the west coast, nor with the HSTs on the east-coast line, where electrification should be complete by 1991. That the line is useful for emergency diversions cannot be denied (but only diesel locomotives can use it), but it is difficult to argue that this alone justifies keeping the route open. keeping the route open.

There is no doubt that the line passes through many isolated communities, where a regular rail service would improve the quality of life. At present, local people do not make significant use of the line: they cannot, for most of the local stations have been closed and trains do not call at those remaining at suitable times for people wanting to travel, especially to work or school or college. Closing the line would undoubtedly make many communities in Cumbria and North Yorkshire even more isolated and dependent on private cars, especially since bus services are already being withdrawn. It has been argued that if the social costs of closing the line are taken into account they would almost equal the operational savings that BR would probably make.

Tourist line

The third argument, which hinges on the line's tourist potential, is the strongest, as BR itself has found. Even as the Notice of Closure was issued, BR increased its marketing efforts, using a few simple techniques such as leaflets, fare offers and so on. The result was an increase in the number of people travelling on the line from about 100,000 people a year in 1983 and before to about 250,000 a year.

Surveys have shown that most passengers on the line have come for the ride; in other words, the line itself is a tourist attraction. But at the moment there is relatively little to do except sit in the train and admire the splendour of the surrounding country. Opening intermediate stations, providing facilities such as guided and self-guided walks, leaflets and publications, an attractive Visitor Centre, educational facilities, an annual festival and regular events, as well as observation cars and maps on the trains, would all help to attract visitors. And these visitors would then stay to spend money in the area, so helping to boost its economy, and thereby the line once more.

It has been said that, on the usage figures for 1984, the line made a small operational profit, whereas most lines in remote places make a considerable loss. With relatively little additional investment, the line could become both an asset for local communities and a valuable tourist attraction, bringing visitors and much-needed income to the area. It must be the hope of everyone that the line stays open.

Britannia 4–6–2 No. 70016 steaming north through the lush Eden valley near Armathwaite with the long line of the Pennines in the background.

Steam on a web of steel: Britannia leaving the locomotive sheds at Carlisle Kingsmoor.

Keighley & Worth Valley Railway

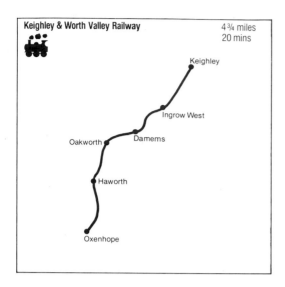

Keighley & Worth Valley Railway
4¾ miles
20 mins

Keighley

Ingrow West

Oakworth — Damems

Haworth

Oxenhope

The route was planned in the late 1840s by local mill- and quarry-owners, but only opened nearly twenty years later, in April 1867. The Midland operated the line right from the start, and took it over formally in 1881. To begin with there was plenty of traffic, and local trade flourished, not to mention the start of the tourist industry in the area, for the Brontë museum in Haworth opened in 1895. By the 1950s, however − the usual story − only the mill-workers still travelled by train.

Celebrity line
A Railway Preservation Society was formed in March 1962, but legal and financial negotiations were so complex that it was four years before a limited company was formed and the first public passenger trains ran. Two years later the line had an unexpected stroke of good fortune.

Broadly speaking, in the south towns merge into the country almost imperceptibly, often through a large band of suburbia, whereas in the north the division is usually sudden and distinct, as this classic Yorkshire branch line demonstrates. The first mile is along the industrial Worth valley, but beyond Ingrow tunnel the line emerges into deep countryside, running at first alongside the pleasant river valley, and then climbing slightly.

It is a difficult route to negotiate. There are some sharp curves, the first on the incline immediately beyond Keighley station, and the average gradient is 1 in 75. At the steepest point, between Ingrow tunnel and Damems, it reaches 1 in 56, and the long final stretch between Haworth and Oxenhope is mostly 1 in 68.

Like many preserved lines, the Keighley & Worth Valley was often used for filming. *The Railway Children,* an enchanting and highly successful film of E. M. Nesbit's book of the same name, hit cinema screens across the world about Christmas in 1970 − and brought the K&WVR instant worldwide renown. The crowds of visitors that arrived during the next few summers put immense demands on the line, which was, and still is, operated and maintained entirely by volunteer labour.

Today a wide variety of steam locomotives (and a few diesels) from many parts of Britain and abroad work the line, which has been restored to a 1950s style. Stations are painted maroon and cream, with maroon coaches and locomotives immaculate in early BR black.

GWR 0-6-0PT No. L89 leaving Haworth through the snow. Owned by London Transport from 1963 to 1970, this locomotive has now been restored to LT lined maroon livery.

USA 2–8–0 Big Jim *at Oakworth station, a typical West Yorkshire country halt which remains unchanged* with gas lamps and Edwardian posters. The station buildings remain unaltered.

Great Central Railway

Great Central Railway

5 miles
20 mins

Loughborough Central

Quorn & Woodhouse

Rothley

But one illustrious line – indeed an entire railway company – has been virtually wiped from the map: the Great Central Railway (GCR). The company had been operating since 1846 in the north and Midlands as the Manchester, Sheffield & Lincolnshire Railway (MS&L). Not for several decades was a route to the capital city considered, and the new line did not open until 1899, two years after the MS&L adopted its grander name.

The route chosen, which ran south from Sheffield via Nottingham, Loughborough, Leicester and Rugby and then through the Chilterns to a new London terminus at Marylebone, was an excellent one: direct, and built for speed. But traffic was never very substantial, and the GCR, unlike the MS&L, never paid a dividend. The problem was that, in its southern section, the line ran through a relatively remote and unpopulated area, while the Midland Railway, its competitor further east, served several biggish towns; and, further north, the two routes were in direct competition between the same centres.

In its heyday, there was everything to be said for choosing the Great Central. The trains were comfortable (the Company's slogan was 'Rapid Travel in Luxury'), fast (GCR trains beat the Midland's by several minutes on the short journey from Leicester to Nottingham), and through services were offered to many different

Even in these days of modern management methods, when British Rail is organized according to types of traffic rather than in the regions of old, the outlines of the former independent railway companies remain faintly discernible. The line west to Bristol retains something of the feel of the GWR; St. Pancras can still remind travellers of the old Midland Railway; while at smaller country halts it is often easy to spot nameboards, decorative features or pieces of station furniture that have been in place since well before Grouping in 1923.

LMS class 5MT 4–6–0 No. 5231 arrives at Quorn and Woodhouse, at present the sole intermediate station.

4–4–0 No. 506 Butler Henderson, *the sole survivor of the Great Central's passenger locomotives, leaves the present Grand Central Railway terminus at Loughborough.*

parts of the country. But such duplication of services could not survive the growth of road transport, and after the Second World War the Great Central line was first downgraded and eventually closed piece by piece during the 1960s. Even Marylebone itself is now threatened with closure. All that now survives is the southernmost portion of the line from Marylebone to Ashendon Junction (midway between Bicester and High Wycombe), along which BR's rather slow and infrequent Marylebone to Banbury services run.

Preserved main line

All, that is, except a 5-mile stretch south from Loughborough. The Great Central Railway of the 1980s is the only preserved main line in Great Britain. The 20-minute ride takes the traveller through the rolling Leicestershire countryside, with some excellent views. Shortly before the present terminus at Rothley (an extension to the completely rebuilt Belgrave & Birstall station on the outskirts of Leicester is due to open in 1988), the train crosses Swithland Reservoir on two fine viaducts.

But landscape is not the principal reason for visiting the Great Central. Rather is it the atmosphere of the line, the smells and the sounds and the look of steam travel. The station at Loughborough with its superb roof is preserved as it was in the 1920s and 1930s, with old timetables and advertisements; a museum on the principal platform contains Great Central memorabilia.

The trains are usually formed of the familiar carmine and cream London Midland region rolling stock of the 1950s; on the sidings opposite rolling stock may be seen awaiting restoration. Some of the line's locomotives date from the same period – including the unique 71000 *Duke of Gloucester* from British Railway's Standard Class – and there is also the only surviving Great Central Railway passenger steam locomotive, 506 *Butler Henderson*. A number of diesel locomotives are also operated, for diesel these days is old enough to have its own enthusiastic devotees. The signal box can also be seen: a highlight of any visit, for it remains a working box and visitors, so long as they do not get in the way, can watch the signalman bringing a train into the station.

WESTERN REGION

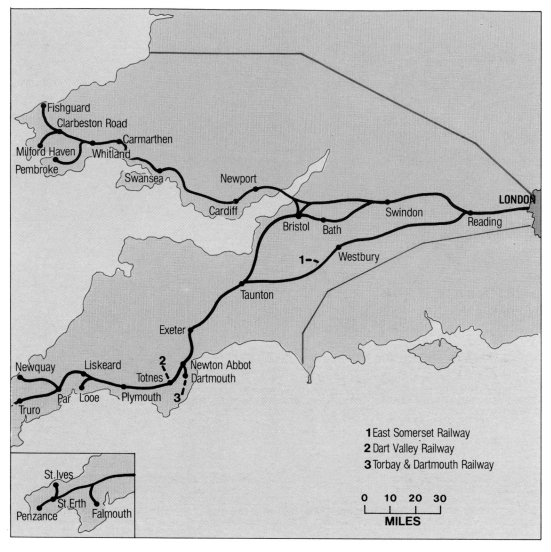

Fishguard
Clarbeston Road
Carmarthen
Milford Haven
Whitland
Pembroke
Swansea
Newport
Cardiff
Bristol
Bath
Swindon
Reading
LONDON
Westbury
Taunton
Exeter
Newquay
Liskeard
Totnes
Newton Abbot
Dartmouth
Truro
Par
Looe
Plymouth

St.Ives
St.Erth
Penzance
Falmouth

1 East Somerset Railway
2 Dart Valley Railway
3 Torbay & Dartmouth Railway

0   10   20   30
MILES

One man and one company have left an indelible mark on today's Western Region. The man was Isambard Kingdom Brunel; the company the Great Western Railway (GWR). Brunel planned and constructed main lines throughout the West Country and South Wales, building them to the broad gauge of 7 feet which he preferred to the 4 foot 8½ inch gauge used in the rest of the country. The GWR rapidly developed its own ethos and way of doing things, and fostered a very special loyalty among both its passengers and its employees. This spirit survived both Grouping in 1923 and nationalization a quarter of a century later, and only began to vanish with the extinction of steam and the imposition by British Rail of a uniform style of management and operations.

It is appropriate that Brunel's and the GWR's original line should have been the first to operate British Rail's new 125 mph High-Speed Trains in 1975. The London to Bristol route strides out along the Thames valley and past the foot of the Berkshire and Wiltshire Downs, touching the edge of the Cotswolds before running alongside the Avon through Bath and into Bristol. Many special moments await the traveller: the magnifi-

cent interior of Paddington station, the fine views of the Downs before Swindon, the entry into Bath and the handsome viaduct across the city and, last of all but not least, Temple Meads station at Bristol, where Brunel's original station, close by the splendid later trainshed, is being carefully and lovingly restored. Further west, there are recollections of one of Brunel's less successful ventures, the atmospheric railway, beyond Exeter; and between that city and Plymouth the train runs close by the coast and then high across the edge of Dartmoor. The entry into Cornwall is heralded by the massive Royal Albert Bridge, still proudly bearing the name of its creator.

Branch lines in the Western region reach to the remotest parts of the country: to westernmost Wales and to several parts of Cornwall, taking the traveller through every aspect of the Duchy's varied landscape. Although broad gauge has of course long since vanished, pockets of steam do survive, most notably on the East Somerset Railway and in south Devon, where two lines – the Dart Valley and the Torbay & Dartmouth – recall the heyday of the Great Western Railway.

GWR 4–6–0S No. 4930 Hagley Hall *and No. 7819*
Hinton Manor *approaching Whiteball tunnel in the*

*Blackdown Hills on Brunel's line from Bristol
to Exeter.*

London to Bristol

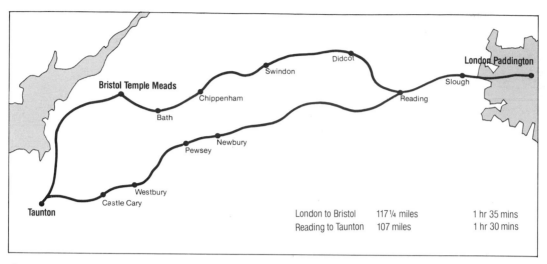

London to Bristol	117¼ miles	1 hr 35 mins
Reading to Taunton	107 miles	1 hr 30 mins

On his appointment as engineer to the Great Western Railway in 1833, it was Isambard Kingdom Brunel's self-confident prediction that his line connecting Bristol and the capital city would be 'the finest work in England'. So it turned out to be. Brunel produced a magnificently engineered line, flat (on all but 4 miles of the 118-mile route the ruling gradient is no greater than 1 in 660), with wide, gentle curves suitable for fast running and, at the western end in particular, with structures of appropriate grandeur.

In appointing Brunel, the merchants of Bristol broke with tradition. Until now, the short history of railway construction had been dominated by men from the north-east of England, with the forceful personalities of George Stephenson and his son Robert towering over all. Brunel was not from the north-east; nor had he ever constructed a railway, or been involved with the early experiments in locomotion. He came to his task without any pre-conceptions, fresh from working on two projects in Bristol – the suspension bridge over the Avon at Clifton and improvements to the docks – and set about it from first principles.

Broad gauge

The principal difference between Brunel's line from Bristol and, say, Robert Stephenson's route between London and Birmingham was the width of the gauge. The north-easterners adopted the traditional 4 foot 8 inch gauge (later extended by half an inch) of the coal-carrying tramways and rail-ways. Brunel chose a 7 foot gauge, saying later, when he gave evidence to the Gauge Commissioners in 1845:

> Looking to the speeds which I contemplated would be adopted on railways and the masses to be moved, it seemed to me that the whole machine was too small for the work to be done, and that it required that the parts should be on a scale more commensurate with the mass and the velocity to be attained.

The advantages of broad gauge, Brunel believed, were that it allowed for more powerful locomotives, larger carriages, and faster, safer and stabler running. He also made innovations in the permanent way. His bridge rails were lighter than the solid rails normally used – 43lb per yard instead of 60lb – and instead of being laid on stone blocks on wooden sleepers were fixed to continuous timbers bolted to wooden transoms that were themselves pegged into the ground by piles. In addition, Brunel used a process known as kyanizing to extend the life of the timbers.

Isambard Kingdom Brunel (1806–59), engineer and ship and railway builder.

*Platform 1 at Paddington, the original departure
platform, during the first part of the twentieth century.*

Building the line

Construction of the new line began in 1835 from
both the London and the Bristol ends. Brunel
travelled frequently between the two stumps of
railway as they slowly advanced towards one
another, involving himself, as was his custom, in
every difficulty and problem, no matter how
small. The strain must have been almost intoler-
able at times; the work did not proceed as
quickly as he had hoped, and in addition he had
to contend with criticisms, first from the GWR's
directors because of rising costs, and then, in
1838, from the so-called Liverpool Party –
GWR shareholders from Lancashire who
questioned his insistence on the broad gauge.
Two independent reports were commissioned,
and locomotive test runs held, before Brunel
finally carried the day at a shareholders' meeting
held in January 1839, after the first part of the
line had already been opened.

The line was completed in sections. The first
part, from London to a little east of Maidenhead,
opened on 4 June 1838; trains were running to
Reading in March 1840, between Bristol and
Bath in August of the same year, and from
London to Wootton Bassett by Christmas. Problems at Box Tunnel delayed completion of the
final section, and it was not until 30 June 1841
that the first through trains ran.

Paddington station

Paddington was not the original terminus,
which until 1854 was at Bishops Road. Initially
there were two platforms only, one for departures, the other for arrivals, separated by several
sets of tracks. Additional platforms were constructed when through services began to Bristol,
before the company eventually agreed to construct a permanent trainshed at Paddington, a
little to the south-east.

There have been many alterations at Paddington since 1854, but fortunately none has succeeded in marring the magnificence of Brunel's
original design. Matthew Digby Wyatt, although generally named as the architect responsible and despite his distinguished reputation,
was invited by Brunel to be his 'assistant for the
ornamentation'.

125

GWR No. 6000 King George V *on a celebration run pulls out of Paddington alongside an HST.*

The new station was in a cutting, and so it was on the interior rather than the exterior that Brunel lavished attention, designing a magnificent glass and iron cathedral. There were three principal spans (the fourth bay, to the right as you face the tracks, was added in 1916), 70 feet, 102 feet 6 inches and 68 feet long respectively, and with two 50-foot transepts, the roof reaching 55 feet at its highest point. The ribs of the roof descended to cross-girders, which were themselves supported by columns; an attractive Moorish trelliswork pattern adorns the lower part of the ribs. Three departure and three arrival platforms were separated by seven tracks, the central five being used to store rolling stock.

Royal departures

The principal departure platform (now number 1, the furthest to the left as you look at the platforms) retains an air of grandeur, with its handsome clock and, above, the attractive oriel windows of the directors' offices. Also in this block are the royal waiting-rooms, which linked the long cab drive and the departure platform.

Queen Victoria arrived at Bishops Road on 13 June 1842, having just experienced her first journey by rail; she complained that the train, which had been driven at 44 mph by Daniel Gooch, whom Brunel had appointed as the GWR's first locomotive superintendent in 1837 and who later served for thirty-four years as chairman of the GWR, had gone rather too fast. As Paddington was the principal London terminus for Windsor, the Queen often arrived here; her funeral train left Paddington as well, as did those of Edward VII, George V and George VI.

The area behind the platforms leading back to the station entrance to the Great Western Hotel is known as the Lawn. Why is uncertain, although the name may refer to a grassy bank by Bishops Road station entrance. A modern statue of Brunel stands in the middle of the Lawn.

Route to Reading

The train leaves Paddington, quickly gathering speed as it sweeps through the inner London suburbs, past Wormwood Scrubs on the left and the Grand Union Canal and Kensal Green Cemetery on the right, and then alongside two sets of sidings, Old Oak Common and Acton, at which a wide variety of locomotives and loads from many parts of the country can be seen. Between the two, a freight-only line connecting with the main lines running into Euston and St. Pancras comes in on the right.

Beyond Southall, the river Brent is crossed on an elegant viaduct, 300 yards long with eight brick arches and named after Lord Wharncliffe, who was chairman of the House of Lords committee that considered the bill to incorporate the GWR; his coat of arms was placed over the central pier. The first fields are reached at Iver, although all the way to Reading it is rather scrappy and uninteresting countryside, the route by-passing the most attractive parts of the Thames Valley.

The exception is at Maidenhead, of which George Measom wrote in his *Illustrated Guide to the Great Western Railway* published in 1852: 'If the passenger will cast a hasty glance in passing, he will behold charming river-scenery bounded by woodlands and pleasant fields.' The comment hardly needs revising today.

The bridge over the Thames gave Brunel some thought. Since the Thames Commissioners insisted that neither the towpath nor the navigation channel should be blocked, only one pier could be used. Brunel, however, wanted to build as low a bridge as possible; the line was already running virtually level on each side of the river, and creating additional gradients for a high bridge would reduce the speed of the trains. The solution was a design with, according to his biographer L. T. C. Rolt: 'two of the largest and flattest arches that have ever been built in brickwork. Each had a span of 128 ft with a rise of only 24 ft 3 in. to the crown.'

Brunel's many detractors were delighted when distortions were spotted in the eastern arch even before a train had crossed, and refused to be mollified when the contractor accepted blame. Brunel had the wooden centres restored until repairs had been made, and then announced that they would remain in place throughout the next winter, while in fact having them eased immediately. Nine months later, the centering was blown down in a storm and, as L. T. C. Rolt says: 'Certainly the fact that the bridge was standing entirely free for nine months while jealous opponents supposed that the centering was still helping to support it was a joke that Brunel must have relished keenly.'

Reading to Swindon

Leaving Reading, the line turns north-west and runs beside the river Thames in delightful country through the Goring Gap. The Chilterns fall quite steeply to the riverside on the right and the Berkshire Downs on the left. The Thames is left behind near Cholsey as the line makes for Didcot and a long, straight stretch through the Vale of the White Horse to Swindon.

The junction with the Oxford line, Didcot is overshadowed by a huge power station, but from then on the countryside is delightful. To the right the wide south Midlands plain stretches out, while to the left the eye is carried up to the ridge of the Downs. The long-distance Ridgeway Path, the modern successor of a prehistoric route, runs along the top of the hills past Wayland's Smithy, a massive long barrow built in about 2800 BC, and the enormous White Horse, 365 feet long and 130 feet tall, thought to have been cut nearly 2,000 years ago. One of the best views of the Horse is to be had from the train.

Swindon

Of Swindon, George Measom asked:

> Who that knows aught of railways, or railway travelling, has not heard of Swindon's world-wide reputation as well for the vastness of its workshops and engine depot, as for the admirable and splendid accommodation that it furnishes for the way-worn traveller?

For many years, trains stopped at Swindon for a short refreshment break. A Mr. Griffiths, the first proprietor of the refreshment rooms, seems not have been a success, prompting Brunel to write to him that: 'I have long since ceased to make complaints at Swindon. I avoid taking anything there when I can help it.' A decade or so later, by contrast, Measom eulogized another proprietor, Mr. Phillips, as: 'that paragon of caterers'.

Like Crewe (see page 64), Swindon was a child of the railway. Gooch and Brunel picked the green fields between the main line and the Cheltenham branch to the west of the station as the site for the Swindon Works, which opened in 1843 with a running shed, an engine house and an erecting shop. The first locomotives were produced three years later. By 1876, 4,500 men were employed in the works; continued expansion brought that total to 12,000 in 1935, when over 1,000 locomotives were repaired and some 100 new ones constructed each year; 5,000 coaches and 8,000 wagons were repaired each year, the totals for new constructions being 275 and 4,750 respectively.

Recently, the works have concentrated on overhauls and refurbishments of diesel multiple units and shunters. However, in May 1985, during the celebrations of the 150th anniversary of the GWR, British Rail announced the closure because of overcapacity of the Swindon Works from March 1986, with the loss of some 2,000 jobs.

Close to the railway line, the GWR erected a model estate of cottages for its workmen and their families, now attractively restored. One cottage is open to the public, with its rooms furnished and decorated as they would have been in the late nineteenth century. The Great Western Railway Museum is next door, with its fascinating collection of GWR memorabilia and locomotives, including a replica of the broad-gauge *North Star*, the Company's earliest reliable locomotive, *Lode Star* from 1907, and a diesel railcar dated 1934.

The flamboyant French Gothic clock tower designed by Sir Matthew Digby Wyatt for the new Bristol Temple Meads station built between 1865 and 1878.

Above: *The western entrance to Box tunnel. The railway policeman on the left worked the signal.*

Below: *Brunel's bridge over the Avon immediately west of Bath station.*

Box Tunnel

Beyond Wootton Bassett, where the direct line to the Severn Tunnel (see page 144) branches off, the line turns south down Dauntsey Bank, where the gradient is an unusual 1 in 100. Beyond Chippenham, the line runs through the southern flank of the Cotswolds, approaching the celebrated Box Tunnel in a deep cutting.

The works at Box were monumental. No less than 247,000 cubic yards of soil were excavated; the tunnel was 2 miles long, all but 300 yards, descending from east to west on a 1 in 100 gradient, through a variety of rocks including clay, blue marl and inferior oolite and, at the eastern end, half a mile of great oolite, or solid Bath stone. In the words of L. T. C. Rolt:

> It was an immense undertaking and the more staggering when we remember that, apart from the steam pumps which kept the workings clear of water and the power of gunpowder which was used to blast away the rock, it was accomplished entirely by the strength of men and horses working by candlelight. For two and a half

years the work consumed a ton of gunpowder and a ton of candles very week.

In December 1840, when the work should already have been finished four months previously, Brunel drafted in no less than 4,000 men and 300 horses, who still had six months labour in front of them before the work was complete. Even when it had been passed by the Inspector General of Railways, many travellers feared to pass through, preferring to leave the train and take a horse-drawn carriage over the hill. The western entrance was decorated with a majestic portal in Bath stone standing between curved wing walls.

Bath and Bristol

A few miles on, at Bathampton Junction, the line meets the river Avon and the Kennet and Avon Canal, and accompanies them into Bath. The city is approached through a series of deep cuttings built of finely dressed masonry and two tunnels, with some attractive bridges above. Once past these, the train suddenly bursts into the open to give a magnificent view of the city stretching out on both sides of the line, with the Abbey in the foreground and the elegant Georgian terraces climbing the hillside behind. The line strides across the city on an elegant viaduct with thirty-seven arches, crosses the river and enters the station. Leaving the station, the train bridges the Avon once more, runs over two viaducts, and then plunges into two tunnels in short succession. The second, Twerton Long Tunnel, has castellated turrets at each end.

And so to Bristol, spiritual home of the Great Western. The present Temple Meads is a joint station built by the Midland, the Great Western and the Bristol & Exeter between 1865 and 1878. The station was constructed on a curve, a fine overall roof embracing a principal and an island platform with ornate ironwork on the end-screens and the arches. The frontage block was built in French Gothic style with a large central tower originally topped by a pinnacle. The refreshment room, close to the original trainshed, is a pleasant place to sit and admire the station.

Brunel's original station, just to the right of the present structure, remained in use until 1965, and has now been carefully restored to its original glory. Two platforms, at first one each for arrivals and departures, were separated by five broad-gauge tracks. The fine timber hammerbeam roof is supported by long arcades of pillars along each platform.

Gauge conversion

It is fitting that, since this majestic line was so successfully engineered by Brunel for speed, British Rail should have chosen to introduce the first High-Speed Trains on it in 1975. One legacy of Brunel's inventive genius is lost, however: the broad gauge.

As early as the mid-1840s, it was clear that most lines were being built on standard gauge; in 1845, the precise figures were 1,901 miles of standard gauge and 274 miles of broad gauge. In that same year the Gauge Commissioners ruled in favour of standard gauge, although the Great Western was allowed to develop broad-gauge lines in those parts of the country where the company had a monopoly.

This anomalous situation could not last for ever, not least because of the problems caused where the two different gauges met. Mixed-gauge lines began to be laid, and in 1861 the line from Reading to Paddington was converted from broad to mixed gauge. Gradually, the Great Western had to admit defeat; a slow programme of conversion began, completed only in 1892 when the last 106 miles of broad gauge, on the main line west from Exeter (see page 130), were lifted. On 20 May 1892, the last broad-gauge express left Penzance for Paddington; it was truly the end of an era.

The roundhouse at the GWR's Swindon works, with, from left to right, a Hall, two Castles and a Grange.

Bristol to Penzance

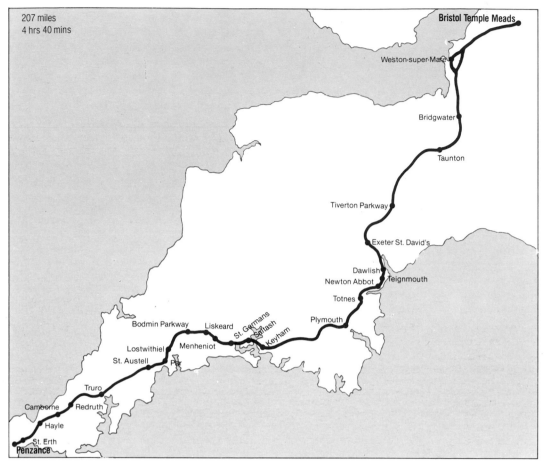

207 miles
4 hrs 40 mins

Bristol Temple Meads
Weston-super-Mare
Bridgwater
Taunton
Tiverton Parkway
Exeter St. David's
Dawlish
Newton Abbot   Teignmouth
Totnes
Plymouth
Bodmin Parkway   Liskeard   St. Germans   Saltash   Keyham
Lostwithiel   Menheniot
St. Austell   Par
Truro
Camborne   Redruth
Hayle
St. Erth
Penzance

The day 14 June 1841 saw not only the start of through services from London to Bristol, but also the opening of the first part of the Bristol & Exeter's line as far as Bridgwater. Again, the engineer was Isambard Kingdom Brunel, although he put the work in the charge of his assistant. Indeed, the first through train from London on that June day did not finish at Bristol, where the Bristol & Exeter had its station in a single-storey timber building nicknamed the 'Cowshed', but ran straight on to Bridgwater.

Although the Cowshed did the company no credit at all, in 1854 the B&E managed to complete a handsome office block commanded by a doorway in what has been described as Jacobean Renaissance style, with two pinnacles above and, inside, a grand staircase with ornate ironwork. The building still stands, and has recently been restored. The B&E was subsequently amalgamated with the Great Western Railway (GWR) in 1876.

Construction of the line to Exeter presented no particular difficulties, although one lengthy tunnel had to be cut through the Blackdown Hills beyond Taunton. The route opened to Taunton in 1842, to Beambridge west of Wellington on May Day 1843, and the inaugural train entered Exeter exactly one year later. The return trip to London was done in only 4 hours 40 minutes, much to Brunel's satisfaction. L. T. C. Rolt writes that the time

represented a performance unparalleled for sustained high speed running, especially when we remember that the time included the frequent stops for water the locomotives of the day, with their small tenders, had to make. It must have given Brunel's narrow gauge rivals furiously to think.

Leaving Bristol

There is an excellent view back over the city centre as the train climbs through the Bristol suburbs, with Brunel's Clifton Suspension Bridge, nowadays magnificently lit at night, clearly visible. Beyond Flax Bourton tunnel the line descends towards the coast, passing the edge of Weston-super-Mare (the town is served by a branch loop, a legacy of the citizens' rejection of the Bristol & Exeter's original route through the town) and then turns south across the edge of the Somerset Levels to Bridgwater. From Bridgwater to Taunton the immediate view from the window is of the Bridgwater & Taunton Canal.

Beyond Taunton, the hills are reached, and there are some attractive views as the train climbs to Whiteball tunnel (1,092 yards) and the summit just beyond. The Wellington Monument, a 75-foot obelisk erected in 1817 to the victor of Waterloo stands clear on the skyline. In steam days, banking engines were often used to assist lengthy trains up the long ascent, known as

Wellington Bank; delays here, especially on summer Saturdays when many thousands of holidaymakers made for the West Country, would cause chaos throughout Devon and beyond.

The descent towards Exeter is much more gentle running briefly alongside another deserted canal, the Grand Western, near Tiverton and then through the lovely Culm valley with fields of rich, red Devon soil. Tiverton Junction, the sole remaining intermediate station, was replaced in May 1986 by a new station a few miles nearer Taunton called Tiverton Parkway close to the M5 and the fast road into North Devon.

Indirect route

London to Exeter via Bristol is not a direct route, and it was not for nothing that the initials GWR were said to stand for Great Way Round. ('God's Wonderful Railway' was the title adopted by GWR loyalists. Grub, Water and Relief was another more scornful suggestion, a phrase used by Adrian Vaughan as the title of the third of his evocative and extremely readable books on the GWR; see bibliography.) Most present-day expresses take the direct Reading to Taunton route through Newbury and Westbury, which was opened in 1906 after two new sections had been built to link existing branch lines.

The river Kennet and the Kennet and Avon Canal accompany the line through Berkshire and Savernake Forest to Pewsey. Then comes a lovely journey through the Vale of Pewsey and beneath the scarp slope of Salisbury Plain to Westbury and Frome. Avoiding lines were built during the 1930s around both these stations. This is a shame as far as Frome is concerned, for the station, designed by a member of Brunel's staff, has a fine overall wooden roof, the only one surviving; this and Newcastle Central (see page 18), which was also built in 1850, are the earliest through trainsheds still in use. A pleasant stretch through Bruton and Somerton brings the line to Somerton tunnel and then on to the Somerset Levels to join the original line from Bristol at Cogload Junction. At Bratton Down near Westbury the celebrated White Horse can be seen, and further west Glastonbury Tor stands out clearly.

Exeter to Plymouth

The journey from Exeter to Plymouth is splendid – one of the finest hours of any British Rail route. After leaving Exeter St. David's station, the line runs beside the estuary of the Exe, where in the best weather the water sparkles in the sun, and the wind rustles the sails as yachts rock on gentle waves; the temptation to leave the train and go for a sail is almost irrestistible. Then comes the well-known stretch of coast through Dawlish, where the line runs on a narrow strip between the beach and the rocks, before making for Newton Abbot alongside the Teign estuary.

The soft coastline is left behind as the train

The line along the coast to Dawlish, one of the most splendid rail journeys in the country.

Above: *Class 50 diesel runs off the Royal Albert Bridge over the Tamar.*

Below: *Class 46 diesel crossing the Lynher viaduct between Saltash and St. Germans.*

Constructing a masonry viaduct near St. Austell in 1908.

turns to the hills, climbing to Dainton tunnel (at one point the ascent is 1 in 37) before descending steeply to the river Dart at Totnes. Another climb follows to the southern flank of Dartmoor, where, especially in winter, you get a real sense of the isolation and bleakness of the Moor. The line twists and turns to take every advantage of geography, running through Bittaford and Ivybridge before dropping to Plymouth.

Atmospheric line

Brunel intended that this route, which he built for the South Devon Railway, should be operated by atmospheric power. David St. John Thomas, historian of West Country railways, explains the system well:

> Stationary engines pumped out the air from a continuous iron pipe laid between the rails. At the top, the pipe had a slot, hinged permanently to one side but opened on the other by a framework of iron plates fitted to the leading vehicle of a train. This vehicle, the piston carriage, had a rod connecting it with a cylinder and close-fitting pistons travelling inside the pipe. Air was let in behind the piston, and its force rushing towards the vacuum in front propelled the train. The pipe was then resealed with pressure from a small roller, and a fresh vacuum was then created by the pumping houses.

Brunel believed that the high cost of the machinery required would be more than offset by savings in operating costs; in addition, steeper gradients could be allowed, which would reduce construction costs. Things went wrong from the start. Delays in installing the apparatus meant that the first trains between Exeter and Teignmouth in May 1846 and on to Newton Abbot the following December were operated by conventional locomotives. Eventually, a service of atmospheric trains was inaugurated: to Teignmouth on 13 September 1847 and to Newton Abbot on 10 January 1848.

Although quite high speeds were attained (a maximum of 68 mph), breakdowns and accidents were frequent; it was impossible to maintain an air-tight seal on the continuous pipe; the leather from which a vital longitudinal valve was made first froze and then disintegrated entirely. In the end, as L. T. C. Rolt writes, Brunel 'faced the fact that he had been responsible for the most costly failure in the history of engineering at that time', and advised the South Devon's directors to abandon the experiment.

The present journey to Plymouth – which might, if things had gone differently, still be operated as an atmospheric railway – provides only two remnants of Brunel's ill-fated experiment. Locomotives still have to tackle remarkably steep gradients originally built for the atmospheric line. And at Starcross, to the right

Great Western steam revived: Nos. 4930 and 7819 near Teignmouth, Devon, on the lovely line between Exeter and Plymouth.

of the line just by the station, there still stands an Italianate pumping station built to service the atmospheric route, now converted into a museum with displays and models of the atmospheric railway that scarcely was. A through service of conventional trains between Exeter and Plymouth began in 1848, and thirty years later the South Devon was absorbed by the GWR.

Cornish line

The Cornwall Railway, which built the 54-mile route west from Plymouth to Truro, opened its line throughout on 4 May 1859, no less than twelve years after construction started. Financial difficulties had plagued the company almost from the start, and work could only be continued because the GWR, the Bristol & Exeter and the South Devon – collectively known as the Associated Companies – bailed the project out. The company never had a truly independent operational existence: a Joint Committee ran it from the start until 1876, when the GWR became sole lessee, and thirteen years later the CR was absorbed into the GWR.

It was not an easy line to build. Apart from the mammoth work of bridging the Tamar (of which more below), many embankments and no less than thirty-four viaducts had to be built over the rivers and streams forging their way from Cornwall's high central plateau towards the sea. Pressed by the company's need to save money, Brunel decided to build these viaducts out of timber rather than cast-iron; the majority were supported on slate piers, although those over St. Germans Creek, just a little into Cornwall, had timber trestles that rested on stone piles.

Kyanized yellow pine from the Baltic was used; this was of excellent quality, relatively inexpensive, and had a life of at least thirty years, all of which meant that the bridges could be readily renewed, especially as they were so designed that single sections could be removed easily. From the 1870s the timber bridges were gradually replaced as the line was doubled, the last one, College Wood viaduct on the Falmouth branch (see page 142), surviving until 1934; some of the old piers can still be seen close to their masonry successors.

Royal Albert Bridge

Considerable problems faced Brunel as he planned the crossing of the Tamar. The river was 1,100 feet wide and 70 feet deep at high tide, and the Admiralty insisted on 100 feet clearance. His eventual solution was to support two principal spans on a single deep-water pier, with foundations that went down into solid rock more than 80 feet below high water. The deck, which for economy's sake was designed to accommodate only a single track (the bridge remains single track to this day), was suspended by hangers and chains from two oval wrought-iron tubes. There were additional spans on each shore, seven on the Devon bank and ten in Cornwall.

While each of the two spans (that is, the tubes, hangers, chains and deck) was prefabricated on shore nearby, construction of the central pier progressed. When the pier was above low-water mark, it was time to float the first span into place. On 1 September 1857, in front of a huge crowd of onlookers, Brunel directed operations as the span was floated out into mid-river on a pontoon and, just at the moment of high tide, was secured into place. L. T. C. Rolt quotes an onlooker: 'With the impressive silence which is the highest evidence of power, it *slid*, as it were, into position without an accident, without any extraordinary mechanical effort, without a "misfit", to the eighth of an inch.' The second span was placed in position in July 1858, whereupon the central pier was slowly built up until it reached its intended height.

Prince Albert travelled to Plymouth in May 1859 to open the bridge that bears his name. Brunel was not there. Ill and exhausted from his attempts to build his massive ship *Great Eastern*, he had gone abroad to recuperate. He visited the bridge but once, when, a sick and dying man, he was slowly drawn across it on a specially prepared wagon.

There are glimpses of the naval yards and the Sound as the train leaves Plymouth station and makes for the bridge. On the approach it slows (the speed limit on the bridge itself is set at 15 mph) and there is a stunning view ahead; as you cross, the views up and downstream are equally magnificent, and from Saltash and beyond, as the train hugs the shore, there are frequent glimpses of the bridge again. It is a superb structure, fully outranking in style and eloquence the road bridge erected alongside just over a century later. It is fitting, too, that the name of its celebrated engineer is commemorated on the shore arches of his bridge.

Cornish countryside

There are three viaducts and a tunnel between Saltash and St. Germans; the last viaduct, just before St. Germans station, strides handsomely over the water, giving splendid views of the Lynher river. The line then leaves the Lynher behind and starts the first of many steep and twisting ascents through pleasant countryside; most of the route to Truro is done at gradients of well under 1 in 100 as it switchbacks across the hills and valleys.

After Liskeard the scenery is delightful, and the line soon joins the river Fowey, descending slowly through a lush landscape with rhododendrons and woods to Bodmin Parkway, past the fine shell keep at Restormel castle, and so first to Lostwithiel and then to the coast again at Par. Of the many viaducts crossed, Moorswater (see also page 140) just beyond Liskeard and St. Pinnock are the most impressive.

Cornwall has many aspects, and the line beyond Par runs through one of the less attractive parts of the county, with huge mountains of china clay rearing up behind the bungalows of St. Austell. China clay forms an important part of freight traffic along the Cornish main line. The line then climbs to Burngullow, descends to cross the river Fal, climbs once more, descends and runs through two tunnels before entering Truro along two viaducts. The view across the town to the cathedral is splendid.

Final stretch

It is a curious fact that of the entire London to Penzance route the first section to be built was in Cornwall. The Hayle Railway's 12-mile line from Hayle to Gwennap was opened in stages, the first on 23 December 1837, with passenger services inaugurated six years later. In 1846 the West Cornwall Railway took over the Hayle company and extended its line both east and west, opening the complete Penzance to Truro route in 1852. Interestingly, this line was laid with narrow-gauge track, and it was not until the West Cornwall Railway Committee, which consisted of representatives of the GWR, the Bristol & Exeter and the South Devon took over in 1865 that broad-gauge rails were laid – only, of course, to be replaced with standard-gauge rails twenty-five years later!

Tin and copper mining is the theme of the next section of the route. A climb brings the line to a high plateau around Chacewater. Around Redruth, where the town is crossed on a dramatic viaduct, and Camborne there are numerous old mine buildings, plus, at Camborne, the well-known School of Mining. Beyond Hayle, the line runs along the edge of the Hayle estuary, through St. Erth, and across the peninsula to the southern coast near Marazion. The final stretch is along the embankment beside Mount's Bay, where there are excellent views of St. Michael's Mount, and into Penzance station.

St. Michael's Mount silhouetted against a winter sky; a fitting climax to the journey by rail through Cornwall.

East Somerset Railway

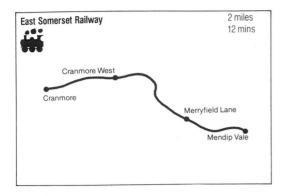

Cranmore West

Cranmore

Merryfield Lane

Mendip Vale

Although the original East Somerset line was almost a storybook route served by a few under-used trains unhurriedly making their way between somnolent villages and little country market towns and other halts, a quite sizeable portion of the line remains open today. But, with one exception, the services operating over the route are mainly freight trains running to the Foster Yeoman stone quarries at Merehead.

The one exception is the trains of the present independent East Somerset Railway, which, largely as a result of the vision of one man, operates a stretch of track almost 2 miles long, running approximately west from Cranmore and connected with the BR route from Reading to Taunton. The man is David Shepherd, who, although best known to the world as an excellent painter of wildlife scenes, is also a lover of steam of long standing. Impelled to record on canvas the final years of steam in the mid and late 1960s, Shepherd not only produced paintings which brilliantly capture the dying glory of the locomotives, but also purchased two locomotives himself.

The search then began for a suitable home. After a long time spent in a fruitless hunt, Cranmore was found in August 1971. The next few years saw the creation of a perfect Victorian railway scene on what had been a derelict piece of land. The original station was restored, and

now looks just as it did some hundred years ago, with posters, nameboards, advertisements, signs, and even a cast-iron Gents sign; porters' barrows and milk churns stand on the platform awaiting the next train. The signalbox dates from 1904, and now serves as an art gallery where it is possible to buy prints of David Shepherd's railway and wildlife paintings.

A little way down the track, near Cranmore West station, a new engine shed was built in 1974, carefully modelled on the layout and design of a Victorian shed. There is also a water tower, a restaurant car where visitors can buy snacks and meals, and a train crew cabin where drivers and firemen take their breaks. The station platform at Cranmore West comes from Athelney in Somerset, a former halt on the Taunton to Reading main line.

For many years, the East Somerset Railway was not permitted to run into Cranmore station, and services on the Company's short line started from Cranmore West. Now, however, the line has been extended at both ends, for Cranmore is the regular terminus, and trains are run beyond Merryfield Lane along a recently opened extension to Mendip Vale. Among the locomotives at work on the line are David Shepherd's *Black Prince*, No. 92203, which he bought after she had worked the last steam-hauled iron-ore train from Liverpool docks to the steel works on the other side of the Dee at Shotton.

The original line, now successfully restored, was opened by the East Somerset Railway between Witham and Shepton Mallet on 9 November 1858, and an extension to Wells was completed in 1892. Although the line was operated independently at first, it was built on the 7-foot broad gauge, and was only taken over by the GWR in 1874, the same year that the tracks were converted to the standard gauge. Passenger services ceased in 1963, but freight traffic continued, and the siding loop to the Merehead stone quarry was opened in 1970.

68005, the tiny Lord Fisher saddletank, heads a train along the line towards Mendip Vale.

South Devon Steam

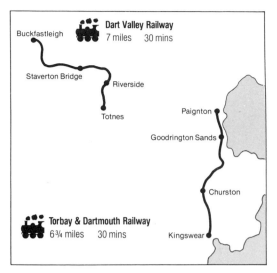

Dart Valley Railway
7 miles   30 mins

Buckfastleigh

Staverton Bridge

Riverside

Totnes

Paignton

Goodrington Sands

Churston

Torbay & Dartmouth Railway
6¾ miles   30 mins

Kingswear

The twentieth century has brought the gradual and now almost total erosion of the individual identities of the pre-Grouping companies. British Rail's image today is a national one – 'This is the Age of the Train', 'We're Getting There' – with merely superficial local variations. Even the special character of the Great Western Railway, which outlasted Grouping and survived almost intact well past nationalization in 1948, has vanished now, and it is to the preserved lines that we must look if we wish to recreate the atmosphere of train travel in the heyday of steam and to understand the loyalties felt for individual railway companies.

Two such lines in south Devon, the Dart Valley and the Torbay & Dartmouth, do much to perpetuate the style of the GWR. Although they are only a few miles apart, they represent very different aspects of that company's operations. Unlike other independent steam lines, they are not run by enthusiasts but as a going commercial concern with a permanent, paid staff; nevertheless, much important assistance is given by volunteers, whose participation is encouraged.

The Dart Valley Railway

The modest route that ran alongside the river Dart from Totnes to Buckfastleigh and Ashburton was a typical GWR branch line. A few passenger trains were operated each day, together with one or two goods trains carrying all manner of freight such as agricultural and horticultural produce, farm machinery, fertilizers and coal. Ashburton was a centre of the wool trade, so woollen goods left the town by train too, and on market days cattle and sheep were loaded on to the wagons. The junction with the main line was at Totnes, where the Ashburton trains (rarely more than a tank engine and two carriages) had to cross the tracks of the main line to reach the platform.

The line was opened in 1872, six years before

A Paignton train leaves Kingswear on the Torbay &
Dartmouth Railway.

137

0–6–0PT No. 1638 at Buckfastleigh, the Dart Valley Railway's northern terminus.

the South Devon Railway amalgamated with the GWR, and survived for considerably less than a century, passenger services ceasing in November 1958 and freight operations almost four years later, in September 1962. Conversion from the original broad gauge to standard gauge took place in May 1892, when the entire system west of Exeter was relaid during the course of a single weekend.

Although it may not have been immediately obvious, there was little hope for the line after motor transport developed on a large scale during the 1920s. The train journey to Newton Abbot, the main commercial centre for Ashburton, took the best part of 2 hours, and involved one change of train; the trip by bus, in contrast, was completed in a matter of 25 minutes.

As soon as the line closed for good in 1962, negotiations to reopen it as a private concern began. They took seven years to complete, and the opening ceremony of the new Dart Valley Railway was conducted by Lord Beeching, who as Dr. Beeching had proposed the closure of so many branch lines; clearly someone involved with the new line had a sense of irony. The new owners had only received permission to operate the line as far as Buckfastleigh; beyond, the land was used for the newly widened A38 trunk route to Plymouth.

From Buckfastleigh, where there is a fascinating steam centre and museum to visit, as well as Buckfast Abbey, a mile outside the town and completed in 1938 after thirty years' work by Benedictine monks, the line crosses first the Mardle and then the Dart itself. The Dart

remains a constant companion as the line runs through delightful pastoral countryside with thick woodlands; in spring, the banks are a riot of wild flowers, while the autumn brings every variation of gold and brown.

Beyond Staverton Bridge, one of two intermediate stations, the line continues alongside the river as it curves round the edge of the Dartington Hall estate. The fine Hall can be visited, as well as attractive gardens and a craft centre, and there is also the well-known public school, where a celebrated summer music school takes place. The river widens towards Totnes, where the Dart Valley trains have recently been allowed to run once again into the British Rail station. Totnes itself is a handsome town that climbs up through narrow streets from the riverside, with many attractive old buildings.

The Torbay & Dartmouth Railway

The contrast between this route and the quiet, rural remoteness of the Dart Valley line could hardly be greater. The Torbay & Dartmouth was a holiday route, accustomed to handling large numbers of people in short periods of time. Unlike the Dart Valley, on which nothing much larger than a tank engine operated, express trains on the Torbay & Dartmouth line used to run through to the terminus at Kingswear. Two named trains arrived every day, the *Torbay Express* from London and the *Devonian* from Leeds, and many other main-line services as well from London and the Midlands.

The Dartmouth & Torbay Railway (the original title put Dartmouth first) opened its line from Torbay to Paignton in 1859, and extended it to Kingswear in 1864, although by that time the South Devon had absorbed the D&TR. In 1972, British Rail cut off the line at Paignton. Most unusually, however, negotiations for the independent operation of the line were already in progress, and the Dart Valley Light Railway Company, owners of the Dart Valley line, took the route over, continuing to operate trains virtually without a break.

The new Railway constructed its own station on what had previously been British Rail's carriage sidings, alongside the existing BR station. The first few hundred yards of the line run parallel to BR's track into Goodrington carriage sidings and are controlled, as far as day-to-day operations are concerned, by British Rail's Paignton South signalbox. The line reaches the sea at Goodrington, and there are fine views across Torbay to Torquay, with Hope's Nose at the top of the peninsula, and south towards Brixham and Berry Head.

The steep ascent to Churston begins, followed by two viaducts, Broadsands and Hookhills, before the line turns inland to Churston station, formerly the junction with the Brixham branch. In terms of scenery, the best part of the route is yet to come. First there is a delightful woodland descent, interspersed with embankments and cuttings, and then the train plunges into Greenway tunnel (495 yards).

On the far side of the tunnel, the view is nothing short of spectacular. The line is now running high above the wide estuary of the Dart, with views upstream to Dittisham and downstream towards Dartmouth. It is an idyllic scene; yachts and motor launches abound, some making their way to or from the open sea, others content to enjoy the peace of the estuary itself. Occasionally, naval vessels are to be seen, and it is easy to understand how safe a haven the estuary is; many craft that sailed across the Channel on D-Day were secluded here during the months of preparation for the invasion.

The route descends to the riverside, and runs along the water's edge into Kingswear station, with fine views across to the Royal Naval College and to Dartmouth town. In Kingswear, two regular ferries – one for foot passengers only, the other for both pedestrians and cars – cross the river to Dartmouth.

One question remains to be asked about this line. Why, since it does not serve Dartmouth itself, does the name of that town appear in the title? The original aim had indeed been to extend the line to Dartmouth, but the House of Lords rejected the idea, and so the original directors of the line had to content themselves with the route to Kingswear and the steam ferry, also later taken over by the GWR, across to Dartmouth.

The majority of locomotives on both of these steam lines was either built by the GWR or are GWR types built by British Railways in the years immediately after 1948. No. 7828, *Lydham Manor*, a 4–6–0 tender locomotive, is popular on the Torbay route, while a 2–8–0 tank is the most powerful preserved tank in Great Britain. Behind the locomotives, painted in the familiar GWR green, run a variety of coaches. Some are ex-British Rail stock in the familiar GWR chocolate and cream livery, while others saw service with the GWR itself; there are a number of interesting special coaches, including a vehicle from a Royal Train and two Pullman-type saloons.

0–4–2T No. 145 with a Torbay & Dartmouth train at Goodrington.

Cornish Branch Lines

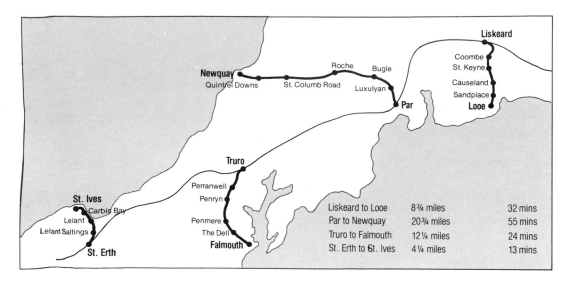

Liskeard to Looe	8¾ miles	32 mins
Par to Newquay	20¾ miles	55 mins
Truro to Falmouth	12¼ miles	24 mins
St. Erth to St. Ives	4¼ miles	13 mins

In contrast with many other parts of the country, Cornwall is still relatively well served by branch lines, remnants of a much larger system of passenger routes and china clay lines. Each has its own distinctive character and to travel on all four (which can be done in a single day if you are determined enough) is to experience many different facets of Cornish life and landscape.

Liskeard to Looe

The Looe trains leave Liskeard from a separate platform set at right angles to the main part of the station. The train faces north to begin with, but soon swings south in a huge curve, running down through the arches of Liskeard viaduct, which carries the main line high above, and descending steeply to Coombe Junction. Here the train reverses, and while the guard climbs down to change the points there is time to admire the view up the valley to Moorswater viaduct, which the main line crosses immediately after leaving Liskeard station. The main part of the route is through deep, luxuriant countryside, past peaceful hamlets and stations remote from the outside world. Eventually the line emerges alongside the East Looe river, and there are pleasant views along the final stretch to Looe station on the edge of the town, just before the East

Main-line Penzance to Paddington train crossing Trewood viaduct near St. Austell, with china clay mountains in the background. The Par to Newquay branch line runs through the heart of the china clay mines, where towering mountains of waste give the landscape a lunar appearance.

Looe to Liskeard train towards the end of its journey.
The train is about to run under Liskeard viaduct.

Looe joins the West Looe and runs on to the sea.

This line has a curious history. The original route was not a railway at all but a canal opened in the late 1820s. Traffic, principally in copper and granite, increased so much that in the late 1850s the canal was converted to a railway; the new line connected with the Liskeard & Caradon Railway, which ran north to the mines and quarries. Freight services began on the new line in 1860, and passenger trains not until 1879, although passengers were permitted to travel in the mineral wagons free so long as they paid for an item of 'freight' – such as their umbrella, for instance! The loop bringing the line from the valley up to the main line at Liskeard was opened in 1901. Mineral traffic was already declining, and the route to Caradon was closed in 1916, all except for a short stump leading north from Coombe Junction, which is still used by china clay trains. Between St. Keyne and Causeland stations remains of the old canal can just be seen to the right of the train.

Par to Newquay

This fascinating route has its origins in the network of lines which, even before the main route out of Cornwall had been completed, were bringing china clay down to the coast. Two sections from Par to Bugle and from St. Dennis (near St. Columb Road station) to Newquay were opened during the 1840s. Although steam locomotion was already well established by this time, both in Cornwall (the Hayle Railway, see page 135, had been operating for some years) and throughout the country, the decision was taken to work the lines with horses, chiefly on the grounds that they were cheaper than locomotives. The two rope inclines, one on each section, were powered by a waterwheel. Between Par and Bugle, the trains (for so they should be called, even though they were horse-drawn) crossed the ten-arch Treffry viaduct, named after J. T. Treffry who built the lines.

Locomotive haulage was not introduced until 1874, when the Cornwall Mineral Railways Company, which had been formed the previous year, opened a dense network of new or reconstructed mineral lines. Considerable improvements were made to the Newquay line; the gaps were joined up, the inclines were by-passed, as was Treffry viaduct, and branch routes added. Two years later a passenger service between Newquay and Fowey was introduced, and in 1879 a link to the main line at Par was built, the GWR having taken over in 1877.

The train branches off the main line immediately after Par station and runs through St. Blazey, where the china clay sidings include part of the original route. Then comes a steep climb past the original Carmears Incline through

North Hill Wood and Luxulyan tunnel, 52 yards long; the line twists and turns on itself through dense greenery, running underneath Treffry viaduct.

Once the summit has been gained, the contrast in the landscape could hardly be greater. The line emerges on to a bare, windswept plateau with a skyline dominated by long mountains of china clay. Beyond Roche the route follows the A30 across part of Bodmin Moor to St. Dennis Junction, where several mineral lines used to branch off.

The final stretch is through pleasant countryside into Newquay, where an incline, now long since abandoned, used to carry mineral wagons down to the harbour. On the outskirts of the town the line crosses Trenance viaduct, a handsome structure built in 1939 to replace a bridge built for the start of locomotive haulage in 1874, which in turn replaced a wooden bridge erected by J. T. Treffry.

Truro to Falmouth

Trains first reached Falmouth in 1863, fifteen years or so later than they should have done. The original plan of the Cornwall Railway (see page 135) had been to build its line from Plymouth to Falmouth. But when the project got into difficulties, not the least of which was the failure of the contractor responsible for the section from Truro to Falmouth, that part of the route was abandoned. Not until 1861 was another Act of Parliament authorizing what was now merely a branch line passed, at the same time that the docks at Falmouth were being improved and extended.

Extensive engineering works were necessary and as a result today the line provides an impressive ride. To begin with there were no less than eight timber viaducts, four now replaced with masonry structures and the other four converted into embankments, and two tunnels. College Wood viaduct, between Penryn and Penmere,

The waterside at Falmouth, where cargo vessels and sailing craft share the magnificent haven.

A St. Ives to St. Erth diesel multiple unit threads its way above the golden sands of Carbis Bay.

was the longest (318 yards) and also the last to be rebuilt, surviving until 1934.

The line leaves the bay platform at Truro station and runs alongside the tracks of the main line as far as Penwithers Junction, where it veers off to the south-west; to begin with, this section provided the unusual sight of a broad-gauge line (the Falmouth branch of the Cornwall Railway) running alongside narrow-gauge tracks (those of the West Cornwall Railway). On its own now, the line runs through attractive countryside through Sparnick tunnel and then over Carnon viaduct which crosses a broad valley made brown and unfertile by tin workings further up-stream. After the second tunnel and two more viaducts the line turns south. There are glimpses of the inlet off Carrick Roads before the train descends through the outskirts of Falmouth, Penmere and The Dell stations following in quick succession, to the terminus. Occasional views of the docks can be caught from the train, and a siding connects with the dockside.

Like the St. Ives branch and the Coombe Junction to Looe section of the Looe line, this line operates according to 'one train working', that is only one train occupying the entire route at any one time.

St. Erth to St. Ives

This last of the Cornish branch lines is also the shortest and one of the finest. The train follows the edge of the Hayle estuary from Lelant Saltings to Carbis Bay, and then runs along a ledge high up the cliff towards St. Ives. The scene is a splendid one. Below, the deep blue waves of the Atlantic roll on to firm, golden sand or hurl themselves against the sheer cliff edge matted with luxuriant vegetation; to the right, the fine Cornish coastline stretches out as far as the eye can see, while ahead the narrow cobbled streets of St. Ives cascade to the harbour. The line is a magnificent approach to the town. Opened in 1877, it was the last line to be built to the 7-foot gauge.

Swindon to Swansea

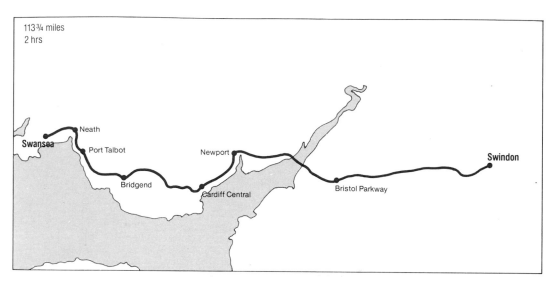

113¾ miles
2 hrs

The estuary of the river Severn – wide, deep and swept by strong tides – was the major obstacle facing railway planners as they considered a route from London to South Wales. To begin with, trains crossed the river high up at Gloucester. Leaving the main London to Bristol line at Swindon (see page 128), the route climbed through the Cotswolds, descended to the river valley and then followed the west bank of the Severn through Chepstow, where the Wye was crossed on Brunel's tubular bridge, now much altered and reconstructed; it was here that Brunel tried out many of the ideas perfected on the Royal Albert Bridge over the Tamar (see page 134). The GWR opened the line from Swindon to Gloucester in 1844, and the South Wales Railway completed the route from Gloucester to Chepstow in 1851, having begun services from Chepstow to Swansea in 1850.

The first company to attempt a more direct route was the Bristol & South Wales Union, which had two lines, an 11½-mile route from

Swindon station in about 1886. The lines through the principal platforms are mixed gauge.

Above: *Broad-gauge locomotives at Swindon, where the GWR locomotives were built.*

Below: *Before the Severn tunnel was built, trains crossed the Severn by way of a bridge at Gloucester.*

Bristol to Aust on the east bank of the Severn and another short spur on the west side linking with the main line at Chepstow. The GWR operated the service, which began in 1863, from the start. Trains ran to the piers on each side of the river, where passengers boarded a steamer for the trip across.

Problems with water

Work on a tunnel began in 1873, and occupied the next thirteen years. Flooding was the principal problem. In 1879, when considerable progress had been made from each bank, the workings were inundated by a fresh-water spring, and tunnelling came to a halt for fifteen months. When it restarted, the bore was redesigned to run 15 feet lower. Even so, there was yet more flooding, first in 1881 and then twice in 1883, when first the Great Spring and then a tidal wave broke through. The Great Spring was eventually tamed by being diverted into a side tunnel where massive beam engines were installed to pump the water away. The original fifteen steam engines were replaced by electric pumps in 1961, which still cope with the 20 million gallons of water welling up from the spring each day. The tunnel was eventually completed in 1885, and opened to regular traffic the following year.

The opening of the tunnel caused considerable congestion on the GWR line through Chippenham, Bath and Bristol, which now became the principal route from the south-east to South Wales. In 1895 work started on a new direct line running from Swindon through Badminton and north of Bristol to the tunnel mouth. This cut-off, which opened in 1903, leaves the original route at Wootton Bassett, a few miles beyond Swindon, and runs across the southern edge of the Cotswolds towards the wide Severn plain. It is a hilly route, and to maintain a reasonably level gradient of not more than 1 in 300 several cuttings and embankments had to be built, as well as Sodbury tunnel, an impressive 2 miles 924 yards long.

Bristol Parkway

All the original stations on the new direct line, which shortened the journey from Newport to London by 10 miles, were closed when local passenger services ceased in 1961, although Badminton retained its station until 1968. Four years later the first of British Rail's Parkway stations was opened. Strategically situated near the M4 and M5, and within easy reach of the large Bristol conurbation, it has been a great success, attracting considerable numbers of London-bound travellers (including regular daily commuters) who might otherwise have gone by road, and also providing a convenient changeover point with trains travelling between the south-west, the Midlands and the north.

Leaving Parkway, the train veers to the right (trains for Temple Meads and the south-west

take the left-hand route) and races towards the river, emerging from Patchway tunnel for a brief moment, when on clear days there may be a good view across to Wales, before plunging once more through a deep cutting which leads straight to the mouth of the Severn tunnel. The descent continues at 1 in 100 for some while within the tunnel, which at 4 miles 628 yards is the longest in Britain. A short level stretch precedes the 1 in 90 ascent to the exit. The view from the Welsh side is dominated by the large marshalling yards at Severn Tunnel Junction, still an important exchange point for freight wagons.

The line enters Newport past the huge Llanwern steel works and over the Usk, where there are good views of the docks. Newport remains an important railway centre. Apart from the east-west line, there are services north to Hereford and Shrewsbury, and a network of freight-only lines leading into the valleys, as well as sidings and dockside lines in the town itself. From the station, the train dives into Hillfield tunnel and emerges to sweep across a stretch of flat grassland by the coast towards Cardiff, where, as in Newport, numerous branches lead off to the docks.

Cardiff to Swansea

The line runs through pleasant pastoral country in the Ely valley, past St. Fagans, where the National Museum of Wales has its open-air Folk Museum. At first there is no sign at all of the hills that lie only a few miles to the north, but they come into view before Bridgend, which is the nodal point of another group of coal lines leading north into the valleys. There are large marshalling yards near the coast at Margam, and a good view ahead of the steel works at Port Talbot, which the train passes, squeezed on to the tiny strip of land between the sea and the steep-sided mountains.

The Talbot who gave his name to Port Talbot lived at Margam Abbey (the grounds are now a pleasant country park just to the right of the line) and was a local industrialist; Chairman of the South Wales Railway, he became a director of the GWR after the two companies amalgamated in 1863. Built as a broad-gauge route, the Newport to Swansea line was among the first GWR lines to go over to standard gauge; conversion took place in 1872.

The final stretch takes the train in a large U-shaped loop up the east side of the river Neath to the town of Neath, and then south into Swansea alongside the river Tawe and over Landore viaduct. Swansea was once a remarkably busy railway centre, with no less than seven termini, including that of the Swansea & Mumbles Railway. When it closed in 1960, the Swansea & Mumbles was the oldest public railway in the world. It was incorporated in 1804 as the Oystermouth Railway, began horse-drawn goods services two years later, and carried its first passengers in 1807.

GWR 4–6–0 No. 7029 Clun Castle *leaves Newport*
for the east across the Usk bridge.

Lines west of Swansea

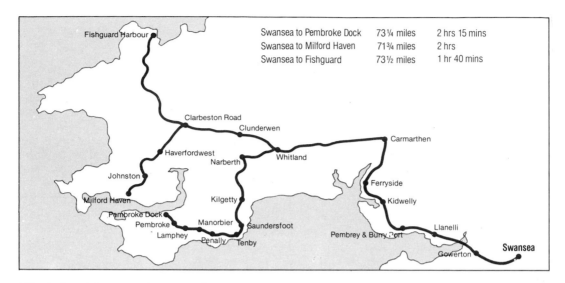

Swansea to Pembroke Dock	73¼ miles	2 hrs 15 mins
Swansea to Milford Haven	71¾ miles	2 hrs
Swansea to Fishguard	73½ miles	1 hr 40 mins

The industrial, urban character of the main line east of Swansea is maintained as the train pushes west, at least for the first few miles. The line runs through Cockett tunnel before descending to the wide mouth of the Loughor, which it crosses on an eighteen-arch viaduct. Brunel's original structure was entirely timber, but the deck was renewed in steel in 1911. At Llandeilo Junction the Heart of Wales line from Shrewsbury (see page 86) comes in from the right, and then it is only a few minutes into Llanelli station.

Now the traveller experiences a complete change of scenery. Gone is the Wales of pitheads, factory chimneys, and terraced houses straggling up hillsides; in its place comes a more pastoral, lyrical scene – the Wales of small farms and little villages grouped around the chapel, with, from time to time, majestic castles that recall the foreign conquests of this lovely land.

The line hugs the coast as far as Burry Port, cuts briefly inland behind Cefn Sidan Sands, and then runs up the delightful Tywi estuary through Kidwelly, where the present castle was built in about 1270 to replace an early twelfth-century earthwork, to Carmarthen. Once upon a time, it was possible to change trains at Carmarthen for all manner of tiny places in central Wales, including Newcastle Emlyn, Lampeter, Aberaeron and Aberystwyth. All these branches have long since been closed, except for the stub of line leading to the station, from which the present-day services have to reverse. Trains not booked to stop at Carmarthen use the main line that by-passes the station.

Line to Fishguard

The South Wales Railway opened its line to Carmarthen on 11 October 1852. The original intention had been to build a direct line to Fishguard, but work stopped in 1851 only 7 miles short of the town as a result of the economic crisis caused by the Irish potato famine; traffic prospects no longer looked so good, and the SWR's Irish partners were unable to proceed with their planned lines in Ireland.

Brunel built south instead, reaching Haverfordwest in 1854 and Neyland two years later. In 1863 the Milford Railway Company built an additional branch from Johnston to Milford Haven, operated by the GWR from the start, and it is this branch that survives today, the Neyland line having closed in 1964.

Construction work on the 50-foot opening span of the bridge over the river Towy in Carmarthen, built in 1908 to replace Brunel's original bridge.

The next line to be opened was to Pembroke Dock. Unlike many small local companies, the Pembroke & Tenby Railway was a genuinely independent concern. It demonstrated its independence by opening a standard-gauge line from Pembroke to Tenby in 1863 in the midst of what was a broad-gauge stronghold; an extension to Pembroke Dock was completed the following year, and to Whitland in 1866, where the broad-gauge main line was joined. An agreement with the GWR (which by now had taken over the South Wales Railway) was reached, whereby one track would be converted to standard-gauge into Carmarthen in return for the P&T abandoning its plans for expansion. This curious arrangement only lasted until 1872, when all the Welsh broad-gauge lines were relaid. The GWR only reached Fishguard at the beginning of the twentieth century, finally opening the line through to the Harbour station in 1906, and inaugurating a ferry service to Rosslare.

Milford Haven and Pembroke Dock

Nowadays, traffic is concentrated on the Milford Haven and Pembroke Dock branches. The latter line provides a delightful ride through lush, deep countryside. There are some steep gradients between Whitland and Saundersfoot, and a 273-yard tunnel just past Narberth station. Tenby has an extremely attractive station built of local stone with a lovely platform awning supported on iron columns, and an equally handsome seven-arch viaduct that strides across the town. There are sea views beyond the town before the line strikes inland again through Manorbier, where the castle has a twelfth-century great tower, to Pembroke; here the cylindrical great tower is the best-known feature of the castle that dominates both the town and the sea approaches. Another 2 miles brings the train to the terminus at Pembroke Dock, where boats leave for Ireland.

The Milford Haven branch runs through a more open landscape, often buffeted by winds from the Atlantic, and with views of the massive oil refineries on the north shore of the Haven. After Johnston the line drops to run beside an attractive inlet towards Milford Haven station. Two freight-only routes lead off, to the Gulf refinery on the left and, on the right, to the Esso and Amoco refineries. Oil trains form an important part of traffic on this branch, which now also sees a regular service of High-Speed Trains.

The Fishguard line runs through wild country below the Preseli hills, passing through a tunnel and several cuttings before descending steeply through Fishguard town to the harbour. Boat trains form the bulk of the traffic on this little-used branch, and ordinary passenger services run only once or twice a day.

Fishguard Harbour station, the end of the line in west Wales. Hopes of developing a substantial trans- *Atlantic traffic were never realized, but sailings continue to Rosslare in Ireland.*

SOUTHERN REGION

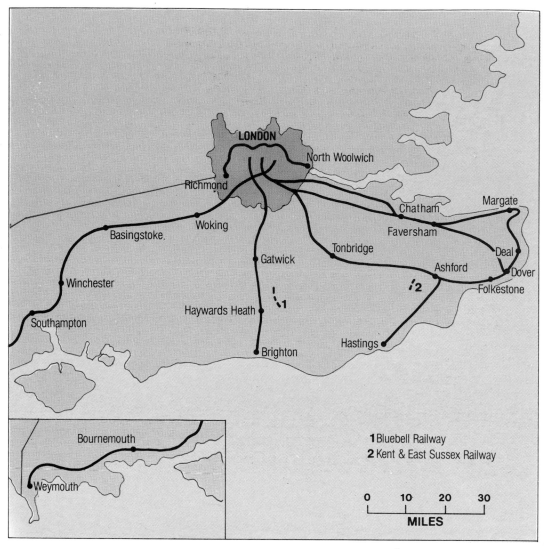

The Southern Region is commuter territory *par excellence*. Every weekday many hundreds of thousands of people pour into London's southern termini from the capital's outer suburbs and from towns and villages throughout Kent, Surrey, Sussex and Hampshire, far more than arrive on the trains of the Western, Midland and Eastern Regions. In addition, despite the phenomenal growth of air travel over the past two decades, there remains a substantial amount of continental traffic from various ports along the Channel coast.

As a result, the Southern Region's operations are characterized by the need to move large numbers of people regularly over relatively short distances. No line reaches much more than 150 miles from the capital, and the majority of services cover less than half that distance. Speeds are relatively slow, for electrification, begun well before nationalization, is on the now old-fashioned third-rail system, and the Region lacks the focus of a few principal arteries.

The landscape in the south offers less drama and fewer surprises than can be found in other regions. Nevertheless there is much to enjoy: the ride through the New Forest between Southampton and Bournemouth on the London

to Weymouth route; the exciting run between Folkestone and Dover straight through Dover's white cliffs and on the very edge of the Channel; the wide skies of the remote Romney Marsh seen from a train on the Ashford to Hastings route, one of the Region's few non-electrified lines. The North and South Downs presented a considerable obstacle to railway builders, as the series of cuttings and tunnels on the journey between London and Brighton demonstrates.

Rail travel within the capital offers many interesting moments. The North London line – which, although included here for the sake of convenience, in fact passes through the territory of four of the five British Rail Regions – reveals a fascinating cross-section of London life, while the journey from London Bridge to Greenwich, which continues along the Thames estuary to beyond Gravesend before swinging south to meet the Medway, was the first line to be built in the capital.

Two of the Region's steam lines are featured, the Kent & East Sussex and the Bluebell Railway. The Bluebell was the first standard-gauge line to be preserved by enthusiasts, setting an example successfully followed throughout the country.

Poster produced by the Southern Railway to attract weekend and holiday custom to its lines and reflecting the enthusiasm for country rambles that grew up between the two World Wars.

The untidy façade of Victoria station before the rebuilding undertaken at the turn of the century.

London to Weymouth

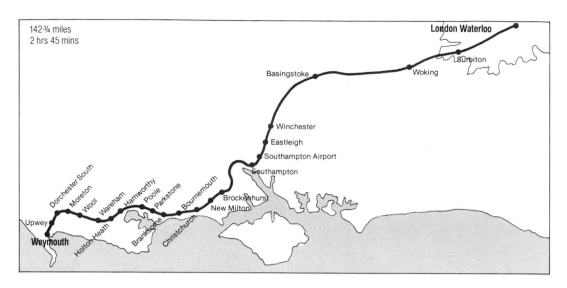

142¾ miles
2 hrs 45 mins

London Waterloo
Surbiton
Woking
Basingstoke
Winchester
Eastleigh
Southampton Airport
Southampton
Brockenhurst
New Milton
Bournemouth
Parkstone
Poole
Hamworthy
Wareham
Wool
Moreton
Dorchester South
Christchurch
Branksome
Holton Heath
Upwey
Weymouth

While St. Pancras, King's Cross and Paddington are characteristically nineteenth-century stations, and Euston is the depressing child of the mid to late twentieth, Waterloo is one of London's few representatives of the early part of the twentieth century. It is certainly a convenient station to use, and the graceful sweep of the concourse (120 feet wide and 770 long) and the high, airy roof above impart a sense of elegance. Yet some element of character appears to be missing; unlike the older termini, the design is all too rational, and there are no nooks and crannies to explore.

Perhaps the destinations served also have something to do with it. With the disappearance of trains beyond Exeter (and even the Exeter line through Salisbury nowadays offers a very rudimentary service) a sense of adventure has been lost; hardly anyone who sets off from Waterloo will sleep the night more than 150 miles from London, and the floods of commuters who take the station over every morning and evening

One of the cab ranks at Waterloo in about 1900, before the station was modernized.

Ivat 2–6–2T No. 41230 crossing the bridge between Lymington and Lymington Pier on the branch from Brockenhurst in 1967, shortly before the end of BR steam.

(Waterloo now ranks as the capital's busiest station) have their homes in the leafiest parts of the stockbroker belt. Even the queues patiently waiting for the Southampton boat train are bound, these days, for a cruise, and not for a new life in the New World.

The growth of Waterloo

The first terminus of the London & Southampton Railway was at Nine Elms, just beyond Vauxhall, where the new Covent Garden Market is now sited. Nine Elms soon proved unsuitable, chiefly because it was too far from the centre of London, and in 1848 the new terminus of the London & South Western Railway (LSWR), as it had now become, opened 1¾ miles further east.

The original station occupied roughly the site of the present platforms 7 to 12 and grew in haphazard fits and starts throughout the rest of the century. A complete reconstruction set in train at the start of the new century occupied the next two decades. As the historian Alan Jackson has pointed out, the most striking part of the new station was the pedestrian entrance through the Victory Arch, the LSWR's memorial to its employees killed in the First World War, and underneath 'a rather masculine Britannia'. The view of the entire frontage block, done in 'the impressively monumental style sometimes called Imperial Baroque', is spoilt by the clutter of low buildings in front.

Trains leave Waterloo along the 1¾-mile viaduct erected in the late 1840s to carry the lines to the new station; as it was, 700 houses had to be pulled down to accommodate the railway. Lambeth Palace can be seen on the right, and beyond it there are glimpses of the Thames. At Clapham Junction the Windsor line veers off to the right and the Brighton line to the left, while we continue south-west, first through Victorian suburbs and then past inter-war developments, and finally out into the plush areas around Esher and Weybridge.

The Basingstoke canal can be seen on the right from time to time from Weybridge through Woking, where Portsmouth trains branch off to the left, and Brookwood. Nowadays better remembered for its racing circuit, Brookwood was the final destination of many a respectable Victorian and Edwardian citizen, for here was the London Necropolis Company's celebrated cemetery. From 1854 until 1941 the LSWR and then the Southern Railway ran funeral trains from a Necropolis station at Waterloo to a private branch line.

Line to Southampton

The countryside begins round about Woking, but until Basingstoke has been passed it is frequently interrupted by small towns much swollen by new building in the last decade. At Worting Junction beyond Basingstoke trains for Salisbury and Exeter continue south-west while the Southampton line veers south over the wide Hampshire Downs through four short tunnels towards Winchester. Then the line runs alongside the river Itchen towards the Southampton conurbation, passing the carriage sidings and works at Eastleigh and Southampton Airport (where a new Parkway station is planned) before entering Southampton station through a recently renovated tunnel.

The line thus far was opened in three stages: from Nine Elms to Woking in May 1838; to Winchfield in September of the same year; and on to Southampton in May 1840. The original Terminus station in Southampton, designed for the LSWR by Sir William Tite and closed as recently as 1966, was a marvellous building of classical, elegant simplicity with a five-bay arcade; fortunately, the façade has survived, although its London counterpart at Nine Elms was destroyed during the construction of the new Covent Garden.

New Forest route

There are good views of the docks as the train heads west out of Southampton, crossing the Test estuary at Totton and almost immediately entering a delightful stretch through the New Forest. As soon as the line to the Esso refinery at Fawley has branched off to the left, the train begins to travel across wild open heathland and then plunges into deeper woodland; in contrast with the motorist, who finds it difficult to escape the crowds of visitors, the train traveller has the chance to appreciate the isolated beauty of the New Forest.

The Avon is crossed at Christchurch, from where it is about seven minutes into the massive station at Bournemouth, opened in 1885. Even though the central part of the roof is missing, it remains an impressive building.

While Southampton owes much of its growth as a port to the coming of the railways, the resort of Bournemouth is their entire creation. As late as the 1840s, when the Southampton & Dorchester route (see below) opened, Bournemouth consisted of only a few houses; forty years on, its population had not yet reached 30,000. It was

The line through the New Forest, one of the most attractive stetches in the Southern Region.

Diesel-hauled Poole to Birmingham train running along the edge of Poole Harbour.

only after the opening of a direct rail service, rather than the awkward branch lines with which the town had previously had to be content, during the 1880s that both the population and the number of visitors began to grow rapidly.

The line between Southampton and Dorchester opened in 1847. The present route was followed as far as Brockenhurst, but then the line swung inland, following an awkward route around the hills and estuaries through Ringwood and Wimborne to Hamworthy. 'The Water Snake' and 'Castleman's Corkscrew' – Castleman being the principal promoter of the Southampton & Dorchester – were the nicknames for this slow, tortuous line. The present route from Brockenhurst to Bournemouth was not finally opened until 1888.

Poole to Weymouth

There is a lovely stretch through Poole with splendid views as the train runs around the edge of Poole Harbour. Beyond Wareham, the line cuts through pleasant countryside towards Dorchester, with the long, low line of the Purbeck Hills on the left and, for much of the

way, the river Frome on the right. Between Wool and Moreton a branch to the United Kingdom Atomic Energy Authority's establishment at Winfrith leads off to the left.

At Dorchester South station there is evidence of the S&D's original intention, never fulfilled, to press on from Dorchester to Exeter. To get to the present-day up and down platforms it is necessary to cross the original platform at which the S&D trains terminated. Just beyond the station, the line meets the former GWR broadgauge route from Castle Cary to Weymouth opened in 1857, and together the two climb to Bincombe tunnel before the final sharp descent into Weymouth. LSWR trains started to run from Dorchester to Weymouth that same year.

Electrification of the line from Waterloo to Bournemouth was completed in 1967, and since then express services have been split at Bournemouth, a diesel locomotive pulling the first four coaches to Weymouth and propelling them back in the other direction. Department of Transport approval is expected shortly for electrification of the entire Bournemouth to Weymouth route, which has a target completion date of 1 January 1988.

London to Brighton

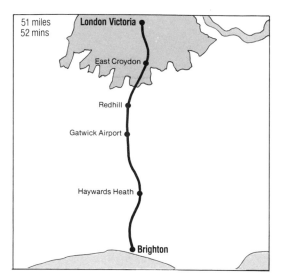

51 miles
52 mins

London Victoria

East Croydon

Redhill

Gatwick Airport

Haywards Heath

Brighton

It really seemed as if London had 'precipitated itself' on Brighton so thick and fast did the living stream pour into town. Thousands who never saw the Queen of Watering Places before seized the opportunity of doing so – hundreds gazed for the first time at the sea, not as they had seen it in grotesque miniature at Deptford or Woolwich but in the full extent of its grandeur and might.

This was the *Brighton Herald*'s description of the Easter holiday 1844, when the first excursion trains were run on the London & Brighton Railway, only two and a half years after the company had inaugurated services between London Bridge and Brighton.

The coming of the railway changed Brighton radically and for good. Before, it had been an elegant, somewhat exclusive resort patronized largely by royalty and the aristocracy, for whom the elegant Regency squares and terraces leading to the shore were constructed. After the railway, while its original patrons did not desert its attractions, they were joined by more raucous, less refined elements out for a happy day (and later, as paid holidays began to be introduced, a week) by the seaside. During the 1830s, only 437 new houses went up; in the next decade the total was more than six times that number. In the mid-1920s, an astonishing 7 million passengers used the station each year, all but 2 million of them during the summer; in the busiest fortnight of the year over 1¼ million people passed through the station, while even today it is one of British Rail's busiest.

Commuting town

There were commuters almost from the first. Season tickets were introduced in 1845 (they cost £50 a year, later reduced to £40, and were available in first class only). The morning up train, which later became famous as the *City Limited*, was scheduled to run non-stop in 75 minutes in 1856; in 1912 timings were reduced to 60 minutes, and today the fastest trains manage the 51 miles in 52 minutes. This is not an especially fast time in comparison with the long-distance routes north and west from London, but the Southern Region's outdated third-rail system of electric working does not make for fast running, and in addition Brighton trains have to negotiate some busy and complex stretches through south London.

There was considerable competition among railway builders for the Brighton route, which

The two London Bridge stations in the 1850s. The façade of the handsome SER building is on the left, *with the entrance to the LB & SCR's less imposing terminus next to it.*

J. U. Rastrick's magnificent viaduct over the Ouse valley, with the winter sun striking through the arches.

promised substantial rewards: in the 1830s, Brighton was the largest town outside London in southern England. In 1835, no less than six schemes were laid before Parliament, none of which met with approval; nor would Parliament give the go-ahead the following year. Other contestants fell away, and in 1837 it was clear that there were only two significant contenders remaining.

These two schemes were supported by two prominent engineers, each with very different ideas about railway construction. Robert Stephenson favoured an indirect route that used river valleys to circumvent the steep slopes of the North and South Downs. John Rennie proposed a direct route through the hills and across the intervening Weald. In the end, it was Rennie's route that was chosen, and construction began in 1838, thousands of navvies congregating to disturb the hitherto unruffled calm of tiny Surrey and Sussex villages. Trains ran from London Bridge as far as Haywards Heath at the end of June 1841 and to Brighton on 22 September of the same year; a short branch from Shoreham to Brighton had already been opened in 1840.

From London Bridge to a point near the present Norwood Junction station trains ran over the metals of the London & Croydon Railway, and until 1868 the route as far as Redhill was shared by the Dover trains of the South Eastern (see page 172). The London & Brighton and the London & Croydon merged in 1846 to form the London, Brighton & South Coast Railway (LB & SCR).

Victoria station

Most Brighton services now run from Victoria station, although some semi-fasts continue to operate to and from London Bridge. Until 1924, Victoria was not one station but two, with separate ticket offices, stationmasters and so on. The grander, western, side, rebuilt in the 1890s and 1900s, belonged to the LB & SCR, while the trains of the London, Chatham & Dover Railway (LC&D; see page 175) left from the eastern side. The LC & D also rebuilt its station, though in somewhat less flamboyant style, in the early twentieth century. The two remain clearly distinguishable today, and while the Chatham side copes with hordes of travellers and their rucksacks queueing for the boat trains, it is the Brighton side that possesses such sophistication as the station can claim.

Today Victoria is something of a visual mess, and, so it seems, permanently overcrowded; as well as large numbers of commuters and travellers bound for the channel ferries at Dover, Folkestone and Newhaven, the station also handles air travellers making for Gatwick on the new non-stop service running every fifteen

A London train runs under the battlemented north portal of Clayton tunnel.

minutes. Considerable redevelopment is taking place, and at present office blocks are being constructed on steel rafts above the platforms on the Brighton side.

Gateway to the south

For the first two years after Victoria opened in 1860, Brighton trains ran via Crystal Palace to Norwood Junction, until the cut-off from Balham to Selhurst was ready. Having crossed the river, the line runs through Battersea and over the tracks leading out of Waterloo, and then descends to run alongside them through Clapham Junction. Balham – that famous 'Gateway to the South' – Streatham and Thornton Heath are soon passed, and then the train runs into East Croydon, now a major commercial centre with many commuters arriving

each morning, along one side of the Gloucester Road triangle. Recently remodelled to eliminate conflicting train movements and increase running speeds, the triangle was formerly a complex tangle of lines where the main lines to and from Victoria and London Bridge and south through Croydon, the West Croydon branch and quite extensive sidings all met. Fast and slow traffic is now segregated as far south as Coulsdon, the slow lines running across the junction in a newly constructed cutting.

South of Croydon the line heads for the North Downs, passing through increasingly prosperous suburbia. Beyond Purley, the original line runs through a lengthy deep cutting and then Merstham tunnel (1 mile 71 yards long), emerging on the far side at Merstham station, while fast trains veer to the left and then cross over the slow line. This fast line, called the Quarry Line, was opened in 1900 to accommodate the increasing amount of traffic making for the south coast. It crosses the Downs through a separate tunnel (Quarry tunnel, 1 mile 353 yards long) before meeting the original line again at Earlswood, 3 miles south of Redhill.

Balcombe viaduct

Now the train makes for Gatwick Airport, where the station was opened in 1958, and then runs through the eastern edge of Crawley New Town, for which Three Bridges is the main-line station. A wooded section brings the line to Balcombe tunnel. Cuttings restrict the view until the train suddenly emerges into a lovely lush valley (the river, more like a stream in size, is the Ouse) which is crossed on a magnificent viaduct with thirty-seven arches. Italianate pavilions stand sentry at each end of the bridge, which also has an elegant balustrade. As one architectural historian has written, 'the structure is an immensely satisfying man-made contribution to the landscape, successful from all distances and angles'.

The final landmark is Clayton tunnel (1 mile 499 yards) through the South Downs, reached by a long 1 in 264 ascent (the standard gradient for the line) from Keymer Junction, where the line for Lewes branches off to the left. The long bare line of the Downs is visible from far off; as the train approaches, it enters a deep cutting leading to the tunnel, whose northern portal is defended by twin battlemented turrets with arrow slits. The cottage in between was probably let to the man in charge of the gas works built to light the tunnel in the early days; the aim, apparently, was to induce 'a feeling of confidence and cheerfulness' in visitors.

Brighton

The last stretch descends through the outskirts of Brighton towards the magnificent station. The large maintenance depot is passed (the locomotive works of the LB & SCR which remained in existence until the early 1960s have since been demolished), and the coast line east to Lewes and Eastbourne can be seen curving across the spectacular London Road viaduct above the cramped streets of the town.

The station is one of the few surviving examples of the work of David Mocatta, the architect engaged by the London & Brighton. Rennie selected a difficult site, on a man-made terrace created from the hillside behind. Mocatta produced an attractive entrance building with a nine-arch arcade in the centre and columned arcades on each side. This still stands, although the impact of the façade is spoilt by the glass and iron *porte-cochère* erected when the station was rebuilt in 1882 and 1883.

The original trainshed was replaced at the same time by the splendid glass and iron temple that the traveller sees today. Two wide spans soar upwards supported on delicate iron columns, and everywhere there is intricate ironwork decoration: a fitting and striking finale to this splendid line.

The frontage block of the terminus at Brighton, built in 1840-1 and still substantially the same, although the trainshed behind and the porte-cochère *in front impede the view.*

Bluebell Railway

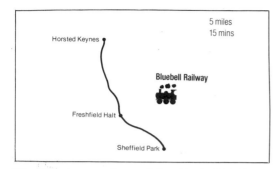

The founder members of the Bluebell Railway Preservation Society can hardly have known what they were starting when they met in March 1959 at Haywards Heath in Sussex to discuss the proposal that the railway between East Grinstead and Lewes should be reopened. For, although a number of narrow-gauge lines such as the Ffestiniog and the Talyllyn (see pages 74–81) were already being operated independently, no group had yet proposed to take responsibility for the far more difficult and complex task of running and maintaining a standard-gauge line, let alone a group composed almost entirely of knowledgeable but none the less amateur enthusiasts. It can now be seen that on their success, not only in winning the Ministry of Transport's go-ahead but also in operating the line successfully and above all safely, hung the development of what has become an extremely healthy and confident preserved steam movement. As soon as enthusiasts and lovers of steam locomotives and country railways had an example of independent operation before them, the establishment of other lines came to seem less daunting.

Perhaps, however, the Bluebell Railway pioneers had some inkling of what was to come, for one major battle had already been won. The route south from East Grinstead to Culver Junction, 3¾ miles north of Lewes, was built by the East Grinstead & Lewes Railway in 1882, but was run from the start by the London, Brighton & South Coast Railway (the major operator in Sussex). The Act of Parliament transferring the line to the LB & SCR obliged that company to maintain a service of four trains a day in each direction in perpetuity.

This grand commitment had unfortunate repercussions for British Railways some seventy years later. The line was closed abruptly in May 1955. Research into the archives revealed that the Act transferring ownership to the LB & SCR had never been repealed; as the LB & SCR's legal successor, though admittedly at one remove, British Railways remained bound to the original conditions. The statutory service had to be resumed, and it was only after a three-day hearing that the line could close for a second time, on this occasion quite legally.

The Bluebell Railway's only ex-GWR locomotive, 4–4–0 No. 3217 Earl of Berkeley.

0–6–0T No. 72 Fenchurch, *the Bluebell Railway's*
oldest locomotive, leaves Horsted Keynes.

BLUEBELL RAILWAY

Museum line

The aim of the Bluebell Railway has been to preserve as a living museum as many aspects of the history and operation of railways in southern England as possible. Almost without exception, the locomotives, which range from *Fenchurch*, an 0–6–0 tank built for the London Brighton & South Coast Railway in 1872, to a massive 2–10–0 built by British Railways as recently as 1958, worked various lines around the south of England.

Some of the coaches were built by the Southern Railway after its formation in 1923, and others by British Railways to Southern Railway designs. But the collection also contains examples from the South Eastern & Chatham Railway, the LB & SCR (a Directors' Saloon car), the London & South Western Railway, the London, Chatham & Dover, and a few interesting 'strays' from outside the region, such as a Great Northern Directors' Saloon. In contrast with many preserved lines, where the lack of available coaches makes it necessary to buy those recently withdrawn from regular service with British Rail, a journey on the Bluebell Railway will always take place in a 'vintage' coach.

The stations have been lovingly restored. Sheffield Park, which takes its name from the former Lord Sheffield's estate close by, has returned to its original identity, a Sussex country station on an LB & SCR branch line smartly painted in that company's maroon and cream livery. It is worth arriving in good time for a train, for there is a great deal to see in and around the station. There is the signal box situated on the principal platform and a small museum, while oil lamps and enamel signs and advertisements help to recreate the atmosphere of Victorian England. Also at Sheffield Park are the Bluebell Railway's locomotive works and running shed, and the collection of vintage locomotives can be viewed.

Painted in the Bluebell Railway's own livery, 0–6–0T No. 323 Bluebell, *built by the South Eastern &* Chatham *in 1910, curves past Freshfield in the winter snow.*

*Firebuckets, period advertisements and a trolley at
Horsted Keynes station.*

Horsted Keynes

Horsted Keynes, at the other end of the 5-mile
line, is a junction station with four platforms and
an altogether busier atmosphere. In 1883, the
year after the line from East Grinstead through
Horsted Keynes was opened, a branch from the
main London to Brighton line (see page 156)
near Haywards Heath was opened to Horsted
Keynes; this line was electrified in 1935 and
closed in 1963. The station at Horsted Keynes is
decorated in the green and white paintwork of
the post 1923 Southern Railway. There are quite
extensive sidings here, and on these and in the
large carriage shed are kept the Railway's collection of coaches and wagons. The Preservation
Society's declared aim is to extend its line north
towards East Grinstead, and in April 1985 a
Light Railway Order and planning permission
for the extension were granted.

The journey lasts for quarter of an hour,
running through some of the most attractive
countryside of the Sussex Weald. Leaving
Sheffield Park, the line crosses the river, curves
to the left and runs through a woodland stretch,
which in late spring is carpeted with the bluebells that give the railway its name. Spring is a
magnificent time of the year to visit the line, for
you are likely to see not only bluebells but banks
of primroses and many other spring flowers.

Then comes the long 1 in 75 ascent up Freshfield Bank where you can see the Ouse valley to
the left. A gentle descent brings the train to
Freshfield Halt, the only intermediate station,
and built by the Bluebell Railway. Another steep
climb follows, with views of the deep and
peaceful countryside, before the train runs on to
an embankment, leaving some waterworks on
the left, and then tackles the final climb into
Horsted Keynes through a deep cutting crossed
by a large bridge.

Kent & East Sussex Railway

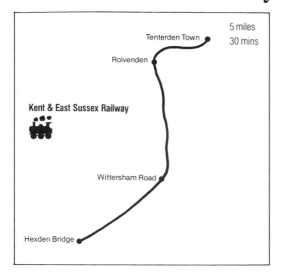

Kent & East Sussex Railway

5 miles
30 mins

Tenterden Town
Rolvenden
Wittersham Road
Hexden Bridge

'Always an eccentric bywater utilizing ramshackle old rolling stock and antique engines.' An extreme description, one might think, but not too extreme to do justice to the Kent & East Sussex, which survived, under-used and neglected, for little more than half a century. The author of these words, who is closely connected with the company that has been operating the line as an independent concern since 1974, goes on to point out, with considerable justice, that only in recent years has the line ever been operated with any degree of success.

The original Kent & East Sussex was one of those lines which make you wonder why they were ever built. By the time the line was authorized by Parliament in 1896, no less than six schemes for a similar route had been proposed, all of which had vanished into thin air. The line ran for 21 miles through remote and relatively unpopulated countryside of the East Sussex and Kent borders from Robertsbridge to Headcorn, passing only three settlements of any size *en route* and missing by some way the other communities it was intended to serve − in one case by as much as 4 miles.

The railway was the first to be officially designated a Light Railway under the terms of the Light Railways Act, passed in the same year that the line was authorized. The Act was passed to encourage the construction of railways in sparsely inhabited rural areas; regulations concerning curves, gradients and signalling were modified to reduce construction and maintenance costs, while lower speed limits and axle loadings were imposed and the frequency of services restricted. To begin with, speeds were restricted to 15 mph, which must, even at the beginning of the century, have seemed a snail's pace; later they were raised to the giddy heights of 25 mph, which remains the maximum speed permitted today; the maximum axle loading was 10 tons.

Origins of the line
The line started operations in 1900 as the Rother Valley Railway between Robertsbridge, where there was a connection with the South Eastern & Chatham's Tonbridge to Hastings line, and Tenterden. Five years later the line, now re-named the Kent & East Sussex, was extended to Headcorn, where a junction was made with another SE & C line, this one the main London to Dover route. At least until 1930, the westernmost section through the Rother valley did run at a profit, albeit not a large one, whereas the eastern extension had begun to make a loss several years before.

After the death in 1931 of Colonel H. F. Stephens, who operated this line as well as a number of other light railways scattered throughout England and Wales, the company became insolvent. The receiver appointed was a Mr. W. H. Austen, who had been the Colonel's assistant, and he managed to keep the line open throughout the 1930s and the Second World War. Despite improved services inaugurated after nationalization in 1948, the line could not hold out much longer in the face of increased road traffic and the general irrelevancy of the route, and passenger services were withdrawn at the beginning of 1954. Freight services survived slightly longer until 1961.

Tenterden Railway Company
In the same year, 1961, the first moves were made towards the revival of the Kent & East Sussex in private hands. Inevitably there were numerous setbacks, plus the usual prolonged financial and legal negotiations. The decision had to be made not to attempt to reopen the line between Robertsbridge and Bodiam, and it was as the owner of some 10 miles of track between Bodiam and Tenterden that the Tenterden Railway Company came into being in 1971. The first short stretch, 2 miles at Tenterden, was opened the following year. Three years later, trains were running for 4 miles to Wittersham Road, and in 1983 a mile-long extension to Hexden Bridge was opened. There are plans to extend the line to Northiam and Bodiam, but

0−6−0T Sutton *heads a train out of Tenterden with the fifteenth-century tower of St. Mildred's church in the background.*

before this project can be tackled the Railway needs to raise sufficient funds.

As on most preserved lines, the bulk of the work has been done by volunteers, supplemented by help from the Royal Engineers and from Job Creation workers and, of course, a good deal of assistance in the form of equipment and advice from local firms and the local authorities. The Society and its members were lucky in that the track itself had not been lifted; but nevertheless every sleeper had to be renewed, and three major bridges had to be replaced, together with a great deal of routine improvement and maintenance. Other major works include the erection of the Tenterden Town signal box, which was originally at Chilham on the Ashford to Canterbury West line; a completely new locomotive depot at Rolvenden; and a new station at Wittersham Road, for which different items were obtained from dismantled stations all over the country.

The journey

The 30-minute journey starts with a steep 1 in 50 descent from Tenterden alongside a small stream and with fine views back towards the pleasant town dominated by the handsome tower of St. Mildred's church. After the train has halted at the first of several road crossings (Ministry of Transport regulations require the train to halt before proceeding over a level crossing except when a crossing-keeper is on duty), it negotiates a very sharp curve before drawing into Rolvenden station. The landscape opens out to the Rother Levels, a flat area that once consisted of little but marshland; now drained, the land is cultivated, although some patches of marshland do remain. Having followed Newmill channel for a way, the line turns into a long straight that takes it through Wittersham Road station (the village of Wittersham is 3 miles away) and on to the present terminus at Hexden Bridge by Hexden channel.

An interesting variety of rolling stock can be seen on the Kent & East Sussex line. Most notable of all is No. 3 *Bodiam*, an 0–6–0 'Brighton Terrier' sidetank built in 1872 and bought by the Rother Valley Railway in 1901, having spent the first part of its long working life hauling London suburban trains; No. 10 *Sutton* is the line's second Terrier. The majority of trains are hauled by one of five 0–6–0 Austerity saddletanks, heavy shunting locomotives developed during the Second World War; also in the collection are a 2–6–0 tender loco from Norway and an 0–6–0 side tank from Southern Railways in the USA. There are some historic coaches, but for day-to-day use British Railways standard passenger coaches are employed.

0–6–0T Bodiam *shunting goods wagons at Rolvenden during the early 1970s.*

Ashford to Hastings

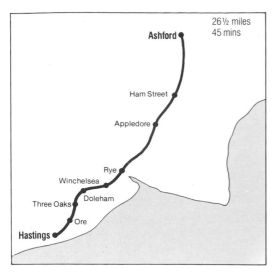

Ashford
Ham Street
Appledore
Rye
Winchelsea
Three Oaks
Doleham
Ore
Hastings

26½ miles
45 mins

It is an attractive ride on this branch route which, unlike most of the Southern Region network, remains unelectrified. The train swings south from the main line at Ashford through pleasant countryside, crossing a belt of woodland around Ham Street. Then the scenery changes, and the line is running through the flat grasslands of Romney Marsh; sheep graze on pastures criss-crossed by the ditches dug when the land was reclaimed from the sea, with only occasional small clumps of trees to break the view to the horizon. In the summer sun, the land seems relatively benign, but in winter, when wind and rain drive in from the sea or else thick fog descends to blot out every feature of the landscape, it becomes sinister and alarming, and it is easy to imagine smugglers quietly rowing ashore with illegal cargoes of silk, tobacco and fine French brandy. Betweem Ham Street and Appledore the line crosses the Royal Military Canal, dug in the early nineteenth century as a defence against Napoleon's expected invasion. Appledore, now some miles inland, was once a busy port on the estuary of the river Rother; a freight-only line to Dungeness nuclear power station branches off to the left.

Rye is the next station after Appledore, and the lovely little hilltop settlement with the Rother winding beneath towards the sea can be seen from miles across the Marsh. The station is an extremely attractive Italianate villa with what has been described as an 'entrance loggia from the Florentine Renaissance'. Beyond Winchelsea and the crossing to the river Brede, the countryside changes, becoming hillier and more fertile. A steep ascent through tiny halts at Doleham and Three Oaks brings the line to Ore tunnel, which is quickly followed by Ore station and Mount Pleasant tunnel before the train draws into Hastings station.

A Hastings train runs through rolling country just west of Winchelsea.

The delightful entrance to Rye over the river Rother and past Gopsall Pottery windmill.

Controversial route

The opening of the route in 1851 was the cause of considerable strife between two rival railway companies. The line had first been proposed six years before by the Brighton, Lewes & Hastings Railway (BL & H) as part of a coastal route from Lewes to Ashford. Parliament gave the go-ahead – not, however, to the BL & H but to its competitor the South Eastern Railway (SER). The trouble arose just west of Hastings at Bopeep Junction (so called because an inn popular with local shepherds stood near the railway) where the lines of the two companies, the SER and the London Brighton & South Coast Railway (which had taken the BL & H over), met. An LB & SCR train was delayed for so long at Bopeep that it had to return to St. Leonards station, and then, a few days later, according to H. P. White, historian of railways in southern England:

> The South Eastern tore up the track at Bopeep, stood a ballast train across the sidings at Hastings, and marooned the Brighton agent in his office there, cutting off the gas . . . . The Brighton hired a bus, a move countered by the South Eastern erecting a barrier across the station approach.

In the end, the LB & SCR won an injunction against the SER, but even so its trains were not permitted to stop at St. Leonards for almost another twenty years.

North London Line

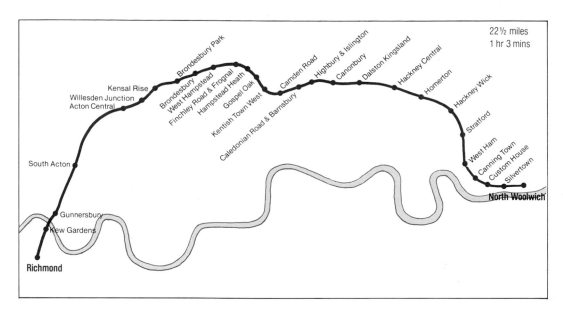

It is easy to travel from the country or suburbs into central London, and vice versa. But, as everyone knows who has tried them, orbital journeys, where both starting-point and destination are outside the central districts of the capital, are a different and much more awkward proposition. British Rail's North London line supplies London's only lengthy passenger rail link that does not run into one or other of the main termini. It is also a fascinating journey through the back gardens of London that reveals to the traveller the absorbing detail of the capital's humdrum, day-to-day existence.

The present line from Richmond in the west to North Woolwich in the east has its origins in the East & West India Docks & Birmingham Junction Railway (E & WID & BJR), whose first line, opened in 1850 between Camden and the West India Docks, accurately reflected the company's long-winded title. Ten years later, by which time the E & WID & BJR had been renamed the North London Railway and come under the control of the London & North Western Railway (LNWR), a link was made with the Hampstead Junction Railway (also nominally independent but in reality controlled by the LNWR) between Camden Town and Old Oak Junction, Willesden.

The prime purpose of these lines was to carry freight: principally manufactured goods to and from the London docks, although there was also some trade in coal both to and from the Midlands and, a more substantial business, from colliers that had run down the east coast and up the Thames from Durham and Northumberland. By the 1860s, however, a large passenger business was also developing, and after trains began to run into the newly opened Broad Street station in 1865 office-workers used the line to travel from their newly constructed villas in north and west London to their City offices. In 1866, 14 million passengers were carried on the route, in 1896 no less than 46.3 million. By the

1860s, there was already a line running from Willesden to Kew, but the more direct route still followed today through South Acton and Gunnersbury to Richmond was opened by the London & South Western Railway in 1869.

Revived route

The heyday of the Richmond to Broad Street line was around the turn of the century. Almost inevitably, as alternative forms of transport developed — motor buses and trams, and especially the rapidly extending Underground network — traffic on the North London line (which was electrified in 1916) declined. By the 1960s it had become one of those lines that BR was trying its hardest to forget. There were several proposals for closure, rolling stock was allowed to run down and travellers often had to suffer vandalized carriages; a general air of decay permeated the line.

In the mid-1980s, all that changed, and the North London line has now taken on a new lease of life and a new stretch of route. Two factors helped to turn the line's fortunes. First there was the enlightened attitude of the Greater London Council, which was committed not only to improving public transport in London but also to extending the infrastructure. Second, there was British Rail's desire to close Broad Street and redevelop that station and Liverpool Street immediately next door (see page 40).

The handsome and compact station at Broad Street has been redundant for many years, used by decreasing numbers of suburban services; such main-line trains that had ever run into the station had long since ceased operating. British Rail's plan is to run trains into Liverpool Street instead along a newly built curve at Hackney connecting the North London line with the Cambridge line from Liverpool Street. The extension to the North London line came about when the GLC funded the electrification of the 8-mile route from Dalston to North Woolwich.

Broad Street, with a gantry in place to provide access to the roof. Now the saddest and least used of London's termini, in the 1900s the station was handling 80,000 passengers and 712 trains a day.

Boarding a train at Gospel Oak station at the foot of Hampstead Heath.

The total cost of the electrification was £9 million, and in addition a new station was opened at Homerton; three other new stations have also been opened as a result of GLC support: Hackney Wick, Hackney Central and Dalston Kingsland.

The line north

The journey starts at Richmond station, operated by the Southern Region, where London Regional Transport trains and Southern Region trains on the Shepperton and Windsor lines share the station. It then strikes north through prosperous, leafy streets marred only by the almost perpetual din of aircraft coming in to land at Heathrow Airport a few miles to the west. Kew Gardens station serves the Botanical Gardens, and then the line runs across the Thames on a fine iron lattice

girder bridge with some attractive decoration. The pleasant little riverside community of Strand-on-the-Green lies on the north bank. Gunnersbury is the next station, and immediately afterwards District Line trains, which have shared the route since Richmond, veer off to the right. Acton is a mixture of less prosperous housing and, especially further north, light industry. At South Acton a freight-only line comes in from the Hounslow loop line.

Some way beyond Acton Central the train emerges on to the western edge of Wormwood Scrubs, an unprepossessing open space bounded on one side by the famous prison and with wide views across central London; the Post Office Tower should be clearly visible. The line then crosses first the main line west from Paddington to Reading (see page 124) and the High Wycombe line and Central Line, which share

the same tracks. The Old Oak Common servicing facilities and maintenance depots used by HSTs on the West Country run are visible on the right, while on the left a major freight-only route branches off. This gives connections with the main lines running north and north-west from Euston, Marylebone and St. Pancras.

North and east London

Beyond Willesden Junction, where the station is built directly above the tracks of the west-coast main line from Euston, there is a long section through pleasant residential districts. Brondesbury follows Kensal Rise; at West Hampstead there are connections with the Underground and the main line from St. Pancras. After Finchley Road & Frognal, Hampstead Heath tunnel takes the line under Belsize Park and southern Hampstead, and the train emerges to run along the foot of the Heath towards Gospel Oak. A sharp turn south brings the route over the main line from St. Pancras for the second time through Camden Town, over the St. Pancras line yet again, and on into Islington, leaving the King's Cross Freightliner Terminal on the right. Islington gives way to Hackney, and in Dalston the junction with the Broad Street line can be seen as the train passes on to the newly electrified stretch.

The houses, shops and lineside communities all reveal a London less prosperous than the districts already passed. Stratford is the next major centre, where travellers alight for the market or to make connections with the Norwich line (see page 42) and the Underground. The final stretch crosses the Underground's District Line and the Fenchurch Street to Southend route at West Ham, and then runs through the East End, alongside the river Lea and through the now deserted Royal Victoria Dock to the riverside at North Woolwich. The ferry crosses the river from here to Woolwich, and there are some good waterside views and a newly opened museum in the handsome Italianate station built for the inauguration of the line by the Eastern Counties Railway in 1847. Exhibits in the museum tell the story of the Great Eastern Railway and include a re-creation of an Edwardian booking office.

The North London line is a significant freight route, as well as operating a regular service of passenger trains. In the west it provides a direct and rapid link between several main lines, while further east some dozen regular freight trains run from the west-coast main line across north London to the Freightliner Terminal at Stratford or further afield to docks at Tilbury, Ipswich, Felixstowe or Parkeston Quay.

The Woolwich Ferry makes its way across the Thames to the landing stage next to North Woolwich station.

Routes to East Kent and Dover

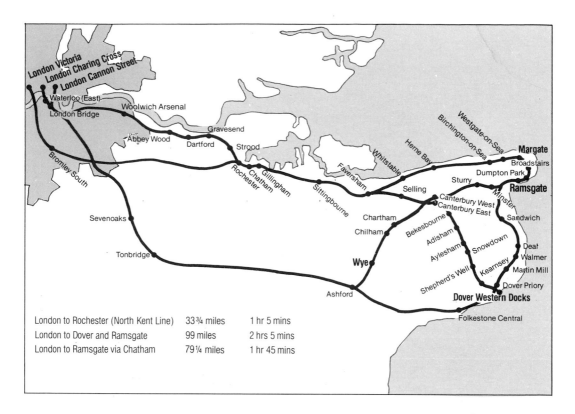

London to Rochester (North Kent Line)	33¾ miles	1 hr 5 mins
London to Dover and Ramsgate	99 miles	2 hrs 5 mins
London to Ramsgate via Chatham	79¼ miles	1 hr 45 mins

Even in the mid-1980s, nearly forty years after nationalization and well over sixty since a unified railway was formed in the south as a result of Grouping, the patterns of the nineteenth-century railway system are still discernible. The two principal companies serving Kent and south-east London were the South Eastern Railway (SER) and the London, Chatham & Dover Railway (LC&D), which, following four decades of bitter and ultimately fruitless rivalry during which each constructed a network of competing lines designed to draw business away from the other, finally came together in 1899 as the South Eastern & Chatham. That two principal routes to Dover remain today, leaving from different London termini and approaching the channel by radically different routes, is just one legacy of this early competition.

Charing Cross to Dover and Ramsgate

This route, today the fastest and by 2 miles the most direct to Dover, is based on the first line built to the Channel ports, opened by the SER in stages between 1842 and 1844. Parliament was adamant that one rail exit from London to the south was all that was required, and so, instead of following a direct line from London Bridge to Kent, the trains shared the metals of the Brighton route (see page 157) as far as Redhill. From Redhill the line struck out for 47 miles straight across the Weald of Kent through Tonbridge to Ashford before reaching the coast at Folkestone and running along the shore to Dover. Competition from the LC & D, as well as

congestion on the line to Redhill, led the South Eastern to apply for and win permission to build a lengthy cut-off between St. John's, near Lewisham in south-east London, through the North Downs to Tonbridge; this line, which reduced the length of the journey to Dover by 12 miles, was opened in 1868.

The train starts at Charing Cross, rumbles slowly over Hungerford Bridge, where there are fine views upstream to the Palace of West-

Cannon Street station and bridge in about the 1870s; the fine roof is now destroyed, the two towers held water tanks which supplied hydraulic power for the lifts.

172

The south side of Hungerford bridge looking across the Thames to Charing Cross station in 1946.

minster and downstream towards Waterloo Bridge and the City beyond, crosses the South Bank arts complex to Waterloo East, and then runs on through Southwark to London Bridge. From its opening in 1838 until 1864 London Bridge was the main terminus for trains from south London and Kent. In 1864 the through lines along and over the river to Charing Cross were opened, with the branch to Cannon Street following two years later; the two cross-river lines meet above Borough Market by Southwark Cathedral.

Designed to run on a viaduct, so as to minimize the amount of property destroyed, the extension nevertheless involved the loss of St. Thomas' Hospital just beyond London Bridge station. Although the South Eastern only needed a small part of the hospital grounds, the medical authorities insisted that the railway should buy the entire site, and were eventually awarded £300,000 compensation, which went a long way towards meeting the cost of the new hospital erected on the south bank of the Thames in Lambeth.

Heading away from the river, the train runs through inner suburbs, with tower blocks gradually giving way to rows of uniform mid and late Victorian terraced houses. At Hither Green the line begins the long ascent towards the North Downs. The former LC & D route to Chatham and Dover (see below) is crossed at Chislehurst; not until 1901, two years after the rivals merged, were connecting spurs built between the two routes. Three tunnels take the line through the

hills, a short one at Chelsfield and two longer ones, Polhill (1 mile 851 yards long) and Sevenoaks (1 mile 1,693 yards). Leafy, prosperous outer suburbia continues well beyond Orpington, and it is not until the train emerges from Sevenoaks tunnel on the southern slope of the Downs that true countryside is reached, when the lovely Weald of Kent stretches out in front of the train. At Tonbridge the original route from London is joined, and the long straight stretch to Ashford runs past orchards and hop fields. Paddock Wood, one of the principal intermediate stations, is named after a wood felled when the station was built.

Ashford was once a major railway town, the SER having founded its locomotive works there in 1847. These closed in 1962, and despite a series of export orders the end came for the wagon works twenty years later; all that remains today is the spring shop, now under Southern Region control. As well as the Hastings line (see page 166), a branch leads north through delightful countryside alongside the Stour to Canterbury, where the attractive single-storey West station is near the terminus of the Canterbury & Whitstable Railway (see page 177), and then on to Minster and Ramsgate.

Two tunnels are required to bring the line through the edge of the Kentish Downs into Folkestone. After crossing the town on a high-level embankment and the massive nineteen-arch Foord viaduct, the line drops to the coast for the spectacular run along the shore into Dover. This was a magnificent piece of engineering: one

*Sandwich, with the station building and footbridge
attractive in their new paintwork.*

entire cliff, the Round Down, was blown up
(18,500 lbs of gunpowder were required) and
two tunnels (Abbotscliff and Shakespeare, 1,942
and 1,387 yards long respectively) dug, between
which the line runs immediately above the waves
on a ledge that forms part of the sea wall. It is an
impressive ride – one of the best in the Southern
Region – with a fine view of the cross-Channel
shipping. Entering the town alongside the
Western Docks, regular passenger trains swing
left through another short tunnel to the town
station, Dover Priory, leaving the Western
Docks station on the right.

Although Dover was already a sizeable cross-
Channel port, it benefited enormously from the
arrival of the railway, while in neighbouring
Folkestone, while the shipping business developed virtually from scratch. By the 1860s,
both companies had bought the steamer fleets,
the LC & D operating out of Dover, the SER
from Folkestone. Dover always retained the
edge, however, and the South Eastern also ran
boat trains there.

Opened in 1881, the extension from Dover to
Deal was the result of a rare alliance between the
SER and the LC & D; until then, Deal had been
served only by trains from Minster along a
branch opened in 1847. Two short tunnels lead
the train to Buckland Junction, where the line to
Canterbury East and Faversham (see below) continues straight on, while trains for Deal and

Ramsgate curve sharply right and then climb
steeply through Guston tunnel to the cliff top a
few miles behind St. Margaret's Bay. A gentle
descent to Walmer and Deal follows and, after a
freight-only line leads off to Betteshanger
colliery, the line runs past the delightful
sixteenth- and seventeenth-century houses of
Sandwich out on to Minster Marshes and across
the river Stour. Another line leads off to
Richborough power station, which is clearly
visible from the train, before the branch through
Canterbury is joined for the final run into
Ramsgate. This route was electrified as far as
Sevenoaks in 1935 and on to Dover and
Ramsgate in 1961.

Victoria to Ramsgate and Dover

The London, Chatham & Dover's route to
Thanet and Dover was an amalgam of relatively
short stretches built by smaller companies. The
line from Faversham to Chatham was opened in
1858; two years later Canterbury was reached (at
the East station, which to this day has no
physical link with the SER's route through
Canterbury West), and Dover in 1861. Along
the coast, the Margate Railway opened from
Faversham to Whitstable in 1860, to Herne Bay
in 1861 and to Ramsgate in 1863; the line was
always operated by the LC & D, which absorbed
the Margate Railway in 1871.

Until Grouping Victoria was the terminus of two separate railways: the LC & D occupied the 'Chatham' side (the left-hand side as you face the platforms), while the London, Brighton & South Coast Railway ran into the right-hand, 'Brighton', portion. Trains for Dover depart from the 'Chatham' side of the station (see page 157). There is an immediate steep ascent to run over Grosvenor Bridge, at the far end of which the train veers left on to the Bromley line, running just to the right of Battersea Power Station and almost immediately above the celebrated Dogs' Home.

The quarter of an hour's ride to Bromley is a journey through the recent social history of London. When the line was built, tracks were pushed out through what was virtually open country, with just a few scattered settlements and substantial country villas. The railway company built its stations and waited for the houses to grow up alongside.

By the outbreak of the First World War in 1914, this part of south London had been developed as far as Penge, with the exception of the Dulwich College Estate, where building was only permitted around the edges, the central sections being preserved (as they remain today) as open space; the College and its extensive lands can be seen to the left of the line. Independent towns such as Beckenham and Bromley experi-enced their own spurt of suburban development in the late nineteenth century, but the gaps in between and the settlements beyond Bromley only evolved in the 1920s and 1930s; still further into Kent most development has taken place during the last two or three decades.

Beyond Swanley a stretch of not especially interesting countryside brings the line to the Medway. There are fine views upstream as the line crosses the river, first of the elegant motorway bridge and then of the massive twelfth-century castle keep, one of the finest in England. A tunnel and a deep cutting precede Chatham station, followed by another two short tunnels to Gillingham, the outer limit of the electrification programme completed in 1939. The line runs across flat countryside through Rainham and Sittingbourne to Faversham, with views on the left over the Swale to the Isle of Sheppey, served by a shuttle service from Sittingbourne.

At Faversham the line divides. The Dover branch runs south-east through attractive countryside to Canterbury. Apple orchards follow and, a complete contrast, coal mines around Snowdown before the train descends through Lydden tunnel (1 mile 609 yards) towards the coast. There is a station at Kearnsey before the line from Deal is joined and the train runs through Dover Priory to terminate at the Western Docks station.

Opening day on the Canterbury & Whitstable Railway with Robert Stephenson's Invicta *climbing towards Tyler Hill from the coast at Whitstable.* Invicta *was not a success.*

*Rochester cathedral, with the railway line and the
Medway estuary behind.*

The Ramsgate train follows the coastline before entering Whitstable station and then runs through a built-up area as far as Herne Bay. A short stretch of country follows, with an excellent view of the massive twelfth-century towers of Reculver church on the cliffs; the church dates from the seventh century, while Reculver itself originated as one of the so-called Saxon Shore forts built to defend the coast from invasions and raids in the third century AD.

Whitstable has an interesting place in railway history, being the northern terminus of the Canterbury & Whitstable Railway, the first public railway in the south of England. Services opened on 3 May 1830, over four months before the Liverpool & Manchester (see page 94), but *Invicta*, the new line's only locomotive, could not manage the steep 1 in 31 ascent out of the city, and until the SER absorbed the line in 1844 trains were operated by stationary steam engines.

For the last part of the journey the line runs along the coast to Birchington and Margate, where the station is just by the sea front, and then cuts across the Thanet peninsula to Broadstairs and Ramsgate. Electrification of this north Kent route to Dover and Ramsgate was completed in 1959.

London to Rochester

Although the most direct route to Rochester is from Victoria (see page 175), the line along the south side of the Thames estuary provides a more interesting journey. The 3¾-mile stretch between London Bridge and Greenwich was the first railway to be built in London. The London & Greenwich opened its line from Spa Road, a temporary terminus in Bermondsey, to Deptford in February 1836, extending the line to the new terminus at London Bridge in October and eastwards to Greenwich in December 1836.

The entire line was built on a viaduct, now much widened, although there is a good view of the original structure on the Lewisham line as it parts from the Greenwich route at North Kent East Junction. The viaduct was constructed in order to avoid demolishing any more than necessary of the slum dwellings through which the line passed, and to enable the London & Greenwich to gain extra revenue from leasing the arches beneath as houses and warehouses. Understandably, the idea of living directly beneath a railway never caught on, but a century and a half later warehouses and workshops continue to occupy the arches.

The first London Bridge station was a simple two-platform affair, unroofed until some tarred canvas was put up in 1840. As other lines were built through what are now the suburbs of south London, but in the mid-nineteenth century was pleasant countryside dotted with villages, the London & Greenwich became very much the junior partner in the station it had originated.

First, the London & Croydon built its own station. Then, in 1844, a Joint Station was opened, shared beween the SER, the London & Brighton Railway and the London & Croydon, the London & Greenwich using the latter's train shed. Only five years later, this almost brand-new station was considered too small and was demolished, to be replaced by two entirely separate stations next door to one another, belonging to the SER and the London, Brighton & South Coast Railway. Not until 1928, five years after Grouping, was a hole knocked in the dividing wall, and the station was only properly unified during the 1970s.

Greenwich link

Having reached Greenwich, the London & Greenwich, which was leased by the SER in 1845 but remained an independent company until Grouping, found that it could go no further. Fearing that the accuracy of the equipment in the Royal Observatory would be damaged, the Admiralty refused to permit an extension through Greenwich towards Charlton, and this section of the present-day route was not opened fully until 1878. The North Kent line, which reached Charlton via Lewisham and Blackheath and continued to Gravesend, was opened in 1849. The Royal Observatory has another interesting link with the railways, for it was not until a rail network began to develop that a uniform time (known as 'railway time' to begin with) was adopted across the country.

The train tunnels under Greenwich, meets the North Kent line at Angerstein Junction shortly before Charlton and then cuts its way through Woolwich in a sequence of four short tunnels. Abbey Wood is the station for the huge housing estate on the river's edge at Thamesmead. Then the line approaches the river at Erith, only to turn inland briefly towards Dartford, where Richard Trevithick, who built some of the earliest steam locomotives, is buried. Around Greenhithe and Northfleet there are views of the factories alongside the widening Thames, and beyond Gravesend the line runs within a few hundred yards of the river bank, before turning across the neck of the Isle of Grain. Two tunnels, Higham and Strood (1,531 and 2,329 yards long respectively) bring the line to the Medway at Strood, and the direct line from Victoria is joined on the river bank at the approach to the bridge.

Higham and Strood tunnels have an interesting history, having been dug not for the railway but for the Thames and Medway Canal, which was opened in 1824. In 1845, the Gravesend & Rochester Railway Company inaugurated a single-track line through the tunnels, one rail being set on the towpath, the other on a wooden platform above the water. Trains and barges shared the tunnel for a few months until the SER bought it in 1846, filled in the canal bed, and built a double-track route.

SCOTLAND

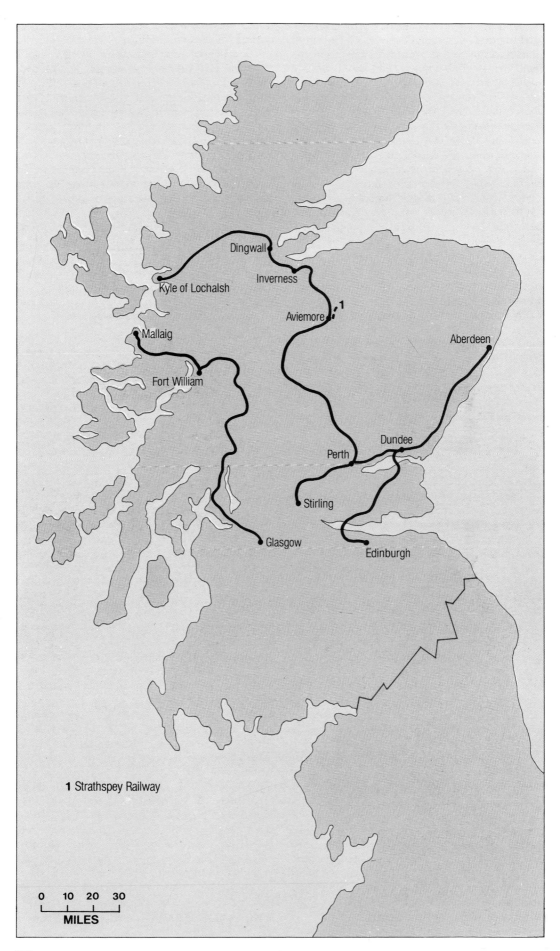

Dingwall

Inverness

Kyle of Lochalsh

Aviemore •••' 1

Mallaig

Aberdeen

Fort William

Dundee

Perth

Stirling

Glasgow

Edinburgh

1 Strathspey Railway

0   10   20   30

MILES

Scotland's railways run through some of the most imposing scenery in Europe. There is little to surpass the view down Loch Lomond or the great sweep of the Horseshoe Curve on the lengthy journey from Glasgow to Fort William and Mallaig, or, further north, the enchanting stretch alongside Loch Carron with the ever-changing panorama of Skye across the sea as the trains heads towards Kyle of Lochalsh. The men who built the Highland lines had to work in bleak and unforgiving terrain, far from creature comforts and often in the most unpleasant weather. The climb over Drumochter, almost 1,500 feet above sea level on the Inverness to Perth route, and the ride across Rannoch Moor south of Fort William, 20 miles of desolate, peaty bog that today remains virtually as inaccessible and inhospitable as when it was conquered after fifteen months of hard and at times desperate labour, demonstrate the achievements and the engineering skills of the men who, with their hands and rudimentary equipment alone, created these northern lines.

Elsewhere in Scotland, other pleasures await the traveller. There is a pleasant run through the gentle hills of Fife and along the east coast between Edinburgh and Aberdeen, with the added bonus of two splendid bridges across the Forth and the Tay. Further south, both the main lines from England (described in the Midland and the Eastern Regions) pass through attractive countryside, the west-coast line striking directly across the hills of the Border Country along the valley of the river Clyde, the east-coast route following the North Sea coast.

Sadly, little remains of Scotland's steam days, although the Strathspey Railway does recreate a short stretch of the original Highland Railway near Aviemore. However, British Rail does run steam excursions along the West Highland extension from Fort William to Mallaig, a majestic journey through splendid scenery.

LMS 'Black Five' 4–6–0 No. 5407 heads a steam excursion into Glenfinnan station above Loch Shiel on one of the finest Scottish routes, from Fort William to Mallaig.

Edinburgh to Aberdeen

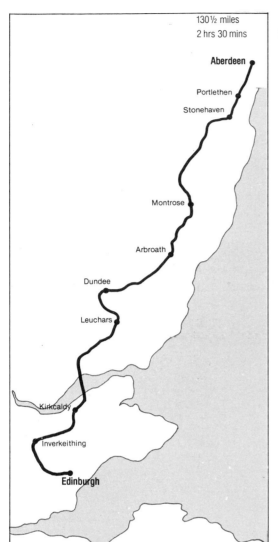

130½ miles
2 hrs 30 mins

Aberdeen
Portlethen
Stonehaven
Montrose
Arbroath
Dundee
Leuchars
Kirkcaldy
Inverkeithing
Edinburgh

Two grand and famous bridges, over the Forth and the Tay, are the highlights of this journey. The Forth Bridge is reached after a ten-minute journey through the suburbs of Edinburgh with occasional glimpses forward to the elegant pylons of the road bridge, opened alongside the rail crossing in 1959. The train climbs up the long approach to the bridge, runs through Dalmeny station and out over the grey waters of the Firth of Forth.

Crossing the bridge is a curious experience. The huge steel ribs of the central cantilevers flash past one after the other, and there is a feeling of being locked in some mid-air prison, until a sudden view of the wide expanse of water is gained as the train enters one of the short trussed spans that link the cantilevers.

Lack of bridges across the two great estuaries hindered the North British Railway's attempts to develop east-coast traffic between Edinburgh, Dundee and Aberdeen. At first their trains had to run a long way round, using lines belonging to the Caledonian Railway for some of the journey. After the first Tay Bridge was opened in 1878, a more direct journey became possible, and a train ferry, the first in the world, was opened across the Forth. But it carried freight services only, and passengers still had to leave their train for the crossing.

The Forth Bridge
When the first Tay Bridge collapsed on 28 December 1879, its architect, Sir Thomas Bouch, had already been working on a suspension bridge across the Forth for five years. The project was soon abandoned: just as well perhaps, for Bouch was planning a span of no less

Waverley station, Edinburgh, built in a narrow valley between the castle and the Old Town on the right and the Georgian New Town on the left. A Deltic Class diesel prepares to leave for the south.

NBR 0–6–0 No. 673 Maude *crosses the Forth Bridge in an intricate maze of steel ribs and supports.*

than 1,600 feet, with four towers each 550 feet high, 38 feet higher than the pylons of the road bridge. One pier had already been built, and is still visible downstream of the present rail bridge, now topped by a lighthouse.

New plans were drawn up by Sir Benjamin Baker and Sir John Fowler for a large cantilever bridge with lengthy viaducts on each side; it remained the largest bridge of its type in the world until the Quebec Bridge in Canada was opened in 1917. Each principal span is 567 yards long, with a total length of 1 mile 1,005 yards. The height to the top of the towers is 361 feet; the Admiralty insisted on a high structure to enable warships to pass beneath.

The bridge was built of mild steel, rather than the iron that had been normal until the 1880s. Steel had several advantages over iron. It was harder and more reliable; and the stresses it created, and thus the different dimensions of each part of the structure, could be more easily calculated. The disadvantage was rust; hence the need continually to paint and repaint the bridge's 145 acres of exposed steel surface.

The best view of the bridge, which was opened in 1890, is from the northern shore, as the train runs near the water's edge between Inverkeithing and Kirkcaldy; the same stretch also offers views of the Edinburgh waterline, with Arthur's Seat rearing up behind. William Morris called the bridge 'the supremest specimen of all ugli-ness', which seems hard on such a splendid structure.

The Tay Bridge

Past Kirkcaldy the line turns inland to run through a lovely stretch of countryside, fertile and rich with gentle hills. Not long after Leuchars, which is now the station for the university town of St. Andrews, the line reaches the southernmost bank of the Firth of Tay. At 10,711 feet long, the Tay Bridge is the longest railway bridge in Britain, and it seems like it too, for the train crosses slowly, and there is plenty of time to admire the views up and down the estuary. The best views of the bridge itself are from the descent towards Dundee station on the north bank and later, past Dundee, as the train gathers speed along the coast towards Arbroath.

The present Tay Bridge was completed in 1885, and replaced the original structure that collapsed in hurricane-strength winds on the night of 28 December 1879, taking a train with it and killing all seventy-five people on board. The winds were unusually strong that night. But it also appears that not enough allowance had been made for wind pressure in the original design of the bridge, and that the high girders in particular were too light and insufficiently braced. Poor design was made worse by bad workmanship badly supervised: faulty columns, for instance, were not re-cast as they should have been.

EDINBURGH TO ABERDEEN

LNER Class A4 No. 4498 Sir Nigel Gresley *heads a train at Wormit at the southern side of the Tay* Bridge, with a view across to the houses of Dundee on the further bank.

Beyond Dundee, the line hugs the coast as far as Arbroath, and then runs a few miles inland from the shore to Montrose. Montrose Basin and the estuary of the South Esk are crossed on an imposing viaduct, of which there is a good view from the attractive new station right by the water's edge. A lengthy inland stretch through pleasant countryside follows until the line returns to the coast along Carron Water at Stonehaven.

The final leg of the journey is mostly along the coast. Porthlethen station was reopened in May 1985 to serve the new housing estates built for North Sea oil workers. The approach to Aberdeen is memorable, with all the sights, sounds and smells of a busy harbour, and gulls cawing and wheeling above. The recently modernized station is marvellously light and airy, and has an attractive overall glass roof.

The race north

The name Kinnaber Junction has little significance in the 1980s. But in pre-nationalization days, when the North British and the Caledonian Railways maintained their traditional rivalry, and in one year in particular, it was a crucial spot for protagonists of each company. The service from Edinburgh to Aberdeen was a North British operation, while the Caledonian approached Aberdeen from the west coast, through Perth and Forfar. The two lines met at Kinnaber Junction, just north of Montrose, and the trains of each company accomplished the final 36 miles to the Granite City along Caledonian metals.

In 1895, the London to Scotland races (see page 66) along the east- and west-coast main lines from King's Cross and Euston resumed, this time to Aberdeen instead of Edinburgh. Two trains, one on each side of the country, thundered through the night; the London & North Western Railway (LNWR) roaring up Shap and Beattock, its east-coast opponents skimming through York, past the Durham coalfields and over the gracious bridge at Berwick, finally crossing the Forth and the Tay on the new bridges. The signal box at Kinnaber Junction was a Caledonian box. But, according to railway custom and practice, whoever reached the junction first would be given prior passage over the line to Aberdeen.

From the start of the contest, the west-coast trains set the pace. This was partly because the LNWR south of the border and the Caledonian in Scotland soon reduced the length of their respective trains to gain faster speeds, and partly because, being the aggressors, they had the determination to do well. The three companies on the east-coast route suffered some humiliating set-backs before they managed to organize themselves sufficiently to avoid unnecessary delays *en route*.

On 19 and 20 August they made immense efforts to beat their rivals, but in vain. On the night of 21 August 1895 they succeeded, reaching Kinnaber Junction no less than 14½ minutes before the west-coast express. The east-coast time for the 523.5 miles to Aberdeen was 520 minutes that night, and when the west-coast train arrived it too had made its fastest run ever: 539.8 miles in 534 minutes. At that, the east-coast companies decided to call it a day, only to find that, the following night, the west-coast train managed the trip in an incredible 512 minutes. The average speed was 63.3 mph, a record for run north from London to Aberdeen that remained unbroken throughout the days of steam.

No. 4498 Sir Nigel Gresley *brings a southbound excursion train out of Aberdeen.*

Perth to Inverness

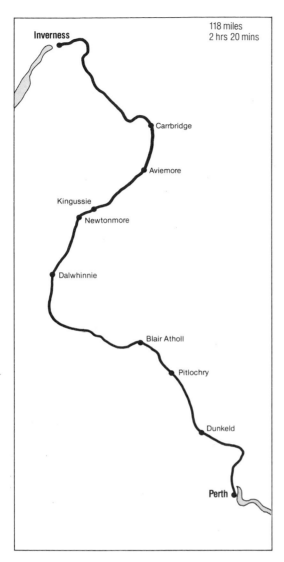

118 miles
2 hrs 20 mins

Even from the insulated comfort of a modern express, there is a sense of anticipation as the train sweeps up from the industrial Lowlands, passes beneath the forbidding walls of Stirling Castle and runs on through Strathallan to Perth. The very thought of the Highlands stirs all but the most unromantic and unadventurous, and this line lives up to expectations, cutting through the heart of the Grampian range across a landscape at some moments bleak and desolate, at others lush and fertile.

The route has a complex history. The principal original section, between Forres and Dunkeld, was opened in 1863 by the Inverness & Perth Junction Railway. At Dunkeld in the south there was a connection to Perth via a line run by the Perth & Dunkeld Railway, and from Forres in the north the trains ran into Inverness along the tracks of the Inverness & Aberdeen Junction Railway. In 1865 the Inverness & Perth and the Inverness & Aberdeen merged to form the Highland Railway.

The Highland Railway

During the last part of the nineteenth century the Highland Railway and its principal rival, the Great North of Scotland Railway (GNSR) based in Aberdeen, were constantly skirmishing, trying to deprive each other of business. As far as the Highland Railway was concerned, the greatest threat came when the GNSR proposed to build a line from Boat of Garten right into the heart of Highland territory at Inverness. The Highland fought back with a counter-proposal for another direct line from Inverness to Aviemore, where it would meet the existing route south. This line won approval and, when it

Pitlochry station, built in 1863 and rebuilt by the Highland Railway twenty-seven years later.

Two diesels head the morning express fron Inverness off Nairn viaduct on Culloden Moor.

was completed in 1898 (construction took six years), the new cut-off became the main line south, and the original route was gradually relegated to a branch, finally closing in 1965. (See Strathspey Railway, page 188.)

Perth to Pitlochry

North of Perth, the line runs through some quite gentle terrain at first, although there is always the view of the mountains in the distance as a reminder that these easy stretches will not last for long. On the other side of the Tay is Scone, where the Scottish monarchs were crowned; Scone Palace, just visible through the trees, is a nineteenth-century mansion built on the site of the Abbey of Scone, destroyed during the Reformation.

Beyond the tunnel, the line runs past Birnam Wood – the Birnam Wood made famous by Shakespeare in *Macbeth* – and crosses the river Bran just past the lovely little cathedral town of Dunkeld. The next 13 miles to Pitlochry continue along lush, thickly wooded river valleys, first the Tay valley and then, after Ballinluig, that of the Tummel. The line crosses bridge with two spans of 210 and 141 feet respectively. The piers at each end and in the centre are decorated with medieval castellated towers.

The train leaves Pitlochry on a route parallel to the main A9 road, which stays close to the railway almost all the way to Inverness; this route through the mountains has always been one of the principal ways north. General Wade's Military Road from Inverness to Dunkeld was the first properly constructed route, but countless thousands of people must have trudged or ridden here before it was built.

Half a century or so later, Thomas Telford laid down his road network throughout the Highlands, over 1,000 miles in not much more than two decades. He built what is now the A9, obliterating some of Wade's route in the process, although a number of stretches do remain. One of Telford's assistants, Joseph Mitchell, was engaged by the Inverness & Perth Junction Railway to build their line.

In recent years, the A9 has been improved to motorway standards. That, combined with the deregulation of bus and coach services and the reduction of government subsidies to unprofitable lines, brought ScotRail (as British Rail in Scotland now calls itself) to the edge of crisis. It was almost as quick to travel by coach from the Lowlands to Inverness, and it was certainly cheaper. The future not only of the Inverness line but of the entire Highland network seemed in question. ScotRail reacted well: fares were dramatically reduced, services improved (High-Speed Trains now run to Inverness) and track

improvements made to allow faster running: on one stretch south of Aviemore 100 mph is permitted. It is too soon, however, to say what long-term results these improvements will bring.

Soldier's Leap

The stretch through Killiecrankie Pass shortly after Pitlochry is most dramatic. The line is hemmed in by trees on each side, with the river tumbling and foaming far below in the bottom of the gorge; at the far end on the left, just before the train enters the tunnel, is the spot known as Soldier's Leap. Here, in 1689, an English government soldier called McBean was being closely pursued by men of the victorious Highland army and, so the story goes, leapt 17 feet across the gorge to safety.

On the other side of the tunnel, the landscape widens and softens again as the line crosses the river Tilt by Blair Atholl station. On the right is Blair Castle set in a beautifully landscaped park. The home of the Dukes of Atholl, the castle is a marvellous example of the nineteenth-century style of architecture known as Scottish baronial; the original castle was built on the same site in 1269.

After Blair Atholl the train begins the long, steep climb up to Drumochter, 1,484 feet above sea level and reached by gradients of up to 1 in 70. This is true Highland country: lonely, remote and with barely a sign of human influence. Even in the best of seasons, in autumn for instance, when the heathers produce a wonderful range of colours, it can seem daunting; when apparently unceasing rain sweeps across the land, or in winter when snow obliterates the view, you are more than relieved to be safe in the warm security of your carriage.

Towards the summit, the line passes Bruar falls on the right, and a disused signal box; a section of General Wade's original road can be seen here, and at one point it crosses the railway on a bridge. There used to be a station at Dalnaspidal, the highest main-line halt in Britain, 1,400 feet up. A large sign announces that the train has reached the summit; the line is hemmed in by mountains, several higher than 3,000 feet.

Long descent

Now the equally long and bleak descent through Dalwhinnie begins. On the left are lovely views of Loch Ericht and another section of Wade's road, and in Dalwhinnie itself there is an attractive nineteenth-century whisky distillery. Once again, the view broadens as the Spey flows in from the west before Newtonmore; the line accompanies the river for the next 15 miles to Aviemore. The valley is lush and green, with thick birch and pine, a sharp contrast with the peaks that stand out all around; ahead and to the right (east) are the Cairngorms, to the left the Monadhliath Mountains, and behind, to the east of the pass along which the line runs, Beinn Dearg (3,307 feet). The train should make good time past little Loch Insh towards Aviemore, for

Blair Castle, a fortified stronghold built in the thirteenth century at the junction of several glens.

*An HST runs through a deep cutting in the rock at
Slochd Summit north of Carrbridge.*

this is a stretch that has been converted to
100 mph running.

On the right in Kingussie stands one of the
most forlorn monuments in Scottish history: the
ruins of Ruthven Barracks. After their defeat at
Culloden in 1746 (see below), the Highland
chiefs assembled here to wait for the call to battle
once more from Bonnie Prince Charlie. The call
never came, for the Prince had taken flight, and
was trying to find a boat in which to escape to
France. The chiefs received a farewell message,
and, before they dispersed, burnt the barracks so
that they should not fall into government hands.
A little way on, also on the right, is the monument to the Duke of Gordon and a cairn com-
memorating the Gordon Highlanders killed at
Waterloo.

Aviemore to Inverness

From the large station at Aviemore, rebuilt for
the opening of the direct line to Inverness, there
are magnificent views back towards the Cairngorms. With luck, if the skies are reasonably
clear, two great peaks will stand out: to the left
(east) Cairngorm itself (4,084 feet), and to the
right Ben Macdui (4,248 feet). On a crisp
winter's day, when the sun plays on the deep-
packed snow, there can hardly be a finer station
view in the entire country.

The Highland Railway's original route to

Grantown and Forres branches off to the right.
The first few miles are operated by the
Strathspey Railway; the station, locomotives and
rolling stock of this preserved line can be seen.

Beyond Carrbridge, the line climbs once
more, passing another stretch of General Wade's
road on the right. The destination is Slochd,
1,315 feet above sea level in a desolate area
known as Black Mount. The descent is equally
steep, 1 in 60 for long stretches, running down to
cross the river Findhorn at Tomatin, where
there is another large distillery. The viaduct is
most impressive: 445 yards long, 143 feet above
the river, with nine spans.

Past Loch Moy on the right, with a ruined
castle romantically set on an island in the lake,
and the little village of Daviot, the line loops
north-east and then west again, crossing the river
Nairn on another magnificent viaduct 600 yards
long and with twenty-eight spans. This is
Culloden Moor, scene of the last battle fought on
British soil and of the final defeat of the
Highlanders by George II's forces, and where
the long-cherished hopes of Scottish independence finally came to nothing.

Inverness is now only a few minutes away.
The track descends through forests to the coast,
meeting the line from Aberdeen, and runs along
the shore, giving good views of the Moray Firth
across to Black Isle, and into Inverness.

Strathspey Railway

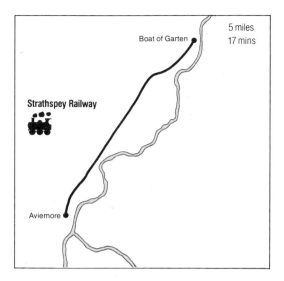

The Strathspey Railway occupies the first five miles of the Highland Railway's former line from Aviemore to Grantown and Forres. The original route, which was gradually displaced after the opening of the direct line from Aviemore over Slochd summit to Inverness in 1898, ran north-east along the lovely Spey valley as far as Grantown. Then it turned north to cross Dava Moor, 1,052 feet above sea level and very prone to drifting snow in winter, descending to the coastal plain near Forres, from where trains ran west to Inverness through Nairn. Present services are between Aviemore and Boat of Garten, although the eventual intention is to run as far as Grantown.

The title of the Railway originated, rather confusingly, in a second line that ran to Boat of Garten. This belonged to the Great North of Scotland Railway, the Highland Railway's rival, and ran south-west from Craigellachie to Grantown and then on to Boat of Garten via Nethy Bridge.

The ride on the present-day Strathspey Railway is a pleasant one through well-wooded and moorland country along the Spey valley. The trees are principally Scots pine and birch; to the west of the line as it approaches Boat of Garten the track of an old road abandoned in the early nineteenth century can be seen. As everywhere on the Highland plateau, the views are magnificent, with fertile country stretching out to the mountains.

Problems of preservation

Legal and financial worries are the besetting problem of every railway preservation group, at least in the early days; when trains finally start to run, operational problems are added. Six years elapsed between the decision to reopen this line and the operation of the first timetabled train. Fortunately, much of the track was in good condition. Not so fortunately, the existing BR station at Aviemore could not be used; the

LMS 4–6–0 No. 5025, one of the stars of the Strathspey Railway's locomotive collection.

principal building at the Strathspey Railway's station has come from Dalnaspidal, 25 miles south on the main line towards Perth (see page 186), and formerly the highest main-line station in Britain. The engine shed, however, is the original one, built for the opening of the direct line in 1898. At Boat of Garten the original station buildings needed considerable restoration, and now appear much as they did thirty years ago; a small museum now occupies part of them. Among the interesting locomotives to be seen on the line is a Stanier Class 4–6–0, built in 1934. She was based at the Perth engine shed, and worked trains on the Caledonian's line to Aberdeen and over Highland Railway tracks to Inverness. The Railway also owns several Ivatt Class 2–6–0s, and a number of industrial and colliery locomotives.

0–6–0ST No. 48 at Boat of Garten. The Strathspey Railway bought her from the National Coal Board.

Inverness to Kyle of Lochalsh

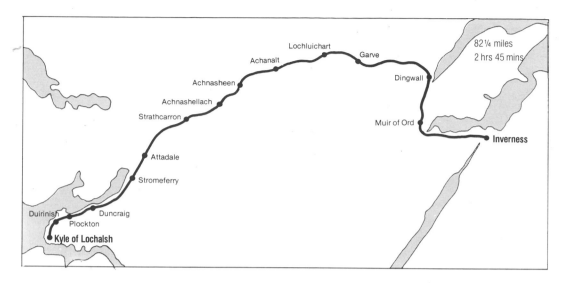

Lochluichart
Achanalt
Garve
Achnasheen
Dingwall
Achnashellach
Strathcarron
Muir of Ord
Attadale
Inverness
Stromeferry
Duirinish   Duncraig
Plockton
Kyle of Lochalsh

82¼ miles
2 hrs 45 mins

To anyone seeking to make economies in British Rail's operating costs, the Kyle line must seem an obvious candidate for closure. A 63-mile line running through one of the most isolated parts of the country, passing nowhere of any importance at all and terminating in a small fishing village is surely at best of marginal value. That certainly seems to have been the thinking behind the Minister of Transport's statement in 1970 that the public service subsidy paid to the line was not 'justified in continuing beyond 1971'.

But the Kyle line is a survivor. It survived that particular threat, and in the mid-1980s its existence seems more secure than it has been for several decades. Passenger traffic is increasing, and British Rail and the various local authorities have all recognized the tourist potential of the line and are making a genuine effort to market it as an attraction for visitors. On the operational side BR has made considerable savings by introducing the newly developed system of Radio Electronic Token Block. Nor should it be overlooked that, scattered and small though the line-side communities may be, the railway does meet a genuine social need; and in winter it is often the only means of access to the outside world.

Radio Electronic Token Block

RETB is worth examining in a little more detail. In essence, the system does away with all conventional trackside signalling, whether semaphore or colour-light, and with all open-wire communication circuits, and hence with the need to renew and maintain equipment and to staff signal boxes and level crossings. All the traffic on the line is controlled electronically, in this case from a single control panel at Dingwall, where the Kyle line branches west off the Far North route to Wick and Thurso. (RETB has been introduced on the Far North line as well.)

In pre-RETB days, as still happens on other single-track routes, a driver was granted permission to proceed along a particular stretch of single track (the technical term is a block) when

the signalman gave him a large brass key. There were four lengthy blocks on the line from Dingwall to Kyle. The key was taken from a key token instrument in the signalbox. The act of removing the key from one box electrically locked all the other keys in that box and in the box at the other end of the block. It was impossible to issue a second key until the first one had been replaced in one of the token instruments at either end of the block.

Under RETB, the driver receives permission to proceed in the form of an electronic display on a panel in his cab, which specifies the precise locations concerned (e.g., at the far end of the line, Strathcarron to Kyle). Interlocking is achieved electronically with the same safety standards and, as before, only one train may occupy a block at any one time. Sophisticated controls provide back-up should the message not be transmitted or received properly, and the driver and signalman at Dingwall also communicate on two-way radios.

RETB, together with the automation of points at passing loops and the installation of automatic open level crossings with flashing lights, produces considerable cost savings. It also increases operating flexibility, making the introduction of additional services easier.

Leaving Inverness

The first part of the line to Kyle, along the shore of Beauly Firth and north across the neck of Black Isle to Dingwall, was opened in 1863 by the Inverness & Aberdeen Junction Railway, which two years later became part of the new Highland Railway. Two bridges follow in short succession on the outskirts of Inverness: the first over the fast-flowing river Ness and then the swing bridge at the northern entrance to the Caledonian Canal, where locks and old boathouses can be seen. The Canal runs along the Great Glen, the deep geological fault in the central Highlands, reaching the Atlantic coast at Banavie, near Fort William (see page 198).

Above: *Kyle of Lochalsh train approaching Achnasheen on one of the remotest and least hospitable stretches of this fine Highland line.*

Below: *The harbour at Kyle of Lochalsh, still an important in-shore fishing port. The station occupies a dramatic position above the water.*

INVERNESS TO KYLE OF LOCHALSH

Descending towards Loch Carron, a train enters Achnashellach station.

The land is pleasant and fertile, with a backdrop of high mountain peaks, and a fine view back of the new road bridge that carries the A9 over Beauly Firth to Black Isle. Near where the line crosses the estuary of the Beauly are Beauly Priory and Castle, and a handsome five-span masonry viaduct crosses the river Conon, just south of Dingwall.

Beyond the attractive station at Dingwall with its fine roof, the line branches west and immediately starts the steep climb to Ravens Rock. The train is now running on the line built by Dingwall & Skye Railway and opened in 1870, although the Highland Railway worked the line from the day it opened, before taking it over altogether in 1880.

The original intention was to drive the line all the way to Kyle of Lochalsh, but funds ran out, and worked stopped at Stromeferry. One of the reasons why money was short was the stretch to Ravens Rock. The original plan was to route the railway through Strathpeffer, which was growing more popular as a spa, but the local landlord objected, and the line had to be diverted. Strathpeffer, visible on the left, did eventually get a branch, now long closed.

On to the moors
There are good views of Ben Wyvis (3,433 feet) to the right and, at the top of the ascent, the fertile coastal plain lies spread out behind, the

wild and forbidding highland in front. The line descends steeply – the gradient is 1 in 50 in places – and runs along the south side of Loch Garve to Garve village, which, with its cottages and pink-painted hotel, seems quite gentle and relaxed in contrast with the country soon to be crossed. Loch Luichart on the left is the next major landmark; after the line crosses the loch the pipes of a hydro-electric scheme can be seen, again to the left.

The next stretch through Achanalt and Achnasheen is the bleakest on the line. Moorland and nothing but moorland, except for a few square clumps of firs on the hillside, stretches out into the distance, seemingly for ever. Luib Summit between Lochs Gowan and Scaven is the highest point on the line; the waters of Gowan flow eastwards, those of Scaven descend to the Atlantic in the west.

Soon a softening in the landscape can be detected. Thick forest accompanies the line; there are deer here although it is unlikely that any will be spotted from the train. The stationmaster's cottage at Achneshellach station is covered with roses, though the stationmaster and his family have long since vanished.

Loch Carron
Past Loch Dughaill on the right, the descent to Strathcarron and the head of Loch Carron is positively lush, with the river Carron flowing

alongside. There are grand views across the loch as the train runs along the southern shore, at one point underneath an avalanche shield, to Stromeferry, the original terminus. Ferries sailed from here to Skye and Stornoway until the railway was extended to Kyle in 1897. A ferry also carried cars across the loch to the northern shore until 1971, for only then was the road built alongside the railway on the southern shore.

The extension to Kyle was a mammoth piece of work. No less than thirty-one cuttings through the rock and twenty-nine bridges had to be built; the rock so displaced was used for ballast to provide a firm foundation for the line. The total cost was a staggering £20,000 per mile, and it is said that gelignite worth as much as £6,000 was used.

Views to Skye

The loch widens once more to give wonderful views across to the Applecross mountains and, further on, across the sound to Rassay and Skye. There is a raised beach on the left as the line crosses Strath Ascaig, left from many centuries ago when the waters of the loch were higher than they are now.

Around Duncraig, where the castle sits high above the line, and the little fishing village of Plockton, the gardens are thick with rhododendrons; this part of Scotland is quite tropical, for the waters benefit from the warmth of the Gulf Stream. Plockton is a delight, and a refreshing contrast with the hard country through which the line has travelled: yachts and motor launches bob up and down in the harbour, and charming cottages are strung out along the water's edge.

The final stretch into Kyle hugs the rocky coast, offering splendid views across the water to Skye. The terminus itself is right on the water's edge, almost a stone's throw from Skye, the hills of which rear up out of the sea, the green at the base turning to brown about halfway up. Even though the ferry for Stornoway now leaves from Ullapool, Kyle is still a busy port, and it becomes clear how remote and inaccessible these islands must have been before the railway came to this part of Scotland.

A morning parcels train for Kyle skirts Loch Carron near Stromeferry.

Glasgow to Mallaig

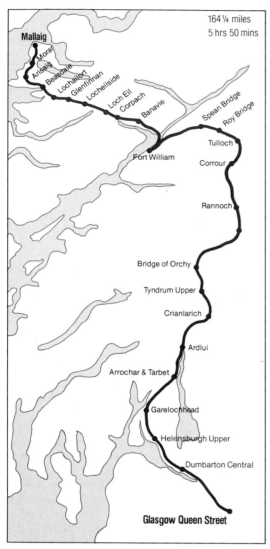

164¼ miles
5 hrs 50 mins

Mallaig
Morar
Arisaig
Beasdale
Lochailort
Glenfinnan
Locheilside
Loch Eil
Corpach
Banavie
Spean Bridge
Roy Bridge
Tulloch
Fort William
Corrour
Rannoch
Bridge of Orchy
Tyndrum Upper
Crianlarich
Ardlui
Arrochar & Tarbet
Garelochhead
Helensburgh Upper
Dumbarton Central
Glasgow Queen Street

Only the most *blasé* travellers will deny themselves a sense of anticipation as they make their way to Queen Street station to start the 164-mile, six-hour journey to Mallaig. For scenery, and for the immensity of the labour required to build it, this is Scotland's – and perhaps Europe's – most awesome line. Skirting lochs and mountains, the line crosses 20 miles of peaty bog, a wilderness almost as remote and inhospitable today as it was when the railway was constructed the best part of a century ago. Beyond Fort William, long stretches had to be carved through hard rock to bring the line to what was, before its development as a railway terminus and an important west-coast harbour, merely a poor and tiny fishing village.

Even with a powerful diesel locomotive at the head of the train, it is a long, slow pull up Cowlairs incline from Queen Street station. For many years after this part of the line opened in 1842 as part of the Edinburgh to Glasgow route, the 1 in 42 gradient was worked by a stationary engine and a cable.

Glasgow to Craigendoran

Quite soon, the train leaves the Glasgow suburbs and runs past the Erskine Road bridge and along the Clyde. Already there are fine views ahead across the estuary to the hills behind Dunoon and Holy Loch. At Craigendoran at the foot of Gare Loch, the local electric services branch off to run into Helensburgh Central, while the Fort William line climbs up steeply behind the town to the Upper station. From 1986, RETB (see page 190) will operate over the entire route to Mallaig, with one short break at Fort William.

As far as Craigendoran, the train has run over

The steamer Maid of the Loch *at Balloch on the southern tip of Loch Lomond. Other than the West*

Highland line, steamers are one of the few means of public transport in the area.

LMS Class 5 4-6-0 No. 5407 waits at Fort William   *to head a British Rail steam excursion to Mallaig.*

what were originally the tracks of the Glasgow, Dumbarton & Helensburgh Railway (GD&H), which opened in 1858 and was taken over by the North British seven years later. It was the North British that lay behind the construction of the Fort William line. It provided financial guarantees and operated the services, although nominally an independent company with its own board of directors, the West Highland Railway, was in charge.

West Highland line
There had been arguments for years about whether a line into the West Highlands was viable, and about which route it should take. The bill authorizing the line only passed through the Commons in 1889, some years after a similar scheme had been thrown out, and construction took another five years. Much of this delay is attributable to the deadly rivalry between the two major Scottish railway companies, the Caledonian and the North British.

Broadly speaking, the Caledonian, together with the Highland Railway, its partner in the north, was pre-eminent on the west side of the country; the North British on the east. The North British's take-over of the GD&H and the main Edinburgh to Glasgow route in 1865 struck straight into the heart of Caledonian territory. The prospect of a North British route opening up a large area of the West Highlands and bringing a rival railway within striking distance of Inverness could not be tolerated.

In the end, the Caledonian's arguments, which centred partly on the number of sheep and fish that the West Highland line would carry south to market; partly on the comparative quality of west-coast and east-coast fish; and

partly on the practicality of the selected route, failed to prevail. Initially, however, the new line was authorized as far as Fort William only; permission for the final section, to Roshven on the Sound of Arisaig, where a terminal and pier would be built to accommodate island steamers and fishing vessels, was refused.

Construction started in October 1889. By June 1892, the route itself was with one long exception complete, apart from the stations, signalling and so forth. This was despite a prolonged dispute in 1891 during which the contractors withdrew their men and plant from the line when the North British, never a generous railway at the best of times, disputed their charges.

The one exception was Rannoch Moor. Like Chat Moss (see page 97), Rannoch Moor seemed bottomless, and, like Chat Moss again, it was eventually crossed by sinking layer after layer of turf and brushwood alternately, along with wagonloads of industrial ash and of soil and debris from excavations elsewhere on the line. Rannoch Moor took fifteen months to conquer, and left the company's finances in such a state that only a private loan from one of the directors staved off financial failure.

North to Fort William
The journey north from Craigendoran to Fort William falls into four sections: loch, mountain, moor and gorge. From Helensburgh the line runs high above Gare Loch, gradually descending towards the northern end, where there is a good view of the large naval establishment. Another climb above Loch Long follows, with more naval bases along the water's edge. This is already true Highland terrain; the forest falls

Above: *A few minutes out of Fort William a train crosses the Caledonian Canal at Banavie in the shadow of Ben Nevis.*

Below: *Southbound train crossing Glenfinnan viaduct on the extension line to Mallaig, dwarfed both by the mountains and by the majesty of the structure.*

steeply down to crystal-clear water sparkling in the rays of the sun, which also illuminates patches of deep green woodland on the opposite slopes, while behind peak after high mountain peak pile up on each other.

The line branches away from the shore for a moment or two, giving a long view down Glen Douglas towards Loch Lomond, then returns briefly to Loch Long before cutting across the narrow neck of land that divides the salt waters of Loch Long from the fresh waters of Loch Lomond. Arrochar & Tarbet is the station between the two lochs. Now there is a splendid stretch along Loch Lomond to Ardlui, with tremendous views up and down the lake and across to Ben Lomond, and later to Rob Roy's cave on the eastern shore.

Now begins the lengthy, laborious climb up Glen Falloch. Even in the worst of weathers, there is something soft and sylvan about the Loch Lomond landscape. The mountains ahead are less forgiving, seeming to hold the individual at a distance. The line crosses the foaming Ben Ghlas Falls, and then runs over Dubh Eas (Gaelic for Black Water) on Glen Falloch viaduct, 118 feet long and 144 feet above the water, emerging at the summit into a moorland landscape of rocks, sparse grassland and rough peaks.

The West Highland built its stations in a uniform Swiss chalet style, facing the overhanging roofs with wooden shingles specially imported from Switzerland. At Crianlarich, trains used to pause for about ten minutes to let passengers pick up the breakfast or lunch baskets they had ordered in advance from the guard. These baskets, and the privately-run dining-room on the platform that supplied them, soon became famous. Like the other stations on the line, Crianlarich looks spruce and well-cared for, and has recently been repainted in its original shades of dark and light green.

Line to Oban

Trains for Oban branch off at Crianlarich, running parallel with the Fort William line as far as Tyndrum and then turning west along Glen Lochy. The Caledonian Railway operated the original line to Oban as an immensely lengthy branch from Stirling and Callander. Although the spur between the two lines was opened as early as 1897, regular Glasgow to Oban services, i.e. using the metals of the two rival companies, only began in 1949, after nationalization; nor was any attempt made before then to align the timetables of the two companies and so provide connections. The Caledonian line east of Crianlarich was closed in 1965.

The train crosses the Oban line on a viaduct, and runs along the side of a wide valley, climbing all the time. Beyond Tyndrum, it cuts through the mountains to one of the highlights of the line: the great Horseshoe Curve between Beinn Odhar (2,948 feet) and Beinn Dorain (3,524 feet). It might have been simpler to build a long viaduct or embankment straight across the valley separating the two peaks. But the West Highland had an eye for economy, and instead swung the line almost due east, built two viaducts, one of five spans and the second a splendid nine spans, and then turned the line first west and then north again. The views are splendid, not only of the line and the viaducts but also of the groups of spruce and fir and the different shades of green where the light strikes the moss and heather.

Rannoch Moor

At Bridge of Orchy, Glen Orchy comes in from the south-west before the line passes Loch Tulla. Now the train approaches Rannoch Moor, that desolate stretch of land which gave the builders of the line so much trouble. The mountains fall away, forming the distant backdrop to an empty world of water, mud and heathery grass, with not a single habitation in sight; even the new plantations of spruce cannot mar this lonely wilderness.

The tiny settlement around Rannoch station, which, except for the lack of a footbridge, remains exactly as it was constructed, was built to house the signalmen and maintenance men who served this part of the line. The station is inaccessible from the west, and only a single road, built by the railway company, reaches it from Loch Rannoch to the east. Immediately beyond the station a nine-span viaduct takes the line over a bog so deep that it was impracticable to fill it with turf and brushwood.

Still climbing, the line strikes across the Moor once again, heading for the summit at Corrour (1,350 feet) and running underneath a snowshed at Cruach Roch, one of the worst spots for drifting snow on the line. The Lochaber mountains draw closer, and Ben Nevis looms in the distance with Aonach Mor, Aonach Beag and the lower peaks of the Grey Corries in the foreground. In the evening, the view of the mountains standing out against the darkening sky is unforgettable.

Loch Ossian lies to the east of Corrour station. Past the station, the train descends to Loch Treig, still as deserted as it was when the line was built, reaching the water's edge at the northern tip of the lake. The landscape changes rapidly along this stretch, and the contrast with the unremitting brown of the Moor makes the greens of this lower country seem all the more vivid.

Beyond Fersit tunnel, the line swings sharply west through Tulloch station, meeting the first road for over 30 miles, and along Glen Spean. The train runs above the river as it thunders and churns through the rocks, cutting its way in an ever narrower gorge. There is a good view down to several waterfalls, the last and most spectacular of all being the long and winding Monessie

Gorge, seemingly only a few feet below the train. The final stretch into Fort William runs alongside the river, wider and less turbulent now that it has reached level ground, with views of the British Aluminium plant and of the huge mass of Ben Nevis.

Route from Fort William

It was never the intention to stop the railway at Fort William, which on its own could not provide sufficient business to make the route profitable. Thwarted in its original plan to run to the coast at Rushven, the West Highland almost immediately started to look round for an alternative destination, and as an earnest of its firm intentions opened a short branch round the bay to Banavie, at the foot of the Caledonian Canal, in 1875. The choice eventually fell on Mallaig. Once again, the lawyers set to work in Parliament, with the added complication that a Guarantee Bill had to be passed, for the North British would not undertake the extension without a substantial subsidy from the government.

Work started in January 1897 with a deadline of July 1902 – a target that the contractors met with well over a year to spare. Not that the route was an easy one. The first dozen miles along the shore of Loch Eil presented no particular chal-lenge, but after that the line cut inland through some difficult country. The rock was hard and difficult to shift; sharp curves and steep gradients of up to 1 in 48 were needed; and, instead of the two originally planned, eleven tunnels had to be built.

Construction was in the hands of Robert McAlpine of the Glasgow firm of the same name (the company remains in existence today), and 'Concrete Bob' had every opportunity to live up to his nickname. Concrete was cheaper than stone, and cheaper to maintain as well, which appealed to the West Highland; in any case the stone excavated to create the track bed was not suitable for use in the bridges and viaducts, and so the Mallaig line boasts some of the earliest large structures built of concrete.

Steam excursions

The pleasure of travelling the line today is doubled if you can do so behind a steam locomotive. The Mallaig extension is one of the lines on which British Rail operates its own extremely successful steam excursions. The return to steam, while undoubtedly enjoyed by passengers and crew alike, has brought its own problems. In summer 1984, one locomotive, the 96-year-old J36 0–6–0 *Maude*, simply could not produce adequate motive power, and when heavily

North British Railway J36 0–6–0 No. 673 Maude *on Loch nam Uamh viaduct.*

The white sands of Morar with distant views of Rhum,
a view shared for several miles by the Mallaig line.

loaded the other locomotives sometimes found it difficult to maintain adhesion on the steepest sections of the route.

The line runs around the bay from Fort William, passing the southern entrance to the Caledonian Canal at Banavie, where there is a good view from the swing bridge of the set of eight interconnected locks known as Neptune's Staircase. Along with the aluminium plant at Fort William, the paper mill at Corpach is the source of most of the freight business on the line from Glasgow; alumina goes into Fort William, and aluminium ingots and other products are despatched south, while from Corpach it is china clay and paper.

The line continues along the loch, and then slowly climbs up into the hills, running through the first tunnel and across the river Finnan as it tumbles down into Loch Shiel, along which there are splendid views. Concrete Bob built the first and most spectacular of his concrete viaducts here; 416 yards long with twenty-one spans, it strides out across the hillside. On the shore below, on the spot where the Prince first raised his standard, is the monument erected to Bonnie Prince Charlie and the Highlanders who joined him in the 1745 uprising.

After two more tunnels, the train descends and first runs along the southern shore of Loch Eilt and then follows the river Ailort to the edge of Loch Ailort. The main camp for the navvies who built the line was at Lochailort; 2,000 men lived here, 40 to a hut, and there was a well-stocked shop and a camp hospital with a permanent staff of a doctor and two nurses.

Line beside the sea

Seascapes are the main feature of the rest of the journey, with views across to Rhum and Eigg, and later to Skye as well. Having crossed the neck of the Ardnish peninsula, the line runs through three tunnels and over another lengthy viaduct, and then accompanies Loch nan Uamh for a while before striking inland to Arisaig where there is a pleasant harbour in which the yachts rock gently in the sea breeze. In summer, the coast here seems almost tropical, with luxuriant vegetation running riot down to the water's edge and the islands in the distance like jewels set in a sparkling blue background.

Beyond Arisaig, the train crosses Keppoch Moss, which had to be conquered in the same way as Rannoch Moor. Then there is another short inland stretch before it emerges on to the coast at Morar, soon crossing Morar viaduct over the river Morar from where there are views down Loch Morar. Now a series of rock cuttings brings the line out on to the coast for the last time, and the train runs past good views across to Skye into Mallaig station.

Gazetteer

As well as the preserved steam lines, there are many Steam Centres and Railway Museums throughout Great Britain. This is a list of the most interesting and significant, with brief details of their operations or contents. Space precludes a more comprehensive list. Opening times vary from year to year; for further details contact the railway or museum in question, especially if you are planning a visit during the week or out of the holiday season.

Eastern Region

Bowes Railway, Springwell, near Gateshead, Tyne & Wear; tel: 091416 1847.
1½-mile stretch of former standard-gauge colliery railway, the oldest part of which was built by George Stephenson and opened in 1826.

Bressingham Steam Museum, Bressingham Hall, Diss, Norfolk; tel: 037988 386.
Collection of locomotives includes 1927 *Royal Scot* and many other standard-gauge examples steamed on demonstration track; also miniature railway and two narrow-gauge lines 2 and 2½ miles long.

Colne Valley Railway, Castle Hedingham Station, near Halstead, Essex; tel: 0787 61174. (See page 50.)

Darlington Railway Museum, North Road Station, Darlington, County Durham; tel: 0325 460532. (See page 26.)

Monkwearmouth Station Museum, North Bridge Street, Sunderland, Tyne & Wear; tel: 0783 77075.
Handsome NER station with classical façade and booking office restored as it was in 1900 and restored footbridge; historical displays.

National Railway Museum, Leeman Road, York; tel: 0904 21261.
The national collection of locomotives and rolling stock is housed in a new building based on a former motive power depot; wide range of displays on history of railways, audio-visual displays etc.

Nene Valley Railway, Wansford Station, Stibbington, near Peterborough, Cambridgeshire PE8 6LR; tel: 0780 782854. (See page 56.)

North Norfolk Railway, Sheringham Station, Sheringham, Norfolk NR26 8RA; tel: 0263 872045. (See page 45.)

North Woolwich Station Museum, Pier Road, North Woolwich, London E16 2JJ; tel: 01-474 7244. (See page 171.)

North Yorkshire Moors Railway, Pickering Station, Pickering, North Yorkshire; tel: 0751 72508. (See page 32.)

South Tynedale Railway, The Railway Station, Alston, Cumbria CA9 3JB; tel: 0498 81696.
2-foot gauge line running along trackbed of former Haltwhistle to Alston line.

Stour Valley Railway Preservation Society, Chappel & Wakes Colne Station, Essex. (See page 48.)

Tanfield Railway, Marley Hill Engine Shed, Marley Hill, Tyne and Wear; tel: 091 274 2002.
1-mile standard-gauge line on route of Tanfield Wagonway, opened in 1725 using colliery locos and non-bogie coaches.

Timothy Hackworth Museum, Soho Street, Shildon, County Durham; tel: 0388 772036. (See page 28.)

Wells-Walsingham Railway, Egmere Road Station, Walsingham, Norfolk.
4-mile 10¼-inch gauge line, claimed to be longest of its gauge anywhere.

Midland Region

Bala Lake Railway, Llanuwchllyn Station, Gwynedd LL23 7DD; tel: 66784 666. (See page 77.)

Birmingham Railway Museum, 670 Warwick Road, Tyseley, Birmingham B11 2HL; tel: 021 707 4696.
Substantial collection of locomotives, rolling stock and workshop equipment; restoration workshops and regular steam days.

Bulmer Railway Centre, Whitecross Road, Hereford; tel: 0272 834430.
Large collection of locomotives including GWR 4–6–0 No. 6000 *King George* and SR 4–6–2 No. 35028 *Clan Line*; regular steam days.

Bury Transport Museum, Castlecroft Road, Bury, Greater Manchester BL9 0LN; tel: 061 746 7790.
Substantial collection of steam and diesel locomotives and rolling stock housed in former goods shed of East Lancashire Railway; regular steam days.

Conwy Valley Railway Museum, Old Goods Yard, Betws-y-Coed, Gwynedd LL24 0AL; tel: 06902 568. (See page 72.)

Dean Forest Railway, Norchard, near Lydney, Forest of Dean, Gloucestershire; tel: 05944 3423.
Large collection of locomotives and rolling stock, including GWR Class 4575s and Hunslet saddletanks, on show at Steam Centre; regular rides along ½-mile track.

Dinting Railway Centre, Dinting Lane, Glossop, Derbyshire; tel: 04574 5596.
Standard-gauge steam centre with collection of locomotives and rolling stock, including LMS 4–6–0 No. 5596 *Bahamas*; regular rides on ¼-mile track.

Fairbourne Railway, Beach Road, Fairbourne, Gwynedd LL38 2EX; tel: 0341 250362.
15-inch gauge line along dunes between Fairbourne and Penrhyn Point, where the former ferry for Barmouth left; rebuilt on 12-inch gauge during 1986. (See page 83.)

Ffestiniog Railway, Porthmadog Harbour Station, Porthmadog, Gwynedd; tel: 0766 2384. (See page 74.)

Gloucestershire-Warwickshire Railway and Cotswold Narrow Gauge Railway, Toddington Station, Gloucestershire; tel: 0242 602946.
Large collection of locomotives (many ex-GWR) and rolling stock from both standard- and narrow-gauge; ⅓-mile rides on both gauges available.

Great Central Railway, Loughborough Central Station, Great Central Road, Loughborough, Leicestershire LE11 6RW; tel: 0509 230726. (See page 120.)

Greater Manchester Museum of Science and Industry, Liverpool Road, Castlefield, Greater Manchester M3 4JP; tel: 061 832 2244. (See page 97.)

Gwili Railway, Bronwydd Arms Station, Bronwydd, near Carmarthen, Dyfed; tel: 0656 732176.
1½-mile standard-gauge steam railway.

Keighley & Worth Valley Railway, Haworth Station, Keighley, West Yorkshire BD22 8NJ; tel: 0535 43629/45214. (See page 118.)

Lakeside & Haverthwaite Railway, Haverthwaite Station, near Newby Bridge, Ulverston, Cumbria; tel: 0448 31594.
3¼-mile standard-gauge railway operating over part of the former Lakeside Railway closed in 1965.

Leighton Buzzard Narrow-Gauge Railway, Pages Park Station, Billington Road, Leighton Buzzard, Bedfordshire LU7 8TN; tel: 0525 373888.
1¾-mile railway on 2 foot-gauge running over part of former Leighton Buzzard Light Railway built to serve sand quarries.

Llanberis Lake Railway, Padarn Country Park, Gilfach Ddu, Llanberis, Gwynedd LL55 4TY; tel: 0286 870549.
2-mile line built in 1971 on 1 foot 11½-inch-gauge running in fine countryside around the edge of Lake Llanberis; steam and diesel haulage.

Llangollen Railway, Llangollen Station, Llangollen, Clwyd; tel: 0978 860951.
1½-mile standard-gauge steam railway on route of former GWR branch from Ruabon to Barmouth.

Market Bosworth Light Railway, Shackerstone Station, near Market Bosworth, Leicestershire.
2¾-mile standard-gauge line running alongside the Ashby Canal.

Midland Railway Centre, Butterley Station, near Ripley, Derbyshire; tel: 0773 44920.
3½-mile standard-gauge steam railway and museum devoted to recreating the heyday of the Midland Railway; line occupies part of the former Ambergate to Pye Bridge branch.

Middleton Railway, Tunstall Road/Moor Road, Leeds LS11 5JY.
1½-mile standard-gauge steam railway that carries freight for local companies during the week and passengers at weekends; based on the former Middleton Railway, where steam locomotives were first used commercially in 1812 and whose horse-drawn predecessor was authorized in 1758.

North Staffordshire Steam Centre, Cheddleton Station, Station Road, Cheddleton, near Leek, Staffordshire; tel: 0538 360522.
Standard-gauge steam centre based on the attractive Cheddleton Station of the former North Staffordshire Railway with collection of locomotives and rolling stock; regular steam days.

Quainton Railway Centre, The Railway Station, Quainton, near Aylesbury, Buckinghamshire HP22 4BY; tel: 029 675 450.
Comprehensive collection of standard-gauge locomotives and rolling stock housed in former Metropolitan and Great Central Railway sidings.

Ravenglass & Eskdale Railway, Ravenglass Station, Ravenglass, Cumbria CA18 1SW; tel: 06577 226.
15-inch gauge steam railway originally constructed to carry iron ore from Eskdale running through attractive Lake District countryside.

Severn Valley Railway, The Railway Station, Bewdley, Worcestershire DY12 1BG; tel: 0299 403816. (See page 90.)

Snowdon Mountain Railway, Llanberis, Gwynedd; tel: 0286 870223.
4¾-mile rack railway (the only example in Great Britain) built on 2 foot 7½ inch gauge and running to the summit of Snowdon.

Steamport, Southport Locomotive and Transport Museum, Derby Road, Southport, Merseyside PR9 0TY; tel: 0704 30693.
Steam museum with collection of standard-gauge locomotives and rolling stock housed in former LMS loco shed; regular steam days.

Steamtown Railway Museum, Warton Road, Carnforth, Lancashire LA5 8HX; tel: 052473 4220.
Live steam museum and preservation centre with substantial collection of standard-gauge main-line and industrial locomotives; housed in former Carnforth Motive Power Depot, where steam locomotives were maintained until 1968, and which contains water columns, turntable, coaling tower, signal box, carriage and wagon shop. Regular rides on 1-mile standard-gauge track and also narrow-gauge line.

Talyllyn Railway, Wharf Station, Tywyn, Gwynedd LL36 9EY; tel: 0654 711297/710472. (See page 78.)

Vale of Rheidol Narrow Gauge Steam Railway, Aberystwyth BR Station, Aberystwyth, Dyfed; tel: 0970 612377. (See page 80.)

Welsh Highland Light Railway, Gelert's Farm Works, Madoc Street West, Porthmadog, Gwynedd LL49 9DY; tel: 0766 3402. (See page 80.)

Welshpool and Llanfair Light Railway, Llanfair Caereinion Station, Powys; tel: 0938 810441. (See page 81.)

Yorkshire Dales Railway, Embsay Station, Embsay, Skipton, North Yorkshire; tel: 0756 4727.
1-mile standard-gauge steam railway running over part of former Skipton-Ilkley route (Midland Railway).

Western Region

Brecon Mountain Railway, Pant Station, Merthyr Tydfil, Mid-Glamorgan; tel: 0685 4854.
2-mile steam railway, built on 1 foot 11¾-inch gauge and running on route of former Brecon & Merthyr Railway, closed in 1962.

Dart Valley Railway, Buckfastleigh Station, Devon TQ11 0DZ: tel: 03644 2338. (See page 136.)

East Somerset Railway, Cranmore Station, Shepton Mallet, Somerset BA4 4QP; Tel: 074988 417. (See page 136.)

Great Western Railway Museum, Faringdon Road, Swindon, Wiltshire SN1 5BQ; tel: 0793 26161 extension 3131. (See page 127.)

Swanage Railway, Swanage Station, Dorset BH19 1HB; tel: 0929 425800.
1½-mile steam standard-gauge line occupying part of the former Swanage to Wareham line.

Swindon Railway Village Museum, Faringdon Road, Swindon, Wiltshire; tel: 0793 26161 extension 3136. (See page 127.)

Torbay & Dartmouth Railway, Paignton Queens Park Station, Paignton, Devon TQ4 6AF; tel: 0803 555872. (See page 138.)

West Somerset Railway, Minehead Station, Minehead, Somerset TA24 5BG; tel: 0643 4996.
20-mile standard-gauge line worked by steam and diesel locomotives over the former West Somerset Railway; the longest private passenger railway in Great Britain.

Southern Region

Bluebell Railway, Sheffield Park Station, Uckfield, West Sussex TN 22 3QL; tel: 082572 2370. (See page 160.)

Isle of Wight Steam Railway, Haven Street Station, near Ryde, Isle of Wight, PO33 4DS; tel: 0983 882204.
1¼-mile standard-gauge steam railway operating over a section of the former Ryde to Newport line.

Kent & East Sussex Railway, Tenterden Town Station, Tenterden, Kent TN30 6HE; tel: 05806 2943. (See page 164.)

Mid-Hants Railway, Alresford Station, Alresford, Hampshire SO24 9JG; tel: 096273 3810.
6¼-mile standard-gauge steam railway ('The Watercress Line') operating on track of former Mid-Hants line.

Romney, Hythe & Dymchurch Railway, New Romney Station, Kent; tel: 06783 2353.
13¾-mile 15-inch gauge railway operating along the Kent coast.

Sittingbourne & Kemsley Light Railway, off Milton Road, Sittingbourne, Kent; tel: 0795 24899 (operating days) or 0634 32320 (other times).

Scotland

Bo'ness & Kinneil Railway, Bo'ness Station, off Union Street, Bo'ness, West Lothian EH51; tel: 0506 822298.
½-mile standard-gauge line along the foreshore at Bo'ness; the 1842 trainshed from Haymarket Station, Edinburgh, has been re-erected.

Strathspey Railway, The Station, Boat of Garten, Inverness-shire PH23 3BH; tel: 047983 692. (See page 188.)

Bibliography

The following were consulted during the preparation of this book:

Baker, S. K., *Rail Atlas of Britain and Ireland*, Oxford Publishing Company, Poole, 4th edition, 1984

Barrie, D. S. M., A Regional History of the Railways of Great Britain, volume XII, *South Wales*, David & Charles, Newton Abbot, 1980

Baughan, Peter E., A Regional History of the Railways of Great Britain, volume XI, *North and Mid Wales*, David & Charles, Newton Abbot, 1980

Beckett, Derrick, *Brunel's Britain*, David & Charles, Newton Abbot, 1980

Beckett, Derrick, *Stephenson's Britain*, David & Charles, Newton Abbot, 1984

Betjeman, John, *London's Historic Railway Stations*, John Murray, London, 1972

Biddle, Gordon, Nock O. S., *et al*, *The Railway Heritage of Britain*, Michael Joseph, London, 1983

Binney, Marcus, and Pearce, David (eds), *Railway Architecture*, Orbis, London, 1979

Binns, Donald, *The Scenic Settle & Carlisle Railway*, Wyvern, Skipton, 1982

Blanchard, L. E., *Bradshaw's Descriptive Guide to the Great Western Railway*, Bradshaw's Railway Publication Office, London, 1845

Body, Geoffrey, *Cornwall Railway*, British Rail (Western) and Avon-AngliA, Weston-super-Mare, 1984

Body, Geoffrey, *Railways of the Southern Region*, Patrick Stephens, Cambridge, 1984

Body, Geoffrey, *Railways of the Western Region*, Patrick Stephens, Cambridge, 1983

Bonavia, Michael R., *The Four Great Railways*, David & Charles, Newton Abbot, 1980

Bowden, Thomas N., and Mills, Bernard, *Brunel's Royal Albert Bridge Saltash*, Peter Watts, Gloucester, n.d.

Brooke, *The Railway Navvy*, David & Charles, Newton Abbot, 1983

Burton, Anthony, *The Rainhill Story*, British Broadcasting Corporation, London, 1980

Burton, Anthony, *The Waterways of Britain*, Collins, London, 1983

Christiansen, Rex, A Regional History of the Railways of Great Britain, volume XIII, *Thames and Severn*, David & Charles, Newton Abbot, 1981

Christiansen, Rex, A Regional History of the Railways of Great Britain, volume VII, *The West Midlands*, 2nd edition, David St. John Thomas/David & Charles, Newton Abbot, 1983

Coghlan, Francis, *The Iron Road Book and Railway Companion*, A. H. Bailey, London, 1838; reprinted E & W Books, 1970

Coles, C. R. L., *Railways Through London*, Ian Allan, Shepperton, 1983

Collins, Michael J., *The East Coast Main Line Today*, Ian Allan, Shepperton, 1985

Conolly, W. Philip, *British Railways Pre-Grouping Atlas and Gazetteer*, Ian Allan, Shepperton, 1976

Cooper, B. K., *Rail Centres: Brighton*, Ian Allan, Shepperton, 1981

Cripps, N., and Hastilow, F. J. (eds), *Midlands by Rail*, Midlands Branch of the Railway Development Society, Birmingham and Sutton Coalfield, n.d.

Crombleholme, Roger, and Kirtland, Terry, *Steam British Isles*, David & Charles, Newton Abbot, 1983

Davies, R., and Grant, M. D., *London and Its Railways*, David & Charles, Newton Abbot, 1983

Day, Lance, *Broad Gauge*, Her Majesty's Stationery Office, London, 1985

Ferneyhough, Frank, *The History of Railways in Great Britain*, Osprey, London, 1975

Freeling, Arthur, *The London and Brimingham Railway Companion*, Whittaker and Company, London, 1838

Garrod, Trevor (ed), *East Anglia by Rail*, 2nd Edition, East Anglian Branch, Railway Development Society/Jarrold and Sons, Norwich, 1985

Garrod, Trevor (ed), *Lincolnshire by Rail*, Lincolnshire Branch Railway Development Society, Lincoln, 1985

Gittins, Rob, and Spencer Davies, Dorian, *The Illustrated Heart of Wales Line*, Gomer, Llandysul, 1985

Gordon, D. I., A Regional History of the Railways of Great Britain, vol. V, *The Eastern Counties*, 2nd edition, David & Charles, Newton Abbot, 1977

Harris, Michael (ed), *Brunel, the GWR & Bristol*, Ian Allan, Weybridge, 1985

Harris, Michael (ed), *Scottish Scenic Routes*, Ian Allan, Weybridge, 1985

Harris, Michael (ed), *The Settle & Carlisle Route*, Ian Allan, Shepperton, 1984

Heap, Christine, and van Riemsdijk, John, *The Pre-Grouping Railways*, parts 1, 2 and 3, London, Her Majesty's Stationery Office, 1972, 1980 and 1985

Holt, Geoffrey O., A Regional History of the Railways of Great Britain, volume X, *The North West*, David & Charles, Newton Abbot, 1978

Hoole, K., A Regional History of the Railways of Great Britain, volume IV, *North East England*, David & Charles, Dawlish/Macdonald, London, 1965

Hoole, K., *Rail Centres: York*, Ian Allan, Shepperton, 1983

Hoole, K., *Railway Stations of the North East*, David & Charles, Newton Abbot, 1985

Hoskins, W. G., *The Making of the English Landscape*, Penguin, Harmondsworth, 1970

Jackson, Alan A., *London's Termini*, 2nd edition, David & Charles, Newton Abbot, 1985

Joby, R. S., *The Railway Builders*, David & Charles, Newton Abbot, 1983

Johnson, Peter, *The Cambrian Lines*, Ian Allan, Shepperton, 1984

Johnson, Peter, *The Welsh Narrow-Gauge Railways*, Ian Allan, Weybridge, 1985

Joy, David, *Main Line Over Shap*, 3rd edition, Dalesman, Clapham, 1979

Joy, David, A Regional History of the Railways of Great Britain, volume VIII, *South & West Yorkshire*, 2nd edition, David St. John Thomas/David & Charles, Newton Abbot, 1984

Leleux, Robin, A Regional History of the Railways of Great Britain, volume IX, *The East Midlands*, 2nd edition, David St. John Thomas/David & Charles, Newton Abbot, 1984

Lloyd, David, *Railway Station Architecture*, 2nd edition, David & Charles, Newton Abbot, 1978

McLagan, Willie, and Shields, Tom, *Glasgow-London: A Travellers' Guide*, Famedram, Gartocharn, 1974

Maggs, Colin G., *Rail Centres: Swindon*, Ian Allan, Shepperton, 1983

Measom, George, *The Illustrated Guide to the Great Western Railway*, W. Marshall and Sons, London, 1852; reprinted by Berkshire County Library in association with Countryside Books, Newbury, 1985

Mitchell, W. R., and Joy, David, *Settle to Carlisle*, 2nd edition, Dalesman, Clapham, 1984

Mogg, E., *Mogg's Brighton Railway Guide*, E. Mogg, London, 1841

Morgan, Bryan, *Civil Engineering: Railways*, Longman, London, 1971

Nock, O. S., *Great Western in Colour*, New Orchard Editions, Poole, n.d.

Nock, O. S., *150 Years of Main Line Railways*, David & Charles, Newton Abbot, 1980

Nock, O. S., *Railway Archaeology*, Patrick Stephens, Cambridge, 1981

Nock, O. S., *Railway Race to the North*, 2nd edition, Ian Allan, Shepperton, 1976

Nock, O. S., *Scottish Railways*, 2nd edition, Thomas Nelson, London, 1961

Nock, O. S., *The Railway Enthusiast's Encyclopaedia*, Arrow, London, 1970

Nock, O. S., *Two Miles a Minute*, Patrick Stephens, Cambridge, 1980

Osborne, E. C., *Osborne's London & Birmingham Railway Guide*, E. C. & W. Osborne, Birmingham, 1840

Pick, Christopher, *Off the Motorway*, Cadogan Books, London, 1984

Richards, J. M., *The National Trust Book of Bridges*, Jonathan Cape, London, 1984

Rolt, L. T. C., *George and Robert Stephenson*, Pelican Books, Harmondsworth, 1978

Rolt, L. T. C., *Isambard Kingdom Brunel*, Penguin Books, Harmondsworth, 1970

Rolt, L. T. C., *Victorian Engineering*, Pelican Books, Harmondsworth, 1974

Semmens, P. W. B., *et al*, *Quest for Speed*, British Rail Eastern Region, 1977

Sprinks, Neil, and Body, Geoffrey, *Heart of Wales Line*, British Rail (Western) and Avon-AngliA, Weston-super-Mare, 1981

Thomas, David St. John, A Regional History of the Railways of Great Britain, volume I, *The West Country*, 5th edition, David & Charles, Newton Abbot, 1981

Thomas, David St. John, and Roxburgh-Smith, Simon, *Summer Saturdays in the West*, David & Charles, Newton Abbot, 197?

Thomas, John, A Regional History of the Railways of Great Britain, volume VI, *Scotland: The Lowlands and the Borders*, 2nd edition, revised and enlarged by Alan J. S. Paterson, David St. John Thomas/David & Charles, Newton Abbot, 1984

Thomas, John, *The West Highland Railway*, David & Charles, Dawlish/Macdonald, London, 1965

Vaughan, Adrian, *Grub, Water and Relief*, John Murray, London, 1985

Vaughan, Adrian, *Signalman's Morning*, John Murray, London, 1981

Vaughan, Adrian, *Signalman's Twilight*, John Murray, London, 1983

Vaughan, John, *This is Paddington*, Ian Allan, Shepperton, 1982

Walker, James Scott, *An Accurate Description of the Liverpool and Manchester Rail-Way*, 3rd edition, J. F. Cannell, Liverpool, 1831

Weir, Tom, *The Highland Line*, Famedram, Gartocharn, n.d.

Weir, Tom, *The Kyle Line*, Famedram, Gartocharn, n.d.

Weir, Tom, *The Mallaig Line*, Famedram, Gartocharn, n.d.

Weir, Tom, *The Oban Line*, Famedram, Gartocharn, n.d.

Westcott-Jones, Kenneth, *Railways for Pleasure*, Lutterworth Press, Guildford and London, 1980

White, H. P., A Regional History of the Railways of Great Britain, volume III, *Greater London*, David & Charles, Newton Abbot, 1971

White, H. P., A Regional History of the Railways of Great Britain, volume II, *Southern England*, 4th edition, David & Charles, Newton Abbot, 1982

Whitehouse, Patrick, and Thomas, David St. John (eds), *The Great Western Railway*, David & Charles, Newton Abbot, 1984

Williams, Herbert, *Railways in Wales*, Christopher Davies, Swansea, 1981

Williams, Hugh, *APT − A Promise Unfulfilled*, Ian Allan, Weybridge, 1985

All Change at Crewe, British Rail (London Midland) Public Affairs Department, Birmingham, 1985

The Rannoch Line, Famedram, Gartocharn, n.d.

Swindon Works and Its Place in Great Western Railway History, The Great Western Railway, London, 1935

Magazines:
  Modern Railways;
  Railway Magazine;
  Railway World.

Index

Page numbers in italics refer to illustrations.

INDEX